RTI & Math:
The Classroom Connection

Estimates Considered,
Logic Required,
Data Imperative

by
Karen A. Kemp
Mary Ann Eaton &
Sharon Poole

DUDE PUBLISHING
A Division of
National Professional Resources, Inc.
Port Chester, New York

Publisher's Cataloging-in-Publication
(Provided by Quality Books, Inc.)

Kemp, Karen A.
RTI & math : the classroom connection / by Karen A.
Kemp, Mary Ann Eaton, Sharon Poole.
p. cm.
ISBN-13: 978-1934032-83-1
ISBN-10: 1934032-83-2

1. Mathematics--Study and teaching (Elementary)--
Handbooks, manuals, etc. 2. Individualized instruction
--Handbooks, manuals, etc.   I. Eaton, Mary Ann.
II. Poole, Sharon, 1947- III. Title. IV. Title: RTI and
math.

QA135.6.K46 2008   372.7'044
               QBI08-600261

Acquisitions Editor: Helene M. Hanson
Associate Editor: Lisa L. Hanson
Production Editor, Cover Design: Andrea Cerone,
National Professional Resources, Inc., Port Chester, NY

Dude Publishing
A Division of National Professional Resources, Inc.
25 South Regent Street
Port Chester, New York 10573
Toll free: (800) 453-7461
Phone: (914) 937-8879

Visit our web site: www.NPRinc.com

Printed in the United States of America

ISBN 978-1934032-83-1

To our children
Corey and Curtis
Thomas, Tara and Lisa
John, Erin and Alex

Acknowledgements

"Wish I didn't know now what I didn't know then."
—Bob Seeger

But I do . . . thanks to the family, friends, colleagues and students who contributed to my collection of knowledge and then endured my wacky, wild and sometimes bright ideas! You are my inspiration and constant support. Without you, who knows what I'd know?

To knowledge... Karen

"Life is chance. Love is infinity. Grace is reality."
—Thomas Bryan Eaton

With appreciation to my family, friends, teachers and students who have laughed, cried, sung and danced with me. I am eternally grateful for the many conversations that have enriched my life. May the dialogue continue as we go forth doing the best we can with what we have available to us on any given day.

To life... Mary Ann

"There's still a lot of faith, trust and warmth when we keep on keeping on."
—Curtis Mayfield

Love and thanks to my children who never fail to support me as I throw myself into yet another project. You keep me going on. Thanks to my colleagues from whom I continue to learn what it means to be an educator, and what it means to be a life-long learner. To the many students I have met over the years, thanks for teaching me that one size does not fit all, and for making me determined to find many sizes.

To perseverance...Sharon

To everyone who has contributed knowledge, life, and perseverance to our existence ~ We Thank You.

Contents

Introduction

"Together we will unite and make the right choice
And fight for education, save the next generation.
Come together as one
I don't understand why it's never been done
So let's change on the count of one."
—Black Eyed Peas, *Union*

The prevailing discourse and discussion among educators tend to focus primarily on reading/literacy proficiency at the elementary and secondary levels. Often overlooked but included in the No Child Left Behind (NCLB) Act is the additional declaration that no child will be left behind in mathematics *(the cognitive process of using numbers and symbols to study measurement, properties, and relationships of quantities and sets).*

While Mary Ann and Karen were writing the book, *RTI: The Classroom Connection for Literacy,* the notion kept surfacing that schools are facing difficulties in the area of mathematics comparable to those in reading. The recurring thought that many students struggle with mathematics, as they do with reading, and that teachers are continuously searching for effective interventions to meet the needs of all students, led the authors to the idea of writing another book. So, before the dust had a chance to settle on laptops or brains, the challenge to provide a similar framework for implementing Response To Intervention (RTI) and research-based techniques for math became a reality. For those of you new to RTI, it is a multi-tiered approach to maximize progress for students who struggle with learning, in which interventions are provided with increasing levels of intensity based on progress monitoring and analysis.

For this book we invited our colleague, Sharon, to join (divide and conquer) in our effort. The three of us set out to scrutinize the recommendations of the National Council of Teachers of Mathematics (NCTM) as well as the National Mathematics Advisory Panel (NMP) and integrate the research regarding best practices for helping students achieve those recommendations.

It is imperative for us to point out that this book is not about "how to teach" mathematics. It is a dialogue about the underlying math concepts and skills that many students lack because they come to school without the required language concepts; they are victims of poor or repeating curriculums, or they moved through grade levels without adequate preparation or practice opportunities for mastery.

This book offers teacher-friendly, research-based techniques (sometimes from countries other than the United States) for students at the primary, elementary and intermediate levels who are struggling with math foundations, specifically whole numbers. Also included are tools to monitor the effectiveness of the techniques based upon student responsiveness and progress.

What You Will Find:

Chapter 1 highlights research that corroborates the reality of the mathematics challenges in our society today. Information from a variety of resources, including the National Mathematics Advisory Panel, provides the reader with a broad perspective of the critical issues schools face.

Chapter 2 presents the Cardinal Questions to be considered by the teacher prior to implementing an intervention. These questions provide a framework for assessing the teacher's knowledge as well as that of the student. (The Cardinal Questions were first introduced in *RTI: The Classroom Connection for Literacy,* Kemp and Eaton (2007).

Chapter 3 provides an overview of a multi-tiered system of intervention most commonly referred to as RTI (Response To Intervention). We have developed tracking forms to assist in the documentation of interventions as they are implemented. These forms become especially useful as the RTI process unfolds.

Chapter 4 explains the essential components of Curriculum Based Measurement (CBM) and how it can be used to monitor student progress and overall growth in each of the critical areas of mathematics.

Chapters 5 through 8 each includes an overview of one of the four key areas of early mathematics instruction and leads teachers through the process of identifying student needs by reflecting on the Cardinal Questions. Techniques for each key area are provided using step-by-step implementation formats along with a suggested curriculum based measurement probe to assess student learning.

Chapter 9 addresses the importance of motivation and persistence in the acquisition of math skills. Techniques for investigating student's personal interests and possible anxieties associated with math are provided.

Chapter 10 discusses the next steps to be taken should students require more intensive intervention, including referral to special education.

Appendix A contains sample Curriculum Based Measurement probes, and directions for their use.

Appendix B contains Reproducible Materials that support and enhance topics in this book.

"You got the numbers—you got no limits,
one day you're out but the next day you're in it.
You find the answers—you know what to say,
give us our reasons for livin' today."
—Billy Squier, *Eye On You*

Chapter 1
About Math

"Math is a wonderful thing, math is a really cool thing,
So get off your "ath", let's do some math."
—Jack Black, *The Math Song*

Math is a very cool thing once you overcome the common misperceptions and begin to think in the language of math. This was just one of our discoveries about mathematics as we waded through all the materials in order to deliver the most relevant information to you, the reader.

This book is based on the same two premises of *RTI: The Classroom Connection to Literacy* (Kemp & Eaton, 2007). They are: first, all students need to develop literacy in math; second, the educators charged with teaching this complex process need to dialogue early and often about how to best reach all students, regardless of race, culture, economic status or disability. In particular, educators at the primary and elementary levels who may have had little or no specific training in how to best teach students the cognitive underpinning of basic math concepts and skills needed to be successful in later years, will find this book to be a helpful resource (National Council on Teacher Quality, 2008).

To begin, we identify the concept areas of mathematics outlined by the National Council of Teacher's of Mathematics (NCTM). The original standards of the NCTM were revised in 2000 and are currently referred to as the Principles and Standards for School Mathematics. The Council has identified the ten standards listed in Table 1 as the basic skills and understandings necessary for students to function effectively in the twenty-first century.

Table 1- NCTM Principles and Standards

Content	Processes
Number and Operations	Problem Solving
Algebra	Reasoning & Proof
Geometry	Connections
Measurement	Communication
Data Analysis & Probability	Representation

In a later document entitled *Adding It Up,* published by the National Research Council in 2001, the same concepts are reiterated but are condensed into five attributes that may be used to guide best practice in the early stages of teaching mathematics. These target areas were identified after careful analysis of the available research was conducted, and relevant information related to mathematics was gathered. To capture what they believed defined successful learning of mathematics, this Council coined the term "mathematical proficiency." Mathematical proficiency, according to the National Research Council, includes the following:

1. Conceptual understanding or understanding— knowing what mathematical symbols, diagrams and procedures mean as well as comprehension of mathematical concepts, operations and relations;

2. Procedural fluency or computing—carrying out procedures such as adding, subtracting, multiplying and dividing numbers flexibly, accurately, efficiently and appropriately;

3. Strategic competence or applying—being able to formulate, represent and devise strategies for solving mathematical problems;

4. Adaptive reasoning or reasoning—using logical thought to reflect, explain and justify solutions to problems;

5. Productive disposition or engaging—seeing mathematics as sensible, useful and worthwhile, coupled with a willingness to do the work and stay with it.

The preceding information, while widely documented, did not provide the necessary platform to "fix" the broken system of mathematics instruction in our country, according to the National Mathematics Advisory Panel report of 2008. This panel, appointed in 2006 at the request of the President, was formed to discern "best available scientific evidence" in order to improve mathematics performance among our students. The most compelling aspect of this report is the recommendation to streamline math curriculum in grades K-8 and emphasize only the most critical topics in the early grades, as is common in higher achieving countries. The panel further advises that what is "known" from rigorous research about how children learn should be embraced immediately. The "known" results include:

> a. Providing children with a strong start;
> b. Focusing on conceptual understanding, procedural fluency and automatic recall of facts;
> c. Recognizing that effort, not inherent talent, is what counts.

The following essential ideas were highlighted in the Executive Summary of the 2008 National Advisory Panel report:

- Students require a focused, coherent progression of mathematics learning with an emphasis on proficiency of key topics. This translates to avoidance of spiraling curriculums, improvements in scope and sequence and attention to automaticity of basic facts and standard algorithms.
- There is a critical need for the development of fluency with whole numbers as a necessary precursor to the study of fractions, geometry and measurement, which are the critical foundations for algebra.
- School must focus on improvement in math knowledge of pre-schoolers and kindergartners, especially those children from lower-income backgrounds.
- There is a need for additional interventions that address social, affective and motivational factors associated with math performance and achievement.
- Additional pre-service and in-service training for educators is essential so they can acquire the knowledge and skills necessary to teach math effectively.

- Effective instructional practices (ie. explicit instruction for lower performers, peer-mediated instruction and formative assessment) should be part of every program.

Although the report does not provide entirely new information, it emphasizes the mathematical areas essential to achievement and reinforces best practices for teaching mathematics. Furthermore, it serves to eliminate the problem of teachers and students getting caught in the crossfire of the different beliefs and curricula currently in vogue.

Another sometimes overlooked critical topic re-addressed in this latest report is the need to change the perception among teachers and students that math is abstract and difficult; that some people have "a head for math" and some do not. The belief that we must have some kind of geek-like tendencies to be any good at math has been perpetuated throughout our society for decades—so much so that many students continue to regard math as a phobia that "... is right up there with snakes, public speaking and heights" (Burns, 1998).

While waiting for the release of the National Advisory Panel's final report, the authors of this book spent extensive time reviewing the available literature in order to compile what we believe to be "must have" information related to math ability, instruction and acquisition. We did this for two reasons: first, to dispel some of the prevailing math myths; and second, to determine the primary reasons students have difficulty learning and achieving mathematic proficiency.

What follows is a discussion of the most significant math myths that have contributed to the social acceptance of math phobia in our schools, and reasons why these myths do not hold true (Smith & Smith, 2006).

Math aptitude is innate.

We are born with a modest amount of innate math ability, such as an idea of basic quantities. As children's brains grow and mature, their capability grows as well. However, higher cognition of mathematics is not innate; rather, its development depends heavily upon the informal and formal learning opportunities available. Traditional methods of math instruction teach math through reading. In this scenario, students who are not proficient in reading will find it difficult or impossible to learn math. It is therefore essential that students learn math through reading the language of math instead of being required to learn math through standard reading (Moursund, 2007).

Being good at math means being good at calculation.

"Being a wiz at figures is not the mark of success in mathematics" (Smith & Smith, 2006). We know that being good at computing is a good start, but math literacy is so much more! Being good at math is about interpreting, estimating, comparing and drawing conclusions using numerical, spatial and quantitative data (Paulos, 1991). It means being good at understanding, applying, reasoning and engaging. In other words, calculating is only one part of mathematics. Think about this analogy: calculating is to mathematics as diagramming sentences is to English. It would be difficult to develop an appreciation of literature if all one was good at was dissecting a sentence; the same is true about being good at calculating.

Math requires only logic and not creativity.

Although it is important to make sense of math in a logical way, the creative process is considered the essence of the discipline. The ability to generate hypotheses, multiple representations, conjectures and solution strategies all require creativity and are mainstays of math (Kogleman and Warren, 1978 as cited in Barlow & Reddish, 2006).

What is important in math is the right answer.

An overemphasis on exact answers may lead students away from the process of math. On the contrary, it is understanding the concepts and language of math that can lead to the answers. Although most problems do have exact answers, as stressed in many testing and classroom situations, there are many circumstances in which approximate answers are just as valuable, especially in the processes of estimating, hypothesizing and conjecturing (Kogleman and Warren 1978 as cited in Barlow & Reddish, 2006).

Males are better at mathematical thinking.

The truth is both males and females can do well at math. What is important is giving all students equal access and the time they need to build their math skills in order to gain understanding (Devlin, 2008). We know that this myth is not valid as female students have already proven themselves in math-related subjects and professions. A recent study published in mid-October, 2008, in the Notices of the American Mathematical Society suggests that while many girls have exceptional talent in math, they are rarely identified in our country because the American culture does not highly value math talent. More about this study can be found in Chapter 9 of this book.

While all of these assumptions or myths can be proven wrong, another area of concern—math phobia or math anxiety—is not as easily pushed aside. Math anxiety is a real phenomenon and the subject of extensive research in the fields of educational and cognitive psychology. It is defined by Tobias (1998 as cited in Curtain-Phillips 2005) as, "feelings of tension and anxiety that interfere with the manipulation of numbers and solving of mathematical problems in a wide variety of ordinary life and academic situations." Many educational approaches to teaching math, combined with the strict emphasis on getting the right answer (and the embarrassment factor when you don't), have produced and perpetuated the notion that math is a risky frontier meant only for the "numbers people."

Recent research (Ashcroft 2007), indicates that math anxiety can become a self-fulfilling prophecy, which disrupts a student's overall performance by interfering with working memory. Working memory is required to solve even the most basic of multi-step processes

> **Ashcroft (2007), indicates that math anxiety can become a self-fulfilling prophecy .**

such as carrying, borrowing or long division. Students who cannot store information in memory due to anxiety will struggle to solve even the most basic problems. This, in turn, creates more self-doubt, more failure, growing anxiety and the continuation of a never-ending cycle (Cavanaugh, 2007).

Whether mythical or real, the math plight in our schools is evident. The available statistics reveal that the math achievement level of students in our country has remained low in comparison to other countries for several years now. For example, the report published in 2003 by the National Assessment of Educational Progress (NAEP) indicated that only 32% of our fourth graders and 29% of eighth graders were at or above a proficient level in math (National Center for Education Statistics, 2003). The survey released late in 2007 by TIMSS (Trends in International Math and Science Study) based on the Program for International Student Assessment (PISA) showed that 15 year old American students achieved sub-par results among developed nations in math literacy and problem solving (Hechinger, 2008). Based on this information, it is clear that we as educators must do something different in order to advance the opportunities of the next generation and to enable ALL individuals, not just a choice few, to compete in a global economic system.

While contemplating the preceding information, liken it to the first orchestral movement of an entire symphony. There is a vast array of information (the symphony) out there and we are providing you with what we believe to be the starting point (the first movement). Educators are continually faced with the challenge of becoming familiar with the newest information and research related to the content specialty. Mathematics is no exception. Disentangling the research information (the symphony) so one can choose optimal interventions for students, implement them with fidelity, assess the usefulness and report the results is a time-consuming process.

The authors, who work with both teachers and students, realize the ever-increasing pressure and time constraints of sorting through the literature and all of the research studies. This book consolidates the latest research, provides teacher-friendly, effective interventions that augment math instruction and offers techniques for data collection that can be used immediately in the classroom.

Furthermore, it provides a convergence of the literature to address what can occur early on so all students have the opportunity to reach the required proficiency levels expected by the No Child Left Behind Act (NCLB). What makes this book different from the dozens of other books on mathematics is its focus on the basic concepts and language of math—issues known to be a stumbling block for many children when it comes to learning mathematics (Ben-Hur, 2004).

This book is formatted in such a way as to provide educators with valuable information that focuses on:

- Techniques for teaching in four areas of mathematics:
  1. concepts and language
  2. numbers sense
  3. computation and fluency of whole numbers
  4. problem solving

- Techniques to identify and address motivation and/or math anxiety,

- Curriculum based measurement probes to assess student progress, and

- Reproducible materials for classroom use.

Chapters 5 – 8 each begin with a definition/description of its particular topic and an explanation of why it is important to math acquisition. In Chapter 9 the conversation about motivating students for success and overcoming math anxiety begins.

The authors now invite you to come and follow along on a ride to their side of teaching students the formative concepts of mathematics.

"Come with me and let's go for a ride,
Follow me to the other side."
—Green Day, *Best Thing in Town*

Suggested Resources

McKellar, D. (2007). *Math doesn't suck.* NY: Hudson Street Press, Penguin Group.

Sousa, D. (2008). *How the brain learns mathematics.* CA: Corwin Press.

Tobias, Shelia. (1993). *Overcoming Math Anxiety.* NY: W.W. Norton & Company, INC.

Adding It Up: Helping Children Learn Mathematics— http://books.nap.edu/catalog

Center on Instruction— http://www.centeroninstruction.org/files/SERP-MathAIR1-07ppt.pdf

Dautrich,B. (2007). *Why is Math So Hard?* EducationCrossing. Available: www. educationcrossing.com/article/index.php?id=470030

Department of Education and Early Childhood Development, Victoria, Australia-Mathematics Domain—http://www.education.vic.gov.au/ studentlearning/teachingresources/maths/research.htm

Improving Math Instruction through Reading Research and Best Practices— http://my-ecoach.com/online/webresourcelist

Math Matters—http://www.wested.org/pub/docs/

Millennium Mathematics Project, University of Cambridge— www.nrich.maths.org

National Center for Improving Student Learning and Achievement in Mathematics and Science (NCISLA)—http://ncisla.wceruw.org/

National Council of Teachers of Mathematics—www.nctm.org

National Mathematics Advisory Panel—www.ed.gov/pubs/edpubs.html

Recalculating K-12 Math— http://www.eschoolnews.com/resources/math-soutions/

Reforming Mathematics Instruction for ESL Literacy Students— http://www.ncela.gwu.edu/pubs/

Chapter 2
The Cardinal Questions

"We've got a lot of questions we've got a lot to learn,
So tired of solving problems too many bridges burned.
We see it all so clearly and still we close our eyes.
Why should we understand it? What good is knowing why?"
—Face to Face, *Everything is Everything*

Accountability is the word most representative of this chapter. If you have already read *RTI: The Classroom Connection for Literacy: Reading Intervention and Measurement* (Kemp & Eaton, 2007) then you are familiar with the Cardinal Questions. For those of you not familiar with the Cardinal Questions, we feel the following scenario is worth repeating; the rest of you can skip two pages ahead to The Cardinal Questions—A General Focus on Math.

The scenario has to do with a Charlie Brown cartoon in which Charlie tells his friends, "I taught my dog to whistle." Snoopy sits there ready to perform as the friends gather around spellbound and nothing happens. Annoyed, his friends state, "We thought you said your dog could whistle." Charlie's quick retort, "I said I taught my dog to whistle; I didn't say he learned!" While this may be Charlie Brown's answer, it is not an acceptable response for educators faced with the challenge of NCLB's requirement of closing the achievement gap, which calls for schools to have all students reach "proficiency" in reading, math and science by the year 2014.

This vignette speaks directly to teacher accountability. Whether related to one's work, gaining knowledge or simply for pleasure, math is a skill that is learned and improves with practice. There is much talk about using high-quality, scientifically based instruction to close the gap that exists between high and low achieving students. This "talk" refers to what and how teachers are instructing the students in their classrooms. Typically, educators implement the protocol they are provided by their administrators and incorporate ideas from their personal "bag of tricks." Some classroom practices for teaching reading and math have proven useful again and again, and these should most certainly be retained. Additionally, it is necessary to assess which strategies are working for which students and intervene accordingly. Waiting for failure is no longer an option. It is just not acceptable!

Think about how many people have experienced the fear of failure in one or more subjects during the course of their school careers. Once fear sets in, learning shuts down. Referral to special education became the answer for students who were not succeeding in the general education classroom. The assumption was that the problem lies within the learner, rather than with the curriculum or instructional delivery. RTI changes this way of thinking. Instead of waiting to find out whether or not a student is learning, progress is assessed early and often. Once it is found that a student is not learning, alternative methods of instruction in the classroom are explored and implemented. Research provides information about what works so there is no reason to apply practices arbitrarily or make referrals unnecessarily. The real "tricks" are:

- determining if all students are receiving the most effective math instruction along with core reading,
- deciding who may need additional instructional intervention,
- choosing and successfully implementing the most appropriate interventions.

Keeping this in mind, the ultimate educational accountability question becomes, "At the very least, can all of our students read and comprehend math for the purpose of problem solving and computing basic math operations that pervade everyday life?" If the answer to this question is not a resounding "yes," then the next logical question is, "Why not?" One really cannot begin to answer this question without first addressing one's own personal pedagogical content knowledge of math and reading. The authors' experience tells us that knowing one's pedagogical strengths is as important as familiarity with the research we consult.

To focus on accountability in education, this book offers the Cardinal Questions to use as a thinking framework. We believe each of these questions has two functions: one, for teacher self-assessment to discover and reflect on personal knowledge and strengths; and two, to utilize the same questions for the purpose of assessing the strengths of students.

Before proceeding to the Cardinal Questions, let's quickly address the misconception that teachers know everything. We are fully aware that deep understanding and wide application of a new practice do not come naturally. Society and the profession itself must acknowledge that teaching requires lifelong learning achieved only by making a commitment to stay abreast of new information and techniques through reading, questioning, staff development, collaboration and coaching. One cannot teach what one does not know and has not practiced. More importantly, people do not always know what they don't know until they engage in self-reflection.

"Teacher, know thyself." We encourage you to self-evaluate your pedagogical content knowledge and be sure to honor what you already know and do what works for you in the classroom. Once you have accomplished this, we suggest continuing this reflection process with the help of the Cardinal Questions.

The Cardinal Questions—A General Focus on Math

1. **What do you know** about your content area—in this case, about culturally responsive, research-based math instruction? In other words, what do you know about teaching math (concepts and language, number sense, operations, computational fluency, reasoning/problem solving and the cognitive processes involved)?

2. **What do you do** about meeting the learning needs of all your students? For example, while teaching math do you teach the vocabulary and syntax linked to math? Do you promote classroom discourse in your mathematics lessons?

3. **How do you learn** in order to meet your optimal learning needs?
   • What are your environmental preferences (i.e., noise, lighting, chairs, workspace, temperature)?

- What is your preferred sensory input modality (i.e., visual, auditory, motor)?
- How are you smart (i.e., logic smart, music smart, body smart, picture smart, word smart, people smart, self smart, nature smart)?
- What are your executive functioning strengths?

4. **How do you approach or react to an unfamiliar task?** When you learn something new, how are you affected by your:
   - cognitive style (i.e., impulsive/reflective, global/particular, leveler/sharpener, synthetic/analytic, inductive/deductive, concrete/abstract, random/sequential);
   - personality type (i.e., introvert/extrovert, sensory-intuitive, thinking/feeling, judging/perceiving);
   - motivation to learn (i.e., intrinsic, extrinsic)?
   - emotional stance (i.e., anxious, inept, fearful, competent, challenged)?

5. **What will you do with the information you gain from answering the first four questions?**

Once you have judiciously answered these questions, share the information with your colleagues in faculty meetings or study groups. Synthesize the knowledge of the entire staff so that, as a professional learning community, you can support and learn from each other, and even more importantly, ensure a strong core math program in every classroom.

"Teachers, know thy students." Ultimately, you will want to apply this Cardinal Question "thinking framework" while getting to know your students. The Cardinal Questions that lead to a better understanding of a student's ability are:

1. **What does the student know?**

2. **What does the student do?**

(Questions 1 and 2 are revisited with more specificity in the chapters that follow.)

3. **How does the student learn?** To meet the student's optimal learning needs:
   - What are the student's environmental preferences (i.e., noise, lighting, chairs, workspace, temperature)?
   - What is the student's preferred sensory input modality (i.e., visual, auditory, motor)?
   - How is the student smart (i.e., logic smart, music smart, body smart, picture smart, word smart, people smart, self smart)?
   - What are the student's executive functioning strengths?

4. **How does the student approach or react to an unfamiliar task?** When the student is learning something new, how is his/her behavior affected by:
   - cognitive style (i.e., impulsive/reflective, global/particular, leveler/sharpener, synthetic/analytic, inductive/deductive, concrete/abstract, random/sequential);
   - personality type (i.e., introvert/extrovert, sensory-intuitive, thinking/feeling, judging/perceiving);
   - motivation to learn (i.e., intrinsic, extrinsic);
   - emotional stance (i.e., anxious, inept, fearful, competent, challenged)?

5. **What will you do with the knowledge gained from answering the previous four questions?**

Educators can use the Cardinal Questions as a starting point for assessing the student's ability in math as well as other subjects. The Cardinal Questions are also valuable as a way to discover more about the student's background knowledge, family, culture, strengths and interests.

This chapter would not be complete if we did not address student accountability. We fully realize the importance of engaging students in the process of learning and holding students accountable for their participation and efforts. As educators, we cannot start encouraging and teaching students to be meta-cognitive early enough. Students who are less sophisticated in applying executive functions must be explicitly taught how to think about and regulate their own "brain" behaviors when it comes to learning new and unfamiliar subject matter (Blakely and Spence, 1990). As we monitor and assess student progress, it is necessary to engage in frequent dialogue with students. This is one of the purposes for which the Cardinal Questions were developed. They can prove invaluable in the process of assisting students with understanding and becoming responsible for their own learning.

Finally, as we wrap up the subject of teacher and student accountability, it makes sense for us to zoom in on the world of Response To Intervention (RTI) and Curriculum Based Measurement (CBM). The next two chapters address ways to advance accountability through adoption of a process that responds to student problems through interventions and measurement techniques that lead to all students acquiring math literacy.

As we reflect back on our friend Charlie Brown, it comes as no surprise that Snoopy will probably never whistle (never say never!), and thank goodness it's not necessary for him to do so. Students, on the other hand, can and must learn math in order to carry out the demands (e.g., organization, deduction, logic and thinking in general) of the society in which we live (Dickman, 2008). Fortunately, attention to math research is gaining momentum and an increasing amount of information about what it takes to attain this goal is available. The remaining challenge becomes utilization of this knowledge in today's classrooms. No more excuses accepted—it's time to pay attention to the signs and learn again.

> *"Here I am, just waiting for a sign.*
> *Asking questions, learning all the time."*
> —Kansas, *Miracles Out Of Nowhere*

Suggested Resources

Brain Connection: The Brain and Learning—www.brainconnection.com

Caine, R.,N., Caine, G., McClinic, C. L., & Klimek, K. J. (2004). *12 brain/ mind learning principles in action: The fieldbook for making connections, teaching, and the human brain.* CA: Corwin Press.

Feurerstein, R., Feurerstein, R., Falik, L., & Rand, Y. (2006). *Creating and enhancing cognitive modifiability: The feuerstein instrumental enrichment program.* Israel: ICELP Publications.

Gardner, H. (1983). *Frames of mind: The theory of multiple intelligences.* New York, NY: Basic Books.

Gardner, H. (1993). *The unschooled mind: How children think and how schools should teach.* New York, New York: Basic Books.

Jensen, E. (1998). *Teaching with the brain in mind.* VA: ASCD Publications.

Leaver, B. L. (1997). *Teaching the whole class.* CA: Corwin Press.

Mamchur, C. (1996). *A teacher's guide to cognitive type theory & learning style.* Alexandria, VA: ASCD.

McCloskey, G., (2007). PDF file. *The Role of Executive Functions in Childhood Learning and Behavior.*

New Horizons for Learning: News from the Neurosciences http://www.newhorizons.org/neuro/front_neuro.html

Chapter 3
Response To Intervention

"Here and now, I believe there are solutions to the problems we see.
We should all take a chance, don't be afraid to lend a helping hand.
This world could be so beautiful, if we just worked together
to make a difference today."
—Shawn Desman, *Difference*

The Response To Intervention (RTI) approach represents a process for assessing and maximizing the "opportunity to learn" for students who are struggling in any content area. It emphasizes the importance of effective, culturally responsive instruction and early intervening services for all students prior to making a referral to special education. Through the use of an RTI approach, instead of the discrepancy model used exclusively in the past, we remove the harmful effects of delaying intervention until a student's achievement is so low that there is little hope of "catching up." In the authors' view, Response To Intervention is a "makes sense" process for addressing the difficulties students have in the classroom. It works because the focus is on identifying students' specific areas of strength as well as need, and intervening early rather than waiting for failure or ignoring the problem and moving the student along according to program timelines.

The attributes of Response To Intervention are underscored in NCLB and the reauthorized IDEA, 2004, law with the expectation that all staff in a school/district are accountable for results. These attributes as they pertain to mathematics include:

1. **High-quality, culturally responsive classroom instruction**—The underlying assumption is that all children are receiving at least **one hour of math instruction daily,** 90 minutes of core reading instruction, as well as ample science instruction. This instruction is delivered

by teachers who are not only highly qualified according to NCLB, but who also have a working knowledge of differentiated instruction which includes the tenets of Universal Design for Learning (UDL) and Understanding by Design (UbD).

2. **Focused and well-sequenced math instruction**—The mathematics instruction/curriculum that is provided to students reflects the accumulation of research on how children best learn math and how to assist those struggling with the acquisition of basic math concepts. This includes systematic, direct instruction of math concepts, language, symbols, the number system, computation and problem solving. Additionally, in order to meet a broad range of students' abilities, the classroom teacher differentiates instruction by providing appropriate choices, real life examples, enrichment and/or intervention to increase student achievement.

3. **Universal Screening and Benchmarking**—Tools such as Curriculum Based Measurement (a direct assessment method) are used to identify levels of proficiency and rate of learning for each student in essential academics. The results should allow for review of both group and individual performance of specific skills. Benchmarking or obtaining snapshots of student learning occur at a minimum three times a year or more often if additional data is needed.

4. **Progress Monitoring**—Brief assessments are used to make informed instructional decisions relative to a student's progress/achievement as a result of instruction or intervention.

5. **Adoption and early implementation of research-based interventions**—This involves making early decisions for the provision of interventions in the classroom or targeted interventions that are in addition to the core mathematics program. These techniques can be standard protocols or individually designed. Most often, the type of intervention to be used is determined with the assistance of a problem-solving team or instructional support team.

6. **Progress Monitoring during intervention**—Student progress is monitored frequently and instruction is fine tuned based on student

response to the intervention. Data that indicates a substantial lack of progress would signal the need for additional instruction at increasing levels of intensity, using interventions that pinpoint and target the specific skill deficit.

7. Fidelity Measures—This speaks to the level of effectiveness of the instruction/intervention that is provided to students. Observational checklists can be used to assess whether the intervention and/or data collection is being implemented as intended and with consistency.

Response To Intervention is best depicted as a model that incorporates the use of a tiered system which emphasizes accountability and academic supports. This tiered system mirrors that used by the Positive Behavioral Intervention Supports (PBIS) model which focuses on a school wide approach to addressing student behavior (Horner & Sugai, 1999). For optimal results, schools that have a PBIS team in place and/or some form of academic support team can combine the members of both teams to address academic and behavioral concerns. Within the constructs of a three-tiered model (see below), the provision of validated curriculum, effective instruction and positive behavioral supports for all students is paramount.

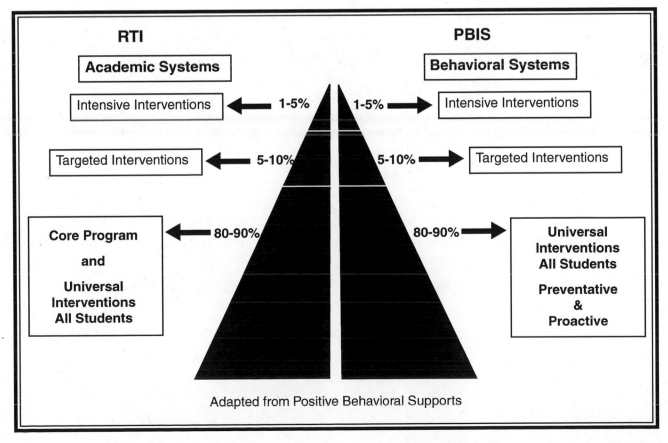

Adapted from Positive Behavioral Supports

Prior to implementation of the RTI process, a school-wide plan should be developed by the building administration in collaboration with their staff. We have provided an RTI Planning Document, Appendix B, to assist in the planning process using the step-by-step sequence below.

RTI Planning Sequence

1. Identify the core math program and determine if the program addresses the essential concepts and standards set forth by the National Council of Teachers of Mathematics. Don't forget to review the core reading program to ensure alignment with the five essential precepts of the National Reading Panel (see *RTI: The Classroom Connection for Literacy,* Kemp & Eaton, 2007).

2. Choose a universal screening tool that reflects the intended purpose and meet the needs of the staff and district.

3. Verify that the math curriculum is being implemented with fidelity and integrity throughout the building. You may want to assess these two facets of your school's math curriculum by using guidelines established in the Effective Practices that Support Teaching and Learning of Mathematics and Science published by the Northwest Regional Educational Laboratory Mathematics and Science Education Center.

4. Identify interventions and supports that are available in the district/school to address the challenges presented by students who are not achieving in mathematics.

5. Categorize the available interventions according to the type and intensity of the services to be provided at each tier.

6. Obtain additional materials and supports wherever gaps exist.

7. Assess the existing building support teams and modify or form a building problem-solving team to assist in the successful implementation of the RTI process.

It is important to stress that intervention at any level should never be a substitute for high-quality classroom instruction. There must be a solid instructional foundation in place at the base of the pyramid (Tier I) for successful implementation of the RTI process.

A Three-Tiered Approach

Universal Screening—Prior to implementing Response To Intervention, school staff must decide what screening tool they will use to obtain data about student performance. This decision requires thoughtful consideration as the chosen screening tool becomes an integral part of the overall RTI process. The assessment tools most suitable for screening an entire school population are those that are quick to administer, efficient to score and valid indicators of general outcomes in the specific content area. These criteria are important as the screening is administered at least three times a year to all students for benchmarking purposes. Some examples of available screening tools include paper/pencil fluency probes and Web-based computer programs (e.g., AIMSweb, MBSP, DIBELS). The data gathered from each screening administration is reviewed in a timely manner to identify the students who have achieved the target benchmarks and those in need of additional instruction/intervention.

There is no right way to "set up" benchmark screenings. Some schools establish an assessment team of five or six staff members who are not classroom teachers (building administrators, psychologists, reading/math specialists, speech therapists, special education teachers, etc.) to administer the screening to all grade levels. This group can then serve as the "review team" to organize the data, communicate the results and make decisions about scheduling and provision of interventions.

Other schools have classroom teachers conduct their own screenings. Loss of instructional time is almost always an issue in this case. Therefore, it often makes sense to have someone other than the classroom teacher conduct the benchmarks three times a year and make the progress-monitoring component the responsibility of the teacher. If the building administrator is not on the assessment team, he/she should become a part of the team when it comes time to share student results with the teachers and plan for interventions.

The availability of alternate formats for progress monitoring students who receive interventions between benchmarks is yet another factor to consider when make a screening tool choice. We suggest taking a look at the National Center on Student Progress Monitoring website (www. studentprogress.org), which is supported by the U.S. Office of Special Education Programs (OSEP). There you will find a guide to data collection tools that can be used to make informed decisions about scientifically-based ways of meeting your school and classroom needs.

Tier I—Classroom Instruction and Interventions

This tier is generally viewed as the base of the pyramid where all students receive instruction in the core math program with differentiation provided to address student variability. Opportunities for students to learn key concepts in a variety of ways are critical at this tier. Best practices such as Universal Design for Learning (UDL) and Understanding by Design (UbD) assist educators in designing instruction to teach the acquisition of mathematic concepts and meet the needs of most of the students in the classroom.

Universal Design for Learning (UDL)

The concept of UDL is one component of Universal Design, which is defined in the Assistive Technology Act of 1998 (P.L. 105-394, S. 2432) as, "A concept or philosophy for designing and delivering products and services that are usable by people with the widest possible range of functional capabilities... includes products and services that are directly usable (without requiring assistive technologies) and... that are made usable with assistive technologies."

The Center for Applied Special Technology (CAST) defines the concept of Universal Design for Learning (UDL) in the following way: "UDL provides a blueprint for creating flexible goals, methods, materials, and assessments that accommodate learner differences." They continue by clarifying that "universal" does not imply a single optimal solution for everyone. Instead, it underscores the need for multiple approaches to meet the needs of diverse learners. A universally designed curriculum calls for the use of the following principles in order to provide equal access to all learners:

- multiple means of representation to give learners various ways of acquiring information and knowledge;

- multiple means of expression to provide learners alternatives for demonstrating what they know;
- multiple means of engagement to tap into learners' interests, challenge them appropriately and motivate them to learn.

Understanding by Design (UbD)

The conceptual framework in Understanding by Design (UbD), developed by Wiggins and McTighe (1998), provides major contributions to instructional models. The premise of the UbD model for planning instruction is based on "backward" design or "beginning with the end in mind." This means first, identifying the desired outcomes of instruction; second, determining acceptable evidence of learning; and then—and only then— planning experiences and instruction. Without this "backward" design for planning, instruction often becomes nice activities or superficial coverage of content. Backward design necessitates an understanding of the big ideas or essential questions underlying knowledge. Embedded in the essential questions are the Six Facets of Understanding which are to explain, interpret, apply, have perspective, empathize and have self-knowledge. This model allows students to deepen their learning and experience an enduring understanding of content. Teachers who desire to accommodate the needs of all learners in their classrooms will be interested in exploring both UDL and UbD in depth.

If instruction is effective and appropriate in Tier I, 80-90 percent of students will respond and achieve the established benchmarks at this tier. The use of the universal screening provides the data needed to determine which students are not reaching established benchmarks. These students then become candidates for classroom interventions. These interventions consist of changing delivery or design of instruction, scaffolding instruction by pre-teaching, using visuals, providing additional practice opportunities, teaching the concept in a different way or even using one of the techniques found in subsequent chapters of this book. Throughout implementation of a classroom intervention, teachers are encouraged to use the Teacher Key Planning Form, Appendix B, p. 250, and one of the Student Tracking Forms, Appendix B, pp. 251-253, provided in this book. These forms are illustrated in some of the techniques in each chapter and serve as documentation of intervention planning and progress monitoring for the teacher. If a student continues to have difficulty after implementation of strategically chosen interventions in the classroom, the planning documentation and data collected will help the building team determine next steps in Tier II.

Tier II—Supplemental Targeted Intervention

At this tier, more often than not, a building problem-solving or assessment review team becomes involved. Determinations for interventions may occur immediately after benchmarks are administered, or teachers may request the assistance of the building team based on a student's lack of progress. If a building team is utilized, the teacher is expected to supply all documentation of attempted Tier I interventions along with relevant data (e.g., checklists, progress monitoring graphs, running records). This information helps team members determine the appropriate course of action. A plan of action is developed to target the specific skill deficit through supplemental instruction or an identified intervention.

Interventions at Tier II should always be research-based and are most often delivered by someone other than the classroom teacher. The intervention is considered to be short term and targeted, lasting for at least six to eight weeks, or longer if necessary. Progress monitoring occurs more frequently (minimally bi-weekly) in order to track the student's response to the intervention. The responsibility for progress monitoring usually shifts to the individual providing the intervention. The length of time a student remains in Tier II is determined by the individual student's response (Atkins et al, 2007). For best results, the intervention must be provided in addition to the core math instruction at least two to three times a week for at least 20-30 minutes each session (Torgesen, 2004).

When deciding on the appropriate intervention, the team will want to clearly identify the specific skill deficit (e.g., concepts, language, numbers, computation) to provide the best possible intervention for that area of concern (Wright, 2007). Students can be grouped for intervention instruction if they share a common skill deficit. Students will not benefit if the needs of the group are varied. If the intervention is a good match, all but five to ten percent of the students should show progress and reintegrate successfully into the classroom instructional program. Students who fail to display meaningful progress at Tier II may be recommended for another intervention at this level or considered for a more intensive intervention at Tier III with the help of a building team.

Tier III—Intensive Intervention

This tier generally requires the utilization of a different systematic research-based approach to math. To promote growth, this highly intensive intervention must continue to address the student's specific area(s) of need. There are many different approaches and/or programs available at this tier. To ensure the best match with the student's deficit, careful deliberation of the most appropriate intervention should occur prior to implementation. Interventions at this level should be delivered for 45-60 minutes a day in addition to the 60 minutes of core math instruction. Tier III interventions can be administered in two blocks of time or all at once. The timeline for implementation at this tier is roughly 8-12 weeks, but can be shortened or extended depending on the student's success or lack thereof. Again, the individual providing the intervention monitors the student at least once a week to obtain the data necessary for making decisions related to skill acquisition and learning. If the intervention is successful, the student may continue at this level until such time as he/she can return to a Tier II status or in some cases return to the classroom math program.

If the student's response data continue to show achievement below that of his/her peers without an appropriate rate of increase, then referral to special education may be considered. The difference between the referral process using RTI and traditional approaches is clearly evident. With RTI, the student does not have to "wait to fail" before obtaining additional support. The substantial amount of information and data that is gathered reveals a great deal about the student's difficulties and is considered an integral part of the evaluation. We are obligated to point out that Response To Intervention should never be used to keep a student in a holding pattern. If interventions implemented with fidelity are not working after a reasonable amount of time, alternate decisions that are in the best interest of the student must be made.

> **Response To Intervention should never be about keeping a student in a holding pattern.**

If a referral to special education is pursued, the need for additional testing is discussed by those conducting the evaluation once all existing information has been submitted and reviewed. RTI in itself does not take the place of a comprehensive evaluation. A social history, physical classroom observation, along with other areas of concern may precipitate the need for further assessments. The parent and/or multi-disciplinary team can determine what additional information is needed and how to obtain it appropriately.

For ease of documentation and to track individual students' profiles throughout the RTI process, we've created a reproducible form entitled Intervention Tracking Form, Appendix B. This form provides a comprehensive view of accommodations, assessments and interventions. The completed form is accompanied by charts or graphs that will help stakeholders make informed decisions about a student's performance and subsequent needs.

Although the RTI process requires time and creativity, the benefits are all encompassing. Neither parents, teachers, nor administrators have to wait for a student to exhibit extreme difficulties before identifying the child as a struggling learner. All students receive high-quality classroom instruction and intervention simultaneously, as needed. Everyone, including the student, is aware of the student's progress at any given time throughout the year. The focus is on teaching students to become competent in math by ensuring adequate opportunity for them to learn and achieve before they fall behind and/or fall prey to the math phobias and anxieties discussed in Chapter 1.

> **RTI requires general education and special education to operate as a seamless system.**

RTI requires general education and special education to operate as a seamless system. The changes called for are not radical, nor are they brand new; however, it is reasonable to assume that, with any refocus of an educational practice, in this case RTI, there will be challenges to overcome. These include planning for professional development, obtaining resources, providing technical assistance, adapting to change and resolving specific issues as they arise.

One way to address these anticipated challenges is to use the interventions presented in this book. These techniques are suggested for use at the classroom level (Tier I), although many can also be implemented during Tier II if delivered with more intensity or for an extended duration. When implemented with fidelity and documented with consistency, these techniques provide teachers with the information and data necessary to demonstrate a student's lack of achievement or success.

And so, the decree to address the learning needs of all students has been issued. Take a chance and step outside your world. Find the time for solutions and embrace the opportunity that finally permits you to focus on results and outcomes for students rather than on testing and eligibility.

"Living in my own world, didn't understand that anything can happen, when you take a chance."
—Vanessa Hudgens, *Start of Something New*

Suggested Resources

Bender, W. & Shores, C. (2007). *Response to intervention: A practical guide for every teacher.* CA: Corwin Press.

Bryant, D. & Bryant, B.R. (2006). *An emerging model: Three-tier mathematics intervention model (K-2).* Austin, Texas: Special Education Research Project: Mathematics. Available: http://www.centeroninstruction.org. files/SERP-MathAIR1-07ppt.pdf.

Hardcastle, B. & Justice, K. (2006). *RTI and the classroom teacher.* Palm Beach Gardens, FL: LRP Publications.

Mallard, D. F.& Johnson, E. (2007). *RTI: A practitioner's guide to implementing response to intervention.* CA: Corwin Press.

Norlander, K. (2007). *RTI Tackles the LD Explosion (video).* Port Chester, NY: National Professional Resources, Inc.

Wiggins, G. & McTighe, J. (2005). *Understanding by design (2nd edition).* Alexandria, VA: Association for Supervision and Curriculum Development.

Wiggins, G. & McTighe, J. (2004). *Understanding by design professional development workbook.* Alexandria, VA: Association for Supervision and Curriculum Development.

Wright, J. (2007). *RTI toolkit: A practical guide for schools.* Port Chester, NY: National Professional Resources, Inc.

Center for Applied Special Technology—http://www.cast.org

IDEA Partnership—http://www.ideapartnership.org

Intervention Central-RTI Readiness Survey and School Based Instructional Teams—http://www.interventioncentral.com

Northwest Regional Educational Laboratory-Mathematics and Science Education Center, Effective Practices that Support Teaching and Learning of Mathematics and Science—http://www.nwrel.org/msec/

RTI Action Network—http://www.rtinetwork.org

The Access Center, Improving Outcomes for All Students K-8—http://www.k8accesscenter.org

Understanding by Design Exchange Website—http://ubd.ascd.org

Chapter 4
Curriculum Based Measurement

"Can you see the magic numbers, falling from the sky,
Trying to get inside my head, but I just don't know why."
—Powergod, *Salvation*

As part of a multi-tiered intervention model, it is more than just good practice to assess student progress on a regular basis—it is essential. Progress monitoring and the collection of data is important for determining the success of an intervention. Questioning and using data for decision making become integral parts of the instructional process. Is the intervention working? Is the student learning? How long should the intervention be continued? These and other questions provide information for both the teacher and the school-based support team which is vital for determining student performance.

The previous chapters emphasize how important it is to provide effective, differentiated instruction and appropriate interventions when students are not making progress. If educators are spending time planning in order to provide the best instruction possible, doesn't it make sense to find out whether that plan is working? Of course it does! Assessment is considered the foundation of the learning process and is key to guiding meaningful instruction. In many cases, assessment of learning occurs at the end of a unit of instruction. Unfortunately, by that point, if teachers find that students missed critical concepts or skills they are usually unable to go back and re-teach the material due to time constraints, curriculum schedules, etc. Because assessment is such a critical part of

> **If educators are spending time planning in order to provide the best instruction possible, doesn't it make sense to find out if that plan is working?**

the instructional cycle, it should not be viewed as a separate activity but as an ongoing part of instruction. Instead of waiting until the end of a chapter, unit or block of instruction to find that a student has not learned, it is best to assess throughout instruction. Results from assessments that are administered frequently allow teachers to base their instruction on multiple data to meet the specific needs of each student. One reliable and valid way to do this is through the use of curriculum based measures.

Curriculum Based Measurement (CBM) is an offspring of a specific set of procedures developed at the University of Minnesota by Stan Deno in 1985 and work done by Ogden Lindsley at the University of Kansas. Curriculum Based Measurement is best defined as direct, repeated assessments, administered frequently in order to make decisions about student learning. This method is not only a valuable decision-making tool for teachers, but it can also be an influential motivator for students. Progress Monitoring (PM) through the use of curriculum based measures is designed to estimate and predict rates of student improvement, identify students who are not demonstrating adequate progress and assist in the development of more effective, individualized instructional programs for struggling learners. To understand how CBM differs from traditional assessments, a comparison of purpose, construct and scoring between these two types of assessment is depicted in Figure 1.

Figure 1: Comparison of Traditional and Curricululm Based Assessments

Assessment	Purpose	Construct	Scoring
Traditional	Summative—administered at the end of a unit	Time and format changes depending on content	Single score or grade usually reported in percent. Cannot be used to predict future learning
Curriculum Based Measures	Formative—administered several times during a unit	Time remains constant and probes are always in the same format with content that is different but similar	Scores reported in terms of fluency rates. Results are charted to determine progress and predict learning

As seen in Table 1, the critical difference between CBM and traditional assessment is that CBM is a formative assessment with the primary purpose of pinpointing skill deficits efficiently, thereby enabling teachers to make decisions about student performance and appropriate instruction. The measures have particular relevance to the classroom in that they are drawn from the curriculum. Additionally, similar forms of a CBM probe can be developed and used as a progress-monitoring tool throughout an intervention. This is because the measures are sensitive enough to be administered more than once during the assessment period without allowing students to become test smart. Scores are reported using fluency rates and can be used to make predictions about student learning based on established local or national norms.

CBM methods are practical and simple in their administration yet yield very useful information including the skill the student needs to learn, the rate at which he works and the conditions under which he is able to complete the tasks (Hosp, Hosp & Howell, 2007). Recording data in chart form provides a valuable record of student progress that is easily interpreted by others (Figure 2). Data Collection Sheet and Chart Templates are available, at the end of Appendix A.

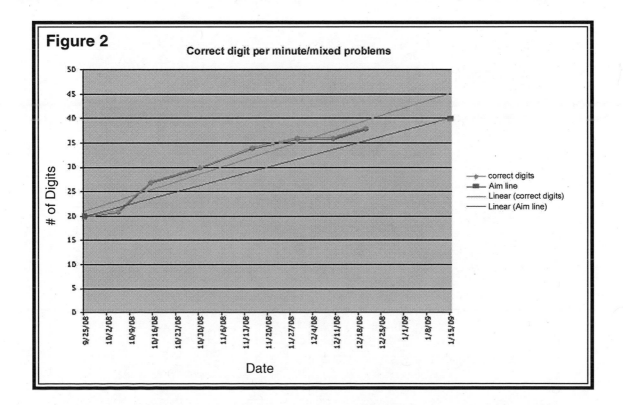

Figure 2

Correct digit per minute/mixed problems

The data derived from the assessments can be used to track the progress of an entire class, assign students to instructional groups or determine the appropriate interventions within an RTI process (Shinn, 2002). Additionally, CBM charts can serve as a powerful communication tool for parent conferences and questions related to student performance (Shinn, Habedank, & Good, 1993).

The process of CBM is important to understand. Students are assessed in different skill areas on a weekly, biweekly or monthly basis. Probes take from one to seven minutes to administer depending on the skill area. The score is reported as the number of correct and incorrect responses during the time period and is an overall indicator of student academic competence. Recording the results on a chart or graph (Figure 3) provides a visual display of how much the student is learning. Each time a score is recorded, the graphic representation becomes a dynamic framework for making decisions about the student's skill acquisition and progress. For example, when the data shows that a student is not learning at the expected rate, a decision can be made to make a change (Fuchs et al., 1993). Changes can include instructional techniques, length or intensity of instruction, different materials, group size and additional practice within the classroom, as well as interventions that may be provided outside the classroom. These changes can be coded on the student's chart to keep track of the type of changes made and when they occurred during the school year. If the student is making progress, the teacher can make

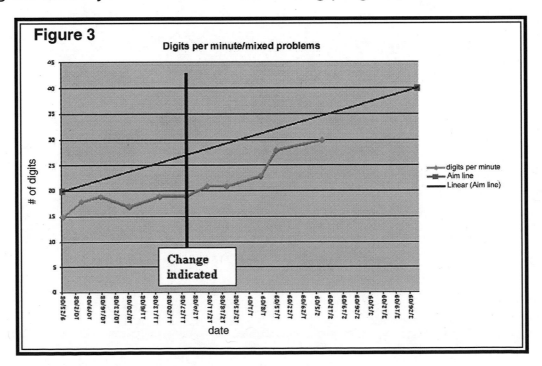

a decision to continue with the current instruction. Decisions about student progress can be viewed in terms of improving, maintaining or declining and always follow explicit decision-making rules. If you are interested in exploring charting and decision making further, it is recommended that you consult the resources listed at the end of the chapter.

There are multiple benefits to CBM. The research conducted in the past 30 years has expanded the use of Curriculum Based Measurement, making it more than just a means of evaluating instruction. It is now widely used as a universal screening, a school wide accountability tool and a method to address disproportionality. Perhaps even more importantly, it can be used as a way to predict student success on high-stakes testing (Stecker et al., 2005). It is important to note that CBM probes are not meant to determine a student's overall knowledge of a content area and as a rule are not diagnostic. However, oral reading probes, writing probes and math probes can identify skill deficits if the person administering the probe effectively documents observations.

CBM probes are published for many skill areas. One of the most widely used tools for math is AIMSweb. Other published probes include Skill Builders from Sopris West and the Fuchs & Fuchs at Vanderbilt/Peabody University. Many of these sources also provide online computer scoring programs that allow the user to keep track of individual benchmarks, determine trend lines, compare results to norms and indicate instructional changes. Additional information about these computer tools can be found at the end of the chapter. If any of these probes or online programs are being used to monitor student progress, they can also serve as the measurement for some of the interventions in this book. Alternatively, if there is no screening or monitoring tool in place for your classroom, this book describes an appropriate probe for each of the interventions along with expected benchmarks. Several of the probes are classroom ready, while others are examples that include directions for development and administration. So remember, "estimates considered, logic required, data imperative," because numbers are what it's all about.

"No miracles or wonders is what life's bringing,
It's all about numbers that'll make the world go round."
—Louise Hoffsten, *All About Numbers*

Suggested Resources

Beck, R., Conrad, D., & Anderson, P., (2008). *Basic skill builders.* Longmont, CO: Sopris West Educational Services.

Hosp, M., Hosp, J., & Howell, K. (2006). *The ABC's of CBM.* New York, NY: The Guilford Press.

Rose, C. M., Minton, L., Arline, C. (2007). *Uncovering student thinking in mathematics.* CA: Corwin Press.

Wright, J. (2007). *RTI Toolkit: A practical guide for schools.* Port Chester, NY: National Professional Resources, Inc.

IDEA Partnership Web-Based Resources for Practitioners: Classroom Assessment, updated in May 2008— http://www.ideapartnership.org/report.cfm?reportid=141

National Center on Student Progress Monitoring— http://www.studentprogress.org

Research Institute on Progress Monitoring— http://www.progressmonitoring.org

The IRIS Center—http://iris.peabody.vanderbilt.edu/

Intervention Central, Jim Wright—http://www.interventioncentral.com

CBM Probes

Computer Based Data Management Programs: AIMSweb from Edformation, Inc.—http://www.edformation.com

DIBELS from Sopris West Inc— http://www.sopriswest.com or http://dibels.uoregon.edu

Edcheckup from WebEdCo—http://www.edcheckup.com

mClass software—http://www.wirelessgeneration.com/products.html

Monitoring Basic Skills Progress (MBSP) from Pro-Ed— http://www.proedinc.com

Using CBM for Progress Monitoring, Lynn Fuchs & Doug Fuchs Vanderbilt University

Utah Personnel Development Center— http://www.updc.org/initiatives/math/CBM_probes.html

Yearly ProgressPro from McGraw-Hill—http://www.mhdigitallearning.com

Chapter 5
About Language and Concepts

"How many seas must the white dove sail,
before she sleeps in the sand?"
—Bob Dylan, *Blowin' in the Wind*

Just what is it about math that seems to present such a challenge to so many? While thinking about this chapter, the fifty basic language concepts of the Boehm Test of Basic Concepts (Boehm, 1976) kept coming to mind. While working with her students, co-author Mary Ann Eaton, a speech and language pathologist, recognized these concepts as "the language of school" or "the language of directions." She realized that many of her students were having difficulty mastering these concepts and applying them in the classroom. Furthermore, it became apparent that the classroom-based language interventions she was using were also relevant to developing early math concepts. Not surprisingly, she then discovered that many of her students with language delays were experiencing challenges in both learning to read and developing math skills. The co-morbidity of language and math deficits is now well documented. Children who demonstrate phonologically based reading difficulties also exhibit difficulties in arithmetic retrieval. Students who display reading comprehension challenges also demonstrate math problem solving difficulties (Light & Defries, 1995).

Further experiences led to the conclusion that students' classroom performance is dependent upon their ability to understand and apply basic language concepts. These concepts appear continuously throughout the school curriculum. They are embedded in the language of directions related to classroom management (sometimes referred to as the hidden curriculum). Consequently, concepts related to the teaching of reading clearly apply to the teaching of mathematics. While the authors recognize the relevance of these concepts to school readiness in general, for the purposes of this book we will address the concepts inherent to the acquisition of math literacy.

While researching techniques for effective mathematics instruction, the notion of mathematics as a language became more evident. It was determined to use the Cardinal Questions as a thinking framework. What do we know about math? What do we do with math? When all is said and done, math is about adding, subtracting, and dividing for the purpose of measurement. We measure quantity, time and space. Adding is about counting things (quantity) as you join them together, subtracting is about counting things (quantity) as you separate them, and dividing is about separating things into equal amounts. Math is about deciphering relationships or comparing and contrasting quantities through the use of numerical symbols and language to communicate. Ultimately, math is about measurements and comparison of those measurements.

Math is the tool that assists us in making sense of how we perceive our world. While reading and spelling are thinking with letters, imagery and language, math is thinking with numbers, imagery and language. Both reading and math are cognitive processes that require dual coding or the assimilation of language and imagery. To become skilled in math fundamentals one must integrate two aspects of imagery: symbol/numeral imagery (parts/details) and concept imagery (whole/gestalt) (Tuley & Bell, 1997). Therefore, it is critical for educators to instruct and assess the language students use to communicate their perceptions of numeric symbol imagery and conceptual imagery.

Educators must think about language and how it evolves as we emerge from our egocentric infant worlds and develop perspectives of our surroundings. Through our five senses we are immersed in making meaning of our surroundings. As infants we cry when we are uncomfortable, when we have too little or too much of something. Inherently, we make comparisons about quantity, space, sound and time. While using our five senses we are also immersed in learning language. Infants in an English-speaking environment are exposed to words that describe the attributes of our existence, such as wet or dry, hungry or not hungry, thirsty or not thirsty, asleep or awake, light or dark, loud or quiet, more or less, etc. Comparisons of what is comfortable and uncomfortable in our lives are made and labeled using sight, hearing and touch as referents. It is important to recognize that the rudiments of math and its associated language are based in the act of comparing and contrasting, thereby using vocabulary to describe these opposite relationships. (See Appendix B, p. 254, for a list of Basic Language Concepts for Math.)

Consider further that the act of comparing is the act that eventually addresses the concept of equal, which is the very underpinning of math equations. The human ability or lack of ability to compare is at the heart of the research of Reuven Feuerstein and forms the basis for his work and research on cognitive modifiability (Feuerstein et al., 2006). It follows that with exposure to, experience with, and instruction in basic language concepts, humans become able to communicate our perceptions of the world. Eventually, we use numbers (mathematics) to refine and define these comparative relationships.

It seems obvious then for educators to wonder about the early language concepts children bring to school. We know we are products of our life experiences (background knowledge) and these are embedded in our personal stories. It therefore stands to reason that educators must first explore students' understanding and use of the basic language concepts that describe their worlds. Conversations with students may provide valuable insight into the language they know and use day to day, as well as the attributes that define their own perceptions.

An effective mathematics curriculum includes explicit language instruction. During instruction of basic language concepts, a discerning teacher will recognize when a student is not demonstrating mastery of essential language skills and will pursue assessment. To assist, we offer the Cardinal Questions as they relate to basic language concepts:

1. **What does the student know** about language that is implicit to describing his/her perceptions of the world?
   - What is the student's first language?
   - How would you describe the student's oral language skills?
   - What basic language concepts does the student know?

2. **What does the student do** when asked to demonstrate understanding of basic language concepts?
   - Does the student identify word opposites or antonyms?
   - Does the student compare and contrast?
   - Does the student sequence and then describe the pattern?
   - Does the student classify utilizing at least one attribute?
   - Does the student classify utilizing more than one attribute?
   - Does the student describe same and different attributes of his/her perceptions of his/her environment when engaging in discourse?
   - Does the student move his/her body appropriately when following directions that incorporate the basic language concepts?
   - Does the student manipulate objects when following directions that incorporate the basic concepts?

Once you have assessed the student's language skills and are ready to begin preparation for intervention, think about the remaining three Cardinal Questions:

3. **How does the student learn?** (See Chapter Two)

4. **How does the student approach or react to an unfamiliar task?** (See Chapter Two)

5. **What will you do with the knowledge gained from answering the previous four questions?**

Armed with this information, the following five techniques will assist you in teaching language concepts:

1. Movin' and Groovin'
2. Do You See What I See?
3. Sequence Sequester
4. Matchmaker
5. Potent Potentials

"So I go sailing, through the rivers of my mind,
I go sailing, be surprised what you can find,
I go sailing, through the rivers of my mind,
Take a chance on your mind, be surprised what you'll find."
—Stevie Wonder, *I Go Sailing*

Math Language and Concepts—1
Movin' and Groovin'—The Power of Opposites

What it is: A technique for developing understanding of and use of word opposites that address direction and space.

When to use it: When students need to learn how to apply word opposites in order to follow classroom instructions (e.g., left/right, top/bottom, forward/backward).

⚠ Prerequisites are the ability to attend and cooperate when asked to follow directions.

Benefit: Students will build their mathematical lexicon.

Materials:
- Blank 3" x 5" and/or 5" x 8" cards, 8" x 10" cardstock
- A variety of age-appropriate manipulatives (e.g., blocks, miniature people, vehicles and animals)
- Pictures from books, magazines, and/or photos of students engaged in activities in and around school or home
- Markers, paper, pencils, pens
- Stopwatch
- Overhead projector and/or easel with large paper
- Teacher Key Planning Form, Appendix B, p. 250
- Tracking Progress Form, Appendix B, p. 251
- Language and Concepts Probe, Appendix A, pp. 203-204

Implementation Steps:
Part A: Movin' and Groovin'—Me, Myself, and I

1. Explain to students that you are going to play a game called Movin' and Groovin'. This game is about moving in opposite directions (forward and backward). You may want to write these words on the blank cards for future use. Conduct this activity in a large area where students can move freely and use climbing apparatus. Don't forget to include the gym teacher in this lesson!

2. Demonstrate and model the following: "I will say, Move forward, start." Start moving forward. Say, "Groove," then stop. Ask, "Am I in the groove?" Reply, "I'm in the groove, 'cause, I moved forward."

3. Continue with the demonstration. Say, "Move backward, start." Start moving backward. Say, "Groove," then stop. Ask, "Am I in the groove?" Reply, "I'm in the groove 'cause, I moved backward."

4. Place students in lines or rows. Have them move and groove with you. Once students have the idea, ask them to follow directions by moving in a variety of ways, always pairing word opposites. The language opposite concepts that we suggest are:
   - forward/backward
   - left/right—left side/right side
   - up/down
   - toward/away from
   - near/far

Variation #1: As students demonstrate understanding of the concepts and use the related vocabulary, you can begin to add more than one language concept to the directions such as, "move forward quickly," "move backward slowly," "circle to the left," "sidestep left," "turn right and move forward."

Variation #2: Have students give the directions.

Note: As students develop number sense (rational counting) include directions utilizing numbers (e.g., "one step forward," or "two steps forward," "three big steps forward").
Planning:
   - Use the Teacher Key to create your plans for this activity. For example:

Teacher Key for Math Language and Concepts
Technique #1: Movin' and Groovin' Students learn to follow directions by moving their bodies in opposite directions. Use the related vocabulary to describe their movements.
Teacher says: "I will ask you to move in a direction and you will move together in that direction until I say 'groove,' and then you will stop where you are. When you have stopped I will ask, 'Are you in the groove?'" Together you will say 'I'm in the groove, 'cause I moved _____.'"

Sample A:
    • Move forward.
    • Move backward.
    • Move forward.
    • Move forward.
    • Move backward.
    • Move left.
    • Move right.
    • Move forward.
    • Move backward.
    • Move left.

Part B: Movin' and Groovin'—My things

Repeat Steps #1 – 4 of Part A, utilizing manipulatives such as miniature people, animals, and vehicles.

Part C: Movin' and Groovin' – Pictures, Paper, and Pencils

1. Select age-appropriate action pictures of interest to the students. Engage in discourse with students by asking them to describe location, direction, and movement in the pictures. Sample questions and statements might be:

   a) "Does anyone have a picture of something or someone that is backward in the picture?"

   b) "I see something that is on the top of the _____."

c) "What do you see at the bottom of the picture?"

d) "What is far away from the _____?"

e) "If the _____ were to move forward in this picture, where would _____ go?

2. Demonstrate how to draw arrows. Explain that arrows are a way to show direction of movement on paper.

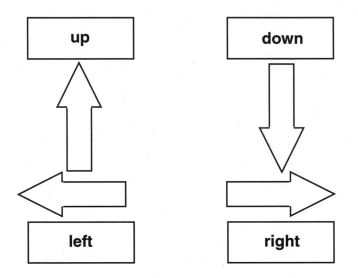

3. Have students draw pictures while you give the directions: "Draw a person on the top left of your paper. Draw a bird on the top right of your paper. Draw an arrow that shows the direction one would walk if walking forward toward the bird." Ask students to describe the direction of the arrows they drew.

4. Provide students with opportunities to draw pictures and arrows going in all directions. Engage them in discourse about their pictures and arrows.

<u>Variation #2</u>: Have students work in pairs and give each other directions.

Progress Tracking:
- Use the Tracking Progress Form to record students' daily progress each time the technique is used. For example:

Tracking Progress for Student: Tom Smith		
Technique #1, Part A: Movin' and Groovin'		
Date:_____ Student:_____		
	Vocabulary	**Moves**
Sample A:		
1. Forward	+	+
2. Backward	+	+
3. Up	+	+
4. Left	+	-
5. Right	+	-
Total	**5/5**	**3/5**

Curriculum Based Measurement: Language and Concepts Probe

Sources:

Marzano, R. (2005). *Preliminary report on the 2004–05 evaluation study of the ASCD program for building academic vocabulary.* Alexandria, VA: Association for Supervision and Curriculum Development.

Powell, W.R. (1986). Teaching vocabulary through opposition. *Journal of Reading*, 29, 617-621.

Penner, E., & Lehrer, R. (2000). The shape of fairness. *Teaching Children Mathematics*, 7(4), 210-214.

Math Language and Concepts—2:
Do You See What I See?—The Power of Perspective

What it is: A technique for developing understanding and application of basic language concepts that pertain to perception.

When to use it: When students need to develop language concepts related to perspective and imagery.

⚠️ Prerequisites are the ability to attend and cooperate when asked to follow directions.

Benefit: Students develop their mathematic lexicon.

Materials:
- Blank colored cards of varied sizes
- A variety of age-appropriate manipulatives (e.g., blocks, miniature people, vehicles and animals)
- Pictures from books, magazines, and/or photos of students engaged in activities in and around school or home
- Self-stick notepads (a variety of colors), colored paper, colored 3" x 5" cards
- Markers, paper, pencils, pens
- Stopwatch
- Overhead projector and/or easel with large paper
- Teacher Key Planning Form, Appendix B, p. 250
- Tracking Progress Form, Appendix B, p. 251
- Language and Concepts Probe, Appendix A, pp. 203-204

Implementation Steps:
Part A: The Power of Perspective—Your eyes, my eyes

1. Tell students you are going to teach them a very powerful word. It is powerful because it is a word that is used in many different ways in life. The word is perspective. Perspective refers to how each person looks at or sees (perceives) things and how they think about things. Have four students stand in a square formation (backs to each other) and have them describe what they see when they look forward

without turning their heads. Record the students' responses. Engage in discourse to explain why they see different things or have different perspectives.

2. Continue this exploration by changing perspective. Ask students to stand or sit in one place and describe what is in front of them.

Note: Developing perspective provides an opportunity to use imagery. As students become competent at describing what they see from different perspectives, introduce the idea of having them describe what they see from memory (visualization/imagery). Ask them to close their eyes and visualize what they would see if their eyes were open. Ask them to describe what they see in their mind. Be sure to use the vocabulary words visualization, imagery and imagine.

3. Explain to students that to understand perspective they must have a clear understanding of the word center. Tell them they are at the center when they stand still and turn all the way around. Tell them to turn to the left. (Demonstrate, if necessary.) Ask, "What do you see?" Repeat this activity until the students have turned all the way around. Record what they say. Compare what they said at different positions. Engage in discourse about what is the same and what is different.

4. Repeat Step #3, this time having students turn to the right, as this is the basis for clockwise, and the left, for counterclockwise. Ask them to describe what they see: what stays the same and what is different.

Note: Relevant to the understanding of perspective is the notion that objects and the environment remain constant. It is a person or the object's placement or movement that changes. This understanding helps students make conceptual connections to number lines, graphs, etc.

5. Emphasize that what they see as they look forward is their perspective from the center. Tell them that this is point zero. Everything in front of them as they look forward is away from the center. Distance is the word we use to describe how close or far away something is. Two words used to describe distance are near and far. Explain that distance can be measured.

6. Continue investigating the impact of distance on perspective. How far or near something is allows one to see the whole or part of something. Compare this to zooming in or out with a telescope or camera lens. Demonstrate whole/part perception by having students hold an object very close to their eyes. Sample questions include:
   • What do you see?
   • Do you see the whole object or only part of it?
   • What part of the object do you see?
   • What part of the object do you see in your mind?

7. Explain to students that they have been exploring perspective from a standing position. A word that can be used to describe standing is upright or vertical. Now have students explore perspective from the supine position, lying on their backs. Tell them the word used to describe lying down is horizontal. Ask them to describe what they see from their horizontal position in space. Sample discourse questions and statements might be:
   • What is above you?
   • Do you see what is above you?
   • What is below you?
   • What do you visualize is below you?

Variation #1: Have students work in pairs to explore perspective. Be sure to include art and physical education teachers in developing perspective.

Variation #2: Place an object in the center of a room or table. Have students look at the object from various places in the room. Have them draw and/or engage in discourse about how the object appears from different perspectives. Emphasize that as students move around the object it remains at the center or point zero.

The language concepts relevant to perspective are:
   • center
   • zero (as a point of reference)
   • above/below
   • front/back,
   • in front/behind

- over/under
- left side/right side
- near/far
- whole/part
- toward/away from
- next to
- beside
- clockwise/counterclockwise
- vertical/horizontal

Planning:

•Use the Teacher Key to create your plans for this activity. For example:

Teacher Key for Math Language and Concepts

Technique #2: Do You See What I See? Students describe things from different perspectives using these language concepts:

Sample A:
1. I see the front of _____.
2. I see the back of _____.
3. I see the top of _____.
4. I see the bottom of _____.
5. I see the side of _____.
6. I see the right side _____.
7. I see the left side _____.
8. I see a part of _____.
9. I see all of _____.
10. I see a piece of _____.

Part B: Do You See What I See?—My Things

1. Tell students you are going to teach them another way to think about perspective. Select miniature people, animals or vehicles. Explain that students will be asked to pretend to be that miniature person, animal or the driver of the miniature vehicle.
2. Repeat Steps #1 – 7 from Part A above.
3. This time, have students describe what their objects might see (e.g., "What would you see if you were sitting in the car?").

🗣✁ <u>Variation #1</u>: Have students use more than one manipulative at a time. Have them describe the perspective for each item they use.

Part C: Do You See What I See?—Pictures, Paper and Pencil

1. Once students have developed the concept of perspective, select age-appropriate pictures and engage in discourse with students as they describe perspective in the picture.
   Sample questions and statements:
   • What is at the center of the picture?
   • What is near/far away in the picture?
   • If you were in the picture where would you be?
   • Do you see the whole picture or part of it?
   • I see the back of the _____.
   • I see the side of the _____.
   • The _____ is very close because I see only a part of it.

2. Ask students to draw pictures from different perspectives and then engage in discourse about their pictures. Sample questions and statements:
   • Draw a person or animal lying on his/her back.
   • Draw a star above the person or animal.
   • Can the person or animal see the star above them?
   • Draw a star below the person or animal.
   • Can the person or animal see the star that is below them? Why?

Progress Tracking:
•Use the Tracking Progress Form to record students' daily progress each time the technique is used. For example:

Tracking Progress for Student: Tom Smith
Technique #2: Do you see what I see? The student uses the vocabulary to describe perspective.
Date: _____

Sample: A

	1. front	+
	2. back	+
	3. right side	+
	4. left side	+
	5. top	+
	6. center	-
	7. near	-
	8. far	+
	9. whole	+
	10. part	–
Total		**7/10**

Curriculum Based Measurement: Language and Concepts Probe

Sources:

Powell, W.R. (1986). Teaching vocabulary through opposition. *Journal of Reading,* 29, 617-62.

Penner, E., & Lehrer, R. (2000). The shape of fairness. *Teaching Children Mathematics,* 7(4), 210-214.

Marzano, R. (2005). *Preliminary report on the 2004–05 evaluation study of the ASCD program for building academic vocabulary.* Alexandria, VA: Association for Supervision and Curriculum Development.

Math Language and Concepts—3: Sequence Sequester—The Power of Order

What it is: A technique for developing understanding and use of basic language concepts pertaining to sequence and patterns.

When to use it: When students need to develop language concepts related to sequence or order and patterns.

⚠️ Prerequisite is the ability to form in a line when directed.

Benefit: Students will develop their mathematical lexicon.

Materials:
- Blank stock cards in various sizes and colors
- A variety of age-apropriate manipulatives (e.g., blocks, miniature people, vehicles and animals). Multiple examples of objects needed.
- Pictures from books, magazines, and/or photos of students engaged in activities in and around school or home environments
- Pictures from discarded books, magazines, catalogs, etc.
- Self-stick notepads (a variety of colors)
- Markers, paper, pencils, pens
- Stopwatch
- Overhead projector and/or easel with large paper
- Teacher Key Planning Form, Appendix B, p. 250
- Tracking Progress Form, Appendix B, p. 251
- Language and Concepts Probe, Appendix A, pp. 203-204

Implementation Steps:
Part A: The Line Up—Boy, Girl, Boy, Girl, Who is next?

1. Tell students you are going to teach them words related to things they already know how to do. Discuss how they line up for lunch or dismissal. Sample questions and comments include:
    - Do you always line up the same way?
    - Who is first?
    - Who is last?

2. Explain to students that you are going to teach them about putting things in a line, in a row, in a column, in order or in sequence. Ask a boy to come up and stand facing the class. Point to him and say, "Boy." Next, ask a girl to come up and stand next to the boy on his left side. Point to each student as you say, "Boy, girl." Now, ask a boy to stand next to the girl. Point to each student and say, "Boy, girl, boy." Explain to students that you are creating a pattern or sequence and that you want a girl to come next. Engage in discussion about why a girl needs to come up next. Sample comments include:
   - A boy is first, then a girl, then another boy, then another girl.
   - A boy is first. Then a girl stood next to him. Then a boy stood next to her. Then a girl stood next to him.
   - Every other student is a boy.

3. Continue until you have created a pattern or sequence that might look like this:

Point as you say, "Boy, girl, boy, girl, boy, girl, boy, girl." Have students say the sequence/pattern in unison with you. Then ask, "Who should come next, a boy or a girl?" Include these language concepts when teaching and discussing patterns and sequence:
   - first
   - second
   - third (and other ordinal numbers as required)
   - next to
   - after
   - between
   - repeat
   - repetition
   - skip
   - same
   - different
   - attribute

4. Demonstrate how to create a new sequence that would look like this:

Say the pattern aloud (girl, girl, boy, girl, girl, boy...) and discuss how it was created. Explain that this pattern is two of the same attributes and then one different attribute. With the students, create a student-friendly definition for the word attribute. For example: An attribute is a quality or element of something that makes it different from other things.

Attributes may include color, size, shape, direction, etc. Point out that tall is an attribute that describes people. Brainstorm other attributes that describe people, such as long hair, short hair, long brown hair, short brown hair, etc.

5. Repeat Step #3, creating sequences that use repeating patterns of three different attributes, then four different attributes.

Note: This is an opportunity to teach, reinforce, and/or review ordinal numbers (first, second, third, fourth, etc.) based on a sequence that repeats itself, starting at a place in the line, row, or column.

Planning:
• Use the Teacher Key to create your plans for this activity. For example:

Teacher Key for Math Language and Concepts

Technique #3: Sequencing and Patterns. Students sequence and utilize the related language.

   Sample A:
      1. Sequence repeat 2 _____
      2. Sequence repeat 3 _____
      3. Sequence repeat 4 _____
      4. Sequence repeat 5 _____
      5. Repeat 2, same 1 different _____
      6. Repeat 2, same 2 different _____
      7. Repeat 3, same 2 different _____
      8. Repeat 2, same 3 different _____
      9. Repeat pattern of 1, 2, 3 _____
      10. Repeat pattern of 3, 2, 1 _____

Part B: The Line Up—My Things

Repeat Steps #1 – 5 of Part A, having students use manipulatives to create sequences.

Note: Be sure to have students create and describe sequences that are vertical (such as towers) as well as horizontal. This will facilitate discussion about questions such as, how does before and after change when you think top to bottom and bottom to top?

Part C: The Line Up—Pictures, Paper and Pencil

Repeat Step #1 - 5 of Part A, having students cut pictures from magazines and create sequences of pictures and/or having them create sequences on paper with crayons or markers. Ask students to explain how they formed patterns in the sequence.

Progress Tracking:
• Use the Tracking Progress Form to record the students' daily progress each time the technique is used. For example:

Tracking Progress for Student: Tom Smith	
Technique #3: Sequencing and Patterns	
Date: _____	
Sample: A	
1. Sequence repeat 2	+
2. Sequence repeat 3	+
3. Sequence repeat 4	+
4. Sequence repeat 5	+
5. Repeat 2, same 1 different	
6. Repeat 2, same 2 different	
7. Repeat 3, same 2 different	
8. Repeat 2, same 3 different	
9. Repeat pattern of 1, 2, 3	
10. Repeat pattern of 3, 2, 1	
Total	**4/10**

• <u>**Curriculum Based Measurement**</u>: Language and Concepts Probe

Sources:

Marzano, R. (2005). *Preliminary report on the 2004–05 evaluation study of the ASCD program for building academic vocabulary.* Alexandria, VA: Association for Supervision and Curriculum Development.

Penner, E., & Lehrer, R. (2000). The shape of fairness. *Teaching Children Mathematics, 7*(4), 210-214.

Khisty, L. L., McLeod, D., and Bertilson, K. (1990). Speaking mathematically in bilingual classrooms: An exploratory study of teacher discourse. In G. Booker, P. Cobb, and T. Mendicutti (Eds.), *Proceedings of the fourteenth international conference for psychology of mathematics education* (Vol. 3). Mexico City: CONACYT.

Khisty, L. L. (1993). A naturalistic look at language factors in mathematics teaching in bilingual classrooms. *Proceedings of the third National Research Symposium on Limited English Proficient Student Issues: Focus on Middle and High School Issues.* Washington, DC: U.D. Department of Education, Office of Bilingual and Minority Language Affairs.

Math Language and Concepts—4: Matchmaker—The Power of Comparison

What it is: A technique for developing understanding of comparing, contrasting, and grouping based on attributes.

When to use it: When students need to develop language concepts related to similarities/differences, comparing/contrasting and grouping.

⚠ Prerequisites are the ability to sort items into at least two categories (e.g., things you wear and things you eat).

Benefit: Students develop their mathematic lexicon.

Materials:
- Blank cards of various sizes and colors
- A variety of age-appropriate manipulatives (e.g., blocks, ,miniature people, vehicles and animals)
- Cut outs or plastic squares, triangles, circles, and rectangles of different sizes and colors
- Pictures from books, magazines, or photos of students engaged in activities in and around the school and home environments
- Self-stick notepads (a variety of colors), colored paper, colored 3" x 5" cards
- Markers, paper, pencils, pens
- Overhead projector and/or easel with large paper
- Stopwatch
- Teacher Key Planning Form, Appendix B, p. 250
- Tracking Progress Form, Appendix B, p. 251
- Language and Concepts Probe, Appendix A, pp. 203-204

Implementation Steps:
Part A: Matchmaker—Me and Others

1. Tell students they will learn about the power of comparison. State, "Comparison is when you take at least two things and look at them, feel them, smell them, listen to them, or taste them to determine how they are the same or different."

2. Have students look at each other and describe how they are similar and different from one another, using the words **compare** and **comparison**. Introduce the words **attributes** and **characteristics** as you discuss tall, short, long blonde hair, short blonde hair, brown eyes, blue eyes, etc. Have fun with comparing. It is a great opportunity to get to know more about your students (favorite foods, songs, books, heroes, TV shows, video games, etc). Have them form groups based on one similar attribute and then see if they can find other similarities within that group. Have them discover ways they can pair up, find a match, or find others who are like or the same as them. Require students to use this language of comparison in their descriptions. Some language concepts relevant to comparing and contrasting include:
   - same/different
   - alike
   - match
   - pair
   - similar/dissimilar
   - compare/contrast

3. When students are adept at identifying their similarities, engage them in identifying the attributes that distinguish them as different or dissimilar from each other. Say, "When you compare and look for attributes that show differences you are looking for **contrasts**."

4. Engage in classroom discourse that communicates ways in which students can be similar and different.

Part B: Matchmaker—My Things

1. Explain to students that you are going to compare and contrast objects. We suggest that you begin with objects that differ in only one attribute; for example, start with a group of blocks that are the same size but are at least three different colors. Sort the blocks one at a time into groups by color. Talk about what you are doing. Say, "This block is red and when I compare it to this block (select another red block), I see that they are the same color. (Be certain that you use the word compare.) I am putting the blocks that are the same color in this group." Repeat the demonstration, asking students to assist you.

Engage in discourse about how many groups (sets) of blocks you have and why you have that many groups. Place all of the blocks in a bin/box and ask each student to take a turn selecting a block. After all students have chosen a block, ask them to compare the colors of the blocks they have chosen with those of their classmates.

2. Repeat comparing colored blocks as described in Step #1, except this time demonstrate how to find a different block, using the word **contrast**.

3. Repeat Steps #1 and 2 for the purpose of comparing and finding same and different attributes such as shape, size, weight, temperature, direction, etc. Be sure to use the vocabulary associated with the attributes.

Note: The concept of pair as two of a kind can be interjected here. You may want to contrast this with the language of a pair of sneakers, shoes, pants.

Note: As students develop the ability to compare and contrast using appropriate vocabulary to describe at least two attributes (e.g., color and shape), you will want to group things in different ways. For example, ask students to separate items into groups based on characteristics of their choosing and then engage in discourse about why they grouped them the way they did. Then ask them to choose another way of grouping the items and continue the discourse.

Variation #1: Have students create sequences (see Technique #3) that include shapes with different attributes (e.g., big blue square, big red square, little blue square, little red square). Ask them to describe the reason for the placement of various shapes in the sequence. Have students point to and say/read their sequence. Emphasize that they need to say/read the sequence from left to right.

Planning:
• Use the Teacher Key to create your plans for this activity.

> **Teacher Key for Math Language and Concepts**
>
> **Technique #4: Comparing and Contrasting Students**
> **Group and compare things based on similar and**
> **different attributes.**
>
> **Sample A: Similar Attributes—same**
>
> 1. **color**
> 2. **shape**
> 3. **color & shape**
> 4. **size & color**
> 5. **weight & size**
> 6. **direction—forward/backward**
> 7. **direction—up/down**

Part C: Matchmaker—Pictures, Paper and Pencil

1. Demonstrate how to draw groupings of similar things. Ask students
   to draw groups or sets of things that are similar. Explain what you are
   doing. For example, draw two circles. In one circle draw a blue, vertical
   line, and in the other circle draw a blue, horizontal line. Ask students
   to tell you what they see. What is similar between the two circles and
   what is different? This activity has many possibilities. Have students
   draw the next lines in your picture, or have them draw their own
   pictures to demonstrate grouping and then ask them to describe their
   groups to you. An overhead projector is useful for this activity.

2. Have students create pictures depicting sequence. Begin with one
   attribute, such as dots or dashes of different colors (e.g., red dot, blue
   dot, yellow dot, red dot, blue dot, yellow dot) and increase the
   number of attributes for each dot or dash (e.g., vary size). Ask them
   to draw these sequences horizontally and vertically on their papers
   and then ask them to describe the sequences. This is a great
   opportunity to have students create sequences that have arrows
   pointing in different directions, and to review left, right, up and down.

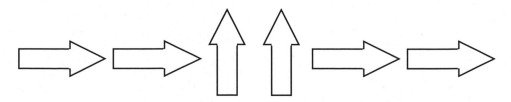

Note: Once students have developed rational counting (1:1 correspondence) and ordinal counting (first, second, third), challenge them to create sequences that depict both of these notions.

Progress Tracking:
• Use the Tracking Progress Form to record students' daily progress each time the technique is used. For example:

Tracking Progress for Student: Tom Smith	
Technique #4: Matchmaker **Student will identify similar and different attributes of things placed in sets or groups.**	
Date: _____	
Sample: A	
1. same color	+
2. same shape	+
3. same size	+
4. different color	+
5. same color & size	-
6. same size & shape	-
7. different color & size	+
Total	5/7

• <u>**Curriculum Based Measurement:**</u> Language and Concepts Probe

<u>Sources</u>:
Marzano, R. (2005). *Preliminary report on the 2004–05 evaluation study of the ASCD program for building academic vocabulary.* Alexandria, VA: Association for Supervision and Curriculum Development.

Penner, E., & Lehrer, R. (2000). The shape of fairness. *Teaching Children Mathematics, 7*(4), 210-214.

Khisty, L. L., McLeod, D., and Bertilson, K. (1990). Speaking mathematically in bilingual classrooms: An exploratory study of teacher discourse. In G. Booker, P. Cobb, and T. Mendicutti (Eds.), *Proceedings of the fourteenth international conference for psychology of mathematics education* (Vol. 3). Mexico City: CONACYT.

Math Language and Concepts—5:
Potent Potentials—All, Nothing, Some and Skip

What it is: A technique for developing understanding and use of the basic language concepts all, nothing, zero, skip, and estimation.

When to use it: When students need to learn how to describe quantities or estimate amounts.

⚠ Prerequisites are the ability to attend and cooperate when asked to follow directions.

Benefit: Students develop their mathematic lexicon.

Materials:
- Blank cardstock of various sizes
- A variety of age-appropriate manipulatives (e.g., blocks, miniature people, vehicles and animals). Have multiple examples of objects.
- Pictures from books, magazines, and/or photos of students engaged in activities in various environments
- Items (props) such as pipe cleaners, miniature flags, tennis balls etc.—at least one for every student
- Containers such as boxes, crates, pans, bowls, hula hoops
- Markers, paper, pencils, pens
- Stopwatch
- Overhead projector and/or easel with large paper
- Masking Tape
- Teacher Key Planning Form, Appendix B, p. 250
- Tracking Progress Form, Appendix B, p. 251
- Language and Concepts Probe, Appendix A, pp. 203-204

Implementation Steps:
Part A: All or Nothing and Guestimation—Me, You, Us, and No One

1. Tell students this discussion is about all or nothing. Ask students to define all and nothing. Record their definitions. Ask them whether there is a numeral that means nothing. Discuss the concept/number of zero. Demonstrate zero for students by showing them what it would

look like if there were zero teachers in the front of the room. Do you dare to show them zero teachers in the room? Only you know your students!

2. Contrast the concept of nothing or zero with the concept of all. For example, say, "I would like all of you to raise your hands. How many students have their hands raised?" (Reinforce the use of the word all). Then say, "I want none of you to raise your hand. How many students have their hands raised?" (Reinforce the use of the words none and zero). A game like Simon Says would work nicely here. Engage students in discourse utilizing the concepts of all and zero. Look up the definition of these words in a variety of dictionaries. Don't forget the online dictionaries! With your students, establish a student-friendly definition for zero and all. For example:
    • Zero means there is nothing.
    • Zero is the absence of all quantity or magnitude.
    • All means the whole amount or quantity

3. Use props such as tennis balls to demonstrate the language concepts. Engage in discourse utilizing the words all, every, whole.
   Sample questions and comments include:
    • Put all the tennis balls in the bowl.
    • Does every student have a pipe cleaner?
    • Will the whole class be able to stand in the hula hoop?

4. Explain that it is time to learn about guestimating! Teach students that to **guestimate** is to estimate the amount or quantity of something based on a reasonable guess. Some of the words used in relation to guestimating are:
    • some
    • a few
    • most
    • more than/less than
    • every

Follow a format of discussion similar to Step #3 above and have students guestimate quantities. Discourse may include statements such as:

- Some students have _____ .
- Most students have _____ .
- More students have _____ than _____ .
- Give a few students a tennis ball.

5. Introduce students to the word/concept of skipping. Ask students to define. Allow them to demonstrate. With students, develop a student-friendly definition such as: skip means to jump from one foot to another over something quickly and lightly.

6. Tell them they will learn to skip count while they skip. Using masking tape, create a number line on the floor with numerals from 0 to 30. Demonstrate different ways of walking on the number line. First, step on every number on the number line. Talk about what you are doing. Then walk without stepping on every number. Say something like, "This time I am not going to step on every number. I am going to skip every other number." Say the numbers as you step on them. Engage in classroom discourse about the numbers that you skipped. Have each student practice walking on the number line, touching every number and then skipping numbers.

Variation # 1: Have students work in pairs to practice skipping numbers on the number line. Ask them to keep track of the numbers they stepped on and the numbers they skipped.

Variation # 2: Have students line up on the number line and give props to every student, every other student, every third student, etc.

Part B: All or Nothing and Guestimation!—My Things

1. Repeat Steps #1 – 5 in Part A, this time using manipulatives.

2. Ask students to describe by "communicating" their movements (what they are doing) with their manipulatives. Sample statements include:
   - I put some _____ in the box.
   - I placed a _____ in front of every _____ .
   - I put a _____ behind every other _____ .

3. Repeat Steps #1 - 5 in Part A, this time using pictures, paper and pencil.

Planning:

- Use the Teacher Key to create your plans for this activity. For example:

Teacher Key for Math Language and Concepts
Technique # 5: Potent Potentials
Sample A: 1. All 2. Nothing 3. Zero 4. No one 5. Nobody 6. Every 7. Every other 8. Every third one 9. Some 10. Few

Progress Tracking:

- Use the Tracking Progress Form to record students' daily progress each time the technique is used. For example:

Tracking Progress for Student: Tom Smith

Technique #5: Potent Potentials

Date: _____

Sample: A	Do	Say
1. All	+	+
2. Nothing	+	+
3. Zero	-	+
4. No one	-	+
5. Nobody	+	-
6. Every	-	+
7. Every other	-	-
8. Every third	+	+
9. Some	+	-
10. Few	—	+
Do/Following Directions	5/10	
Say (Vocabulary Usage)		7/10

- **Curriculum Based Measurement**: Language and Concepts Probe

Sources:

Khisty, L. L., McLeod, D., and Bertilson, K. (1990). Speaking mathematically in bilingual classrooms: An exploratory study of teacher discourse. In G. Booker, P. Cobb, and T. Mendicutti (Eds.), *Proceedings of the fourteenth international conference for psychology of mathematics education* (Vol. 3). Mexico City: CONACYT.

Khisty, L. L. (1993). A naturalistic look at language factors in mathematics teaching in bilingual classrooms. *Proceedings of the third National Research Symposium on Limited English Proficient Student Issues: Focus on Middle and High School Issues.* Washington, DC: U.D. Department of Education, Office of Bilingual and Minority Language Affairs.

Marzano, R. (2005). *Preliminary report on the 2004–05 evaluation study of the ASCD program for building academic vocabulary.* Alexandria, VA: Association for Supervision and Curriculum Development.

Penner, E., & Lehrer, R. (2000). The shape of fairness. *Teaching Children Mathematics, 7*(4), 210-214.

Suggested Resources

Allen, J. (1999). *Words, words, words: Teaching vocabulary in grades 4–12.* Portland, ME: Stenhouse Publishers.

Bell, N. & Tuley, K. (1997). *On cloud nine visualizing and verbalizing for math.* CA: Gander Publishing.

Blachowicz, C. & Fisher, P.J. (2002). *Teaching vocabulary in all classrooms* (Second Edition). New Jersey: Pearson.

Boehm, A. (2008). *Boehm test of basic concepts-Third edition (Boehm-3).* San Antonio, TX: Pearson Education, Inc.

Bracken, B. (2006). *Bracken basic concept scale-Third edition: Receptive (BBCS-3:R).* San Antonio, Texas: Harcourt Assessment.

Bracken, B (2006). *Bracken basic concept scale: expressive (BBCS:E).* San Antonio, TX: Pearson Education, Inc.

Coxhead, A. (2000). A new academic word list. *TESOL Quarterly,* 34, (2), 213-238. Reprinted in W. Teubert and R. Krishnamurthy (Eds.) (2007) Corpus linguistics: critical concepts in linguistics, pp. 123-149. Oxford: Routledge.

Fister, S., & Kemp, K. (1995). *TGIF: But what will I do on monday.* Longmont, Co: Sopris West, Inc.

Marzano, R. J. (2004). *Building background knowledge for academic achievement: Research on what works in schools.* Alexandria, VA: Association for Supervision and Curriculum Development.

Marzano, R. J., & Pickering, D. J. (2005). *Building academic vocabulary: Teacher's manual.* Alexandria, VA: Association for Supervision and Curriculum Development.

Romberg, T.A. (2001). *Mathematical literacy: What does it mean for school mathematics?* Wisconsin School News, 5-8, 31.

Secord, W., & Wiig, E. (2003). *Classroom performance assessment: Appendix C.* AZ: Red Rock Educational Publications, Inc.

Wiig, E. (2004). *WIIG assessment of basic concepts, (WABC).* Greenville, SC: Super Duper Publications.

Chapter 6
About Number Sense:
Numbers, Numerals, & Number Lines

*"One little, two little, three little Indians,
four little, five little, six little Indians."*
—Public Domain (Author unknown), *Ten Little Indians*

What is number sense? We think of it as an astute understanding of numbers, their many uses and their many interpretations. Number sense encompasses the ability to make connections between three interdependent aspectss: quantities, the spoken words that define quantities, and the symbols of mathematics. The symbols of mathematics can be broken into three strands: the numerals (written numbers) that represent the quantities, the symbols that signify relationships between numbers, and the symbols that define the math operations that are performed using numbers. Students need to construct strong connections between the three aspects that delineate number sense in order to be successful in mathematics.

Let's first consider quantity. Quantity is *how much* or *how many* of something we are measuring. Infants are born with the innate ability to discriminate between small quantities of things without formal instruction. Researchers refer to this as subitizing. This intuitive ability of subitizing is the essence of number sense. Scientists have recently established a link between a young child's intuitive number sense and later performance in math class (Stein, 2008). As children mature, the need to communicate the other aspects of number sense becomes an integral piece of math acquisition. With exposure to rote and rational counting, children learn to define quantity (more or less of something) as they acquire the language of math.

Rational counting (pointing to one object at a time while assigning a number in sequence), also known as one to one correspondence, is how students learn the concept of a set or finite group. When counting objects using one to one correspondence (rational counting), the last number counted in the set represents the total number or quantity of objects in the set. This is referred to as a cardinal number. An example for determining the quantity of a set would be to first ask the student, "How many toes (quantity) are on my left foot?" As you point to each toe on your left foot you assign one number to each toe (count rationally). You stop when you have assigned a number to each toe. The last number assigned is five. Therefore, five is the cardinal number that determines the number/quantity of toes on your left foot.

In order for children to count rationally to determine the cardinal number for a set, they must first learn a second interdependent element of number sense: rote counting, the ability to say number words sequentially. Children learn the number words in sequence as they develop language. Some of this may be attributed to the language associated with the repetition of number words in songs and nursery rhymes, etc. One can compare rote counting to learning to say and sing the alphabet long before understanding that each of the twenty-six letters of the alphabet have phonemes attached to them.

Once students can rote count to ten they are ready to attach these numbers to things or objects (rational counting). Through instruction and practice, children learn that the number of things in a set can be determined by connecting the numbers (words) they are saying as they count, with the things they are touching. To develop this understanding, students move through four stages of counting. The four stages of counting are:

Stage 1. Counting individual objects by touching
Stage 2. Counting sets (e.g., how many different shapes, colors, sizes, etc.)
Stage 3. Counting items not readily perceivable
Stage 4. Abbreviated, rapid counting leading to addition and subtraction (Ben Hur, 2004)

The third notion of number sense is developing an understanding of coding using mathematical symbols. These symbols demarcate three aspects of numbers:

1. Numerals, which represent quantities or cardinal numbers;
2. Relationships between cardinal numbers (e.g., more than, less than, equal to);
3. Mathematical operations (addition, subtraction, multiplication, division).

Quantity (how many of something or a cardinal number) is coded by a symbol known as a numeral. Each numeral, which depicts a cardinal number, has its own unique concrete representation. Learning to recognize and write the numerals is one strand of the third notion of number sense. Learning the symbols (numerals) that represent cardinal numbers appears to be more user-friendly than learning the symbols necessary to read and spell. Think about this: we only have to learn the numerals 1, 2, 3, 4, 5, 6, 7, 8, 9, and 0! With those ten symbols, we can then code all other numerals.

Furthermore, each numeral connects to one quantity and therefore leaves no room for interpretation, which is another way that mathematics is very user-friendly. Compare this to the twenty-six (26) symbols (letters) of the alphabet that are used to represent forty-four (44)+ sounds (phonemes) used for coding written and spoken language, which enables us to read and write. The same letters can be used to represent different phonemes.

The idea of comparing quantities between two or more sets necessitates the understanding of the mathematical symbols that depict relationships between numbers. These symbols indicate whether a number is equal to, more than, or less than another number. These three symbols, =, <, and >, are used to write mathematical statements such as $2 > 1$.

As number sense develops, students realize it is advantageous to determine quantities in more efficient ways than 1:1 rational counting. Enter the world of mathematical operations! Students learn to compute or perform operations (adding, subtracting, multiplying, and dividing) as they go about measuring and quantifying the world. These operations are coded with their own symbols, used to communicate the computation of quantity. Think of these symbols as math shorthand, so you don't have to write the words.

The current research conducted at Johns Hopkins University supports the link between number sense and math achievement, making it clear that a well-developed number sense is a necessary base for becoming proficient in mathematics. Embedded in the development of number sense is the opportunity to teach students to use imagery. Imagery or visualization is the ability to form mental pictures in one's mind connected to numbers and language (mathematics) or letters and language (reading and writing). "Imagery is fundamental to the process of thinking with numbers" (Tuley & Bell, 1997). Math requires two aspects of imagery:

1. *symbol imagery,* the parts/details of number sense;
2. *concept imagery,* the whole/gestalt of what is being measured.

A valuable tool that can be used to teach imagery is the number line (a line of infinite extent whose points correspond to the real numbers according to their distance in a positive or negative direction from a point arbitrarily established as zero). A number line is one way to address the parts/detail and the whole/gestalt of mathematics.

An effective mathematics curriculum provides for the development of number sense. The techniques described in this chapter address number sense by delving into connections among quantity, the numerals (numbers) that define quantity, and the related mathematical operations that assist students in communicating measurements.

During instruction of number sense development, a discerning teacher will recognize when a student is not grasping connections between quantity, the numbers that define the quantity, and the related operations that communicate measurements, and will pursue assessment. To assist, we offer the Cardinal Questions as they relate to developing number sense:

1. **What does the student know** about number sense?
   - What does the student know about rote counting?
   - What does the student know about rational counting?
   - What does the student know about sets?
   - What does the student know about cardinal numbers?
   - What does the student know about number lines?
   - What does the student know about the symbols of mathematics?
   - What does the student know about the operations of mathematics?

2. **What does the student do** when asked to demonstrate number sense?
   - Does the student rote count?
   - Does the student 1:1 count (rational count)?

- Does the student count beginning with a number other than one?
- Does the student count backward?
- Does the student count using ordinal numbers (i.e., first, second, third, etc.)?
- Does the student skip count?
- Does the student use number lines?
- Does the student use imagery?
- Does the student understand part/whole and whole/part relationships?
- Does the student understand that rational counting is a component skill of adding?
- Does the student understand that counting backwards is a component skill of subtracting?
- Does the student understand ordinality and cardinality of numbers?

Once you have assessed the student's number sense and are ready to begin preparation for intervention, think about the remaining three Cardinal Questions:

3. **How does the student learn?** (See Chapter Two)

4. **How does the student approach or react to an unfamiliar task?** (See Chapter Two)

5. **What will you do with the knowledge gained from answering the previous four questions?**

Armed with this information, the following five techniques will assist you in the instruction of number sense:
1. How High Can You Count?
2. Quantity Detective
3. Linear Connections
4. Rank and File
5. Deciphering Ciphers

> *"You went to school to learn, girl,*
> *things you never, never knew before...*
> *Like I before E except after C...*
> *and why two plus two makes four."*
> —Jackson Five, *ABC*

Number Sense—1
How High Can You Count?—Rote Counting

What it is: A technique to develop rote counting, the ability to sequence consecutively ordered numbers.

When to use it: When students are unable to rote count from one to one hundred, to count from a number other than one, or to count backward.

⚠️ Prerequisites are the ability to pay attention and to imitate.

Benefit: Students develop number sense.

Materials:
- Blank 3" x 5" or 5" x 8" cards
- Markers, paper, pencils, pens
- Stopwatch
- Overhead projector and/or easel with large paper
- Masking tape
- A conductor's "baton"
- Teacher Key Planning Form, Appendix B, p. 250
- Tracking Progress Form, Appendix B, p. 251
- Counting in Sequence Probe, Appendix A, pp. 205-207

Implementation Steps:
Part A: Counting forward from 1 to 100—Crank up the band!

1. Explain to students that they are going to learn to rote count or say numbers in order from one to ten. Demonstrate: Say, "One, two, three, four, five, six, seven, eight, nine, ten." Tell them they are going to mimic count by repeating each number after you say it, just like you say it. Say, "You will respond when I point to you with my baton." Compare this activity to playing an instrument in an orchestra or band. Demonstrate holding the baton up in the air and say, "one." Point to them with the baton and they say, "one." Say, "two." Baton back in the air and they say "two." Continue to ten. Incorporate variety by saying the numbers slowly, quickly, high pitched, low pitched, quietly,

thunderously, etc. Have fun conducting your students as they mimic rote counting from one to ten.

Note This is an opportunity to coordinate with the music teacher to expose students to the role of music conductors.

Variation: Consider substituting a magic wand for the conductor's baton.

2. When students can mimic count without error, challenge them to synchronize count or say the numbers simultaneously with you. Continue to use the baton to establish the synchronization or the timing of voices.

3. As students become adept at synchronized rote counting, tell them that it is time for them to synchronize count themselves with you playing the role of conductor. Challenge them to rote count without cues.

4. Repeat Steps #1-3 as students expand their rote counting ability up to 100.

Variation 2: Have students who are competent at rote counting become the conductors.

Note: For more exposure and practice in repeating numbers in an ordered sequence, teach songs, nursery rhymes and other age-appropriate poems that feature counting.

Planning:
• Use the Teacher Key to create your plans for this activity. For example:

```
┌─────────────────────────────────────────────────┐
│  Teacher Key: Making Sense of Number Sense        │
├─────────────────────────────────────────────────┤
│  Technique #1: Rote Counting                      │
├─────────────────────────────────────────────────┤
│         Sample A:                                 │
│              1. Mimic Count 1 – 10                │
│              2. Sync Count 1 – 10                 │
│              3. Mimic Count 1- 20                 │
│              4. Sync Count  1 – 20                │
│              5. Mimic Count 20 – 30               │
│              6. Sync Count 20 - 30                │
│              7. Mimic Count 1 - 30                │
│              8. Sync Count 1 - 30                 │
│              9. Mimic Count 30 – 40               │
│             10. Sync Count 30 - 40                │
│             11. Mimic Count 1 - 40                │
└─────────────────────────────────────────────────┘
```

Part B: Kick Off—Counting forward from a number other than one

1. Explain to students that it is possible to start counting from any number and that you are going to teach them how to do so. Review (see Chapter 5, Technique #1: Movin' and Groovin') or establish a student friendly definition for the word forward.

2. Repeat Steps #1–4 from Part A above, while teaching counting forward from numbers.

Note: Students who are fluent rote counters from one to ten can begin with counting to ten starting from any number between one and nine.

Part C: Blast Off—Countdown

1. Explain to students that now that they know how to count forward, they are ready to learn how to count backward. Explain that counting backward is the same as a countdown. Connect this to countdowns for rockets blasting off. Review (see Chapter 5 Technique #1 Movin' and Groovin') or establish a student friendly definition for backward. This is an opportunity to connect this act of forward and backward counting to the notion of opposite concepts (See Chapter 5, Technique #1).

2. Repeat Steps #1- 4 above while teaching counting backward from numbers.

Note: Students who are fluent rote counters from one to ten can start with counting backward from ten. You may want to start from five for the initial countdown.

Variation #3: Have students work in pairs to practice counting down or counting backward. Encourage them to role play scenarios of countdowns in real life.

Progress Tracking:
- Use the Tracking Progress Form to record the student's progress each time the technique is used. For example:

Tracking Progress for Student: Tom Smith
Technique #1: How High Can You Count?
Date: _____

Sample: A — Rote Counting Forward	
1. 1 – 5	+
2. 1 – 10	+
3. 1 – 20	+
4. 1 – 30	+
5. 1 – 40	
6. 1 – 50	
7. 1 – 60	
8. 1 – 70	
9. 1 – 80	
10. 1 – 100	
Total	**4/10**

- **Curriculum Based Measurement**: Counting in Sequence Probe

Sources:
Adetula, L.O. (1996). Effects of counting and thinking strategies in teaching addition and subtraction problems. *Educational Research,* 38(2), 183-195.

Askew, M., Brown, M., Rhodes, V., Wiliam, D., & Johnson, D. (1997). *Effective teachers of numeracy: A report of a study carried out for the Teacher Training Agency.* London: King's College, University of London.

Number Sense—2:
Quantity Detective—Rational Counting & Cardinality

What it is: A technique for developing rational counting, the ability to connect rote counting with touching discreet entities, also referred to as 1:1 correspondence.

When to use it: When students are unable to count the number of entities in a set thereby establishing the cardinal number or the total number of entities in the set.

 Prerequisite is the ability to count to ten.

Benefit: Students develop number sense.

Materials:
- Blank 3" x 5" or 5" x 8" cards
- A variety of age-appropriate manipulatives
- Hula hoops and/or boxes big enough for students to stand or sit in
- Pages from newspaper advertisements, catalogs, etc. that display items that can be counted
- Markers, paper, pencils, pens
- Stopwatch
- Overhead projector and/or easel with large paper
- Masking tape
- Teacher Key Planning Form, Appendix B, p. 250
- Tracking Progress Form, Appendix B, p. 251
- Quantity Array Probe, Appendix A, pp. 208-210

Implementation Steps:
Part A: Quantity Detective—Understanding cardinal numbers

1. Explain to students that they are going to become Quantity Detectives. Be sure students know about detectives. You may have to diverge here briefly to explain the role of a detective. Clarify that as Quantity Detectives they will be able to detect and answer quantity questions that begin with the words "how many" (e.g., how many students are in this room, how many teachers are in this room, how many chairs are

in this room, how many people are in your family, etc.). Brainstorm "how many" questions with your students.

2. Explain that being able to answer "how many" or quantity questions is a very important skill to learn because it is used in many ways and in many places such as school, home, stores, etc. Create a student-friendly definition for *quantity*. For example: *quantity* is an amount or number of something that is measurable. Brainstorm with your students what they might want to measure or count as a Quantity Detective. Then take the opportunity to assess their ability by having them answer some of the "how many" questions they generated.

3. Demonstrate how to be a Quantity Detective by first asking a question related to the quantity of one. For example, have one student hold something that is different from what all the other students are holding. Ask, "How many students in this room are holding a _____?" Model the answer by saying, "I'm a Quantity Detective and I have found one student holding a _____." Point to the student while you say, "one." Now ask the students quantity questions for which the answer is one, using the same format. Emphasize pointing to and counting one.

4. Repeat this demonstration asking quantity questions for which the answer is two. Emphasize pointing and counting simultaneously, *one, two.*

5. Compare quantity counting and rote counting. In *rote counting*, you count as high as you are able to. In *quantity counting*, you have to answer a "how many" question and stop counting once you have assigned one number to each element. The number that you stop at is the number that tells how many or the amount. In other words, it answers the "how many" question. That number is called a **cardinal number**.

Note: Clarify for students that a "how many" question asks you to count a certain number of elements that are grouped together. This is known as a set.

6. Practice having students detect answers to "how many'" questions for quantities from zero to ten.

7. Now, following Steps #1–6, use manipulatives and/or marks to represent objects (e.g., dots, tallies) to apply Quantity Detective work to counting elements.

Note: When asking how many questions for which the answer is zero, you have an opportunity to demonstrate the notion of absurdity into your classroom by asking funny questions such as, "How many teachers have a pink elephant standing on their shoulders?" Humor is (almost) always appropriate in the classroom!

<u>Variation</u>: Have students work in pairs, taking turns asking "how many" questions.

8. The last step of Part A is to apply Quantity Detective work to counting elements in sets that are not readily perceivable e.g. sounds and visualizations, following Steps# 1-6.

Part B: Quantity Detective—Operation: Addition

1. Once students are competent at rational counting (counting elements in one set), introduce the idea of combining and counting the number of elements in two sets.

2. Demonstrate by establishing two sets, such as one set of students with sunglasses and one set of students with hats. Then explain that the students need to detect how many students there are all together. Point and count to each element in one set and continue counting as you point to each element in the other set. Say, "When you combine (put together) sets and detect how many elements you have all together, you are adding, which is known as a math operation."

3. Practice detecting the total number (up to ten) of elements in the two groups. Demonstrate that it does not matter which group is counted first; the quantity or total number is always the same.

4. Repeat Steps #1 – 6 from Part A, applying the operation of addition (e.g., detecting the number of elements in two or more sets).

Note: Remember, rational counting is to determine the number of elements in a set OR is the operation of adding one.

Planning:
• Use the Teacher Key to create your plans for this activity. For example:

Teacher Key: Making Sense of Number Sense
Technique #2: Quantity Detective—Rational Counting—Adding
Sample A: 1. 1-5 2. 1-10 3. 1-15 4. 1-20 5. add 2 sets sum=5 6. add 2 sets sum=10 7. add 3 sets sum=5 8. add 3 sets sum=10 9. add 2 sets sum=20 10. add 3 sets sum=20

Progress Tracking:
• Use the Tracking Progress Form to record students' daily progress each time the technique is used. For example:

```
┌─────────────────────────────────────────────┐
│ Tracking Progress for Student                │
├─────────────────────────────────────────────┤
│ Technique #2: Quantity Detective—Rational Counting │
│ Date: _____  Student: _____ │
├─────────────────────────────────────────────┤
│        Sample: A — Rational Counting         │
│              1. To one      +                │
│              2. To two      +                │
│              3. To three    +                │
│              4. To four     +                │
│              5. To five     +                │
│              6. To six      -                │
│              7. To seven    -                │
│              8. To eight                     │
│              9. To nine                      │
│             10. To ten                       │
│                                              │
│              Total        5/10               │
│                                              │
└─────────────────────────────────────────────┘
```

- **Curriculum Based Measurement**: Quantity Array Probe

Sources:

Hannula, M. M., Rasanen, P. & Lehtinen, E. (2007). Development of counting skills: Role of spontaneous focusing on numerosity and subitizing-based enumeration. *Mathematical Thinking and Learning* (Vol. 9, Issue 1, pp. 51 – 57). USA: Routledge, Taylor & Francis.

Norbert W. Maertens, Rowen C. Jones and Ardis Waite (1977). Elemental groupings help children perceive cardinality: A two-phase research study. *Journal for Research in Mathematics Education* (Vol. 8, No. 3, pp. 181-193). Reston, VA: National Council of Teachers of Mathematics.

Number Sense—3:
Linear Connections—Number Lines

What it is: A technique for conjuring images of a number line in order to use it as a personal, internal mathematical tool.

When to use it: When students are unable to access an internal number line to visualize which numbers are before or after other numbers, which numbers are near to or far away from other numbers, how to count forward and backward, how to skip count for adding and subtracting.

 Prerequisite is the ability to count quantities from 1 to 100.

Benefit: Students understand the gestalt or whole and its related parts. Assists students in understanding adding, subtracting, and point zero.

Materials:
- Blank 3" x 5" or 5" x 8" cards
- Ten each of ten varieties of 8" x 10" cardstock
- A variety of age-appropriate manipulatives such as Blocksblocks
- A variety of 10 different self-stick notepads or colored 3" x 5" cards
- 20" segments of white cotton rope for each student
- Markers, paper, pencils, pens
- Graph paper
- Stopwatch
- Overhead projector and/or easel with large paper
- Masking tape
- Teacher Key Planning Form, Appendix B, p. 250
- Tracking Progress Form, Appendix B, p. 251
- Missing Number Probe, Appendix A, pp. 211-214

Implementation Steps:
Part A: The Line Up—The Human Number Line

1. Tell students that they are going to participate in a line up. Explain that they will be creating a human number line which will help them visualize or picture a number line in their heads. Explain further that picturing an imaginary number line in their heads can help

them understand relationships between numbers. If you have access to a hallway long enough to line up students, use it. Otherwise, place a straight strip of masking tape across the longest dimension of floor space in your room. Tell students you are going to ask them to stand in a line on that tape. Select your first variety of ten 8" x 10" pieces of cardstock, and ask the first student to come and stand on the left end of the masking tape (reinforcing left to right concepts of print, hence movement forward). Write the numeral 1 on one piece of cardstock and ask the student to hold it as he/she stands in place on the line. Ask the second student to come up and stand next to the first student on the masking tape. Write the numeral 2 on the second piece of cardstock and hand it to him/her. Repeat until there are ten students standing in a line holding number cards in order from one to ten. Compare this line up to a number line made up of people—a human number line!

Note: You must consider the number of students you will be including to create the human number line. The goal is to have some students observe the number line and then alternate the observers and participants.

2. Engage in classroom discourse regarding everyone's placement on the number line. Sample questions and statements include:
    • Who is next to the student holding the number one (Student #1)?
    • Who is closest to Student #1?
    • Who is farthest away from Student # 1?
    • Who is farther away from Student #1: Student #4 or Student #9? How do you know that?
    • Who is between Student #7 and Student #9?
    • What did we have to do to make the human number line longer?
    • Were we counting forward or backward when we added more students to make the number line longer?
    • How could we make the number line shorter?

3. Have the students close their eyes and picture in their minds their human number line. Ask them to visualize their classmates and their respective numbers. Then ask them to answer questions similar to Step #2 above while their eyes are closed.

4. When students are able to answer questions related to position and sequence on the number line, explain that more students are going to join the line up to make it longer. Engage in discourse about where the next student should stand and what number should be given to that student. Determine with students that the next student should be #11 and should stand next to Student #10. Use the next variety of cardstock and line up Students #11–20.

Note: If you have limited space to create a longer human number line or a limited number of students, have the students place their number cards next to each other on the masking tape, creating a cardstock number line. Continue making the number line longer by either lining up students in placements 11–20 or create numeral cards on 8" x 10" cardstock and place them in sequence.

Variation: Take photos of the human number line and use the photos to engage in discourse similar to Step #2.

5. Engage in discourse similar to what is suggested in Step # 2.

6. When students are able to answer questions related to position and sequence with numbers 1 – 20, challenge them to visualize a human number line with 30, 40, 100 students standing in it.

7. Once students are able to describe the number line they see in their heads, engage them in discourse about the number that comes before Student #1. Identify this spot or placement as point zero. Explain that point zero is the point from which you begin or start counting placements in the number line. To further demonstrate point zero, place a new strip of masking tape on the floor starting at point zero. Have students stand shoulder to shoulder. Tell Student #1 that he/she must stay in place. Ask the other students to move forward, keeping their shoulders touching, until they are all standing on the new strip of masking tape. Discuss what happened. Point out that point zero remained the same and the rest of the numbers stayed in place. Repeat to demonstrate that the positions of the numbers in the number line stay the same no matter how far forward one moves.

Note: You should consider repeating this demonstration of point zero at least four times, representing each of the perpendicular intersections. This is also a way to demonstrate radius, diameter and circumference.

Variation: Instead of using masking tape, use rope. Have students mark their spots using colored tape as they hold the rope. Label the rope segments #1, #2, etc.

8. Challenge students to visualize a human number line in which Student #1 stands next to point zero and Student #2 stands on the shoulders of Student #1, etc. Identify this as a vertical number line. Contrast this to the horizontal number line they created while standing side by side. Engage in discourse similar to Step #2 above.

Note: If students are unable to visualize and describe this vertical human number line, create a vertical number line using pictures of the students taped to blocks, which can be stacked.

Part B: The Line Up—Blocks and Stickies

1. Repeat Steps #1–8 above using three dimensional objects such as blocks or other age-appropriate items.

2. As you proceed through each step in Part B, have students create a representation of the number lines on paper by having them trace around blocks or stickies. Engage in discourse about how much paper they would need to create a number line made up of 100 blocks, etc.

Part C: The Line Up—Paper and Pencil

1. Explain to students that it is now time to create number lines on paper. Tell students that one way to create number lines on paper is to use special paper called graph paper. Give each student a sheet of graph paper. Demonstrate how to locate or identify point zero.

2. Create horizontal and vertical number lines by repeating Steps #1 - 8 above, using graph paper.

Planning:
- Use the Teacher Key to create your plans for this activity.

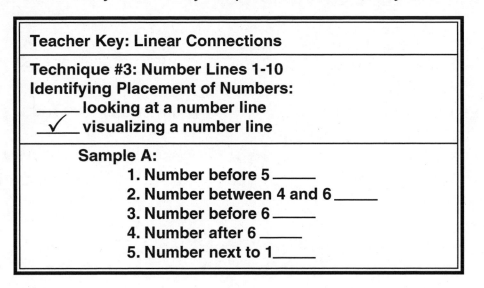

Teacher Key: Linear Connections

Technique #3: Number Lines 1-10
Identifying Placement of Numbers:
_____ **looking at a number line**
___✓___ **visualizing a number line**

Sample A:
1. **Number before 5** _____
2. **Number between 4 and 6** _____
3. **Number before 6** _____
4. **Number after 6** _____
5. **Number next to 1** _____

Progress Tracking:
- Use the Tracking Progress Form to record students' daily progress each time the technique is used. For example:

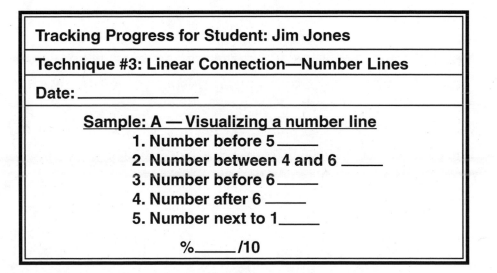

Tracking Progress for Student: Jim Jones

Technique #3: Linear Connection—Number Lines

Date: _____

Sample: A — Visualizing a number line
1. **Number before 5** _____
2. **Number between 4 and 6** _____
3. **Number before 6** _____
4. **Number after 6** _____
5. **Number next to 1** _____

% _____ /10

- **Curriculum Based Measurement**: Missing Number Probe

Source:
Bobis, J. (1996). Visualisation and the development of number sense with kindergarten children. In J.T. Mulligan & M.T. Mitchelmore (Eds.), *Children's number learning* (pp. 17-33). Adelaide: Australian Association of Mathematics Teachers.

Number Sense—4:
Rank and File—Ordinal Numbers

What it is: A technique for developing ordinal counting or counting associated with position in space and time.

When to use it: When students need to follow directions that require comprehension of sequence and order.

⚠ Prerequisites are the ability to count to 20 and identify the cardinal number for a group.

Benefit: Students become competent in following directions and comprehending the sequence of algorithms.

Materials:
- Blank card stock of different sizes
- Markers, paper, pencils, pens
- Stopwatch
- A variety of age-appropriate manipulatives such as blocks
- Model train(s), cars, trucks, etc.
- Dolls, stuffed animals, or other age-appropriate living creature facsimiles
- Pictures of athletes racing, children lined up to go somewhere, etc.
- Overhead projector and/or easel with large paper
- Teacher Key Planning Form, Appendix B, p. 250
- Ordinal Counting Probe, Appendix A, pp. 215-216

Implementation Steps:
Part A: First or Last—Direction dependent

1. Explain to students that they are going to learn ordinal counting. Explain that understanding ordinal numbers and ordinal counting will assist them in understanding time, order, sequence, and importance. It will help them follow directions. Demonstrate ordinal counting: Say, "This is ordinal counting: first, second, third, fourth, fifth, sixth, seventh, eighth, ninth, tenth." Ask the students to say the ordinal numbers with you.

2. Engage students in discourse about the topic of racing. Sample questions and statements include:
   - What does it mean win a race?
   - What does it mean to be second?
   - If you are not first or last, what are you?
   - What does it mean to be first?

Variation: Engage students in discourse about trains. For example, ask them what they know about trains, which car is first, which car is last, what about all the other cars between the engine and the caboose, etc.

3. Compare rational counting to ordinal counting. Place a piece of masking tape (approximately 6 feet in length) between two places in your classroom (e.g., between the door and a window). Ask one student to stand on the line facing the door. Ask, "How many students are lined up to go out the door?" Have the class count. Point and say, "One; one student." (Refer to Technique #2 – Quantity Detective.)

4. Demonstrate how to create a number card. Use a piece of cardstock and write the numeral *1* on it. Hand it to the student standing first in line, asking her to hold it so other students can see it. Explain to students that this student, who is number 1, will be the first student to go out the door. Demonstrate how to change the numeral *1* to the ordinal number. Turn the card over and write another numeral *1* on the other side. Change it to an ordinal number by writing 'st' after the 1 (**1**st). Ask the first student to hold the card showing the side with *1*st.

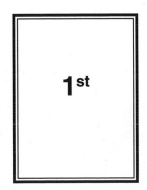

5. Next, ask another student to stand behind the student facing the door or the first student. Repeat Step #4, creating a number card with 2 and 2nd on it.

6. Review with students that in order to answer a question that begins with the words how many (a quantity question), they count rationally(one, two, etc.) and determine the cardinal number in the set. Differentiate between cardinal numbers (one, two, three, etc.) that refer to quantity, and ordinal numbers (first, second, third, etc.) that refer to time and position. Engage in discourse about time and position using underlying key language concepts such as before/after, in front/behind, first/last, follow/lead. Sample questions and comments include:
   - Who is in front?
   - Where is _____?
   - Who will lead going out the door?
   - The leader going out the door will be first.
   - When will the second student go out the door?
   - The second student will go out the door after the leader.

7. Continue repeating Steps #3 and 4 above until your masking tape line is filled with students holding number cards representing their place in the line.

8. When the masking tape line is completely filled, you will introduce the concept of last. Explain to students that the number that determines the answer to how many in a set is the last number because it is the last element that you counted.

9. Explain to students that ordinal numbers are direction and time dependent; in other words, ordinal numbers assist you in describing when and how you move towards something (forward) and away from something else. To demonstrate this, ask the students to stay in place and turn around to face whatever is at the opposite end of the line from the door. Engage in discourse about what changed, and have students exchange their number cards accordingly. Sample questions and statements include:

- If we were going to climb out the window, who would be first?
- Who would be second?
- Who would be last?

10. Further clarify with students that ordinal numbers may be used to establish a time reference for movement (e.g., when a student does something first, he/she does it before anyone else does it). This is a great opportunity to collaborate with the physical education teacher. Utilize a stopwatch while students engage in activities (e.g., walking around the gym, running the length of a room). Engage in discourse about the relationship between ordinal numbers and time.

11. Sample questions and comments include:
- Who was first?
- Why was _____ first?
- Who was second?
- Who was faster?
- Why was _____ last?
- Who was third?
- _____ was between _____ and _____. Who was in the middle?

Part B: First or Last—Following directions using manipulatives

1. Explain to students that you will now use ordinal numbers to describe placement of things and to follow directions. Demonstrate by creating a line of toy cars, animals, and/or people all facing in the same direction. Engage in discourse about who/what is first, second, third, last, etc.

2. Ask students to create lines of things. Sample directions include:
- Place a blue block on your desk. Create a line of miniature vehicles facing the block.
- Point to the vehicle that is first in line facing the block.
- Describe the vehicle that is third in line.

3. Practice creating lines of things in order from first place to twenty-first place as you give directions and engage in discourse as described

in Step# 2, above. Be certain to count the things in line using ordinal numbers. Discuss how the way we say the numbers changes.

Part C: First or Last—Pencil and paper challenge

1. Explain to students that once they understand ordinal counting, they can use this skill to follow directions with paper and pencil tasks. Clarify that when they write or read words on paper, the first word or number is written at the top left side of the paper. The second, third and fourth words/numbers are written across the page from left to right.

2. Demonstrate creating lines/sequences of letters/numbers going from top to bottom and left to right on the page. Engage in discourse that utilizes and emphasizes the ordinal numbers and their respective places.

3. Engage in discourse as you view pictures of people in lines, races, etc.

Teacher Key: Number Sense

Technique #4: Rank and File—Ordinal Numbers

Sample A: Attributes—same
1. first
2. second
3. last
4. third
5. middle
6. fourteenth
7. ninth
8. tenth
9. seventeenth
10. twenty-first

• **Curriculum Based Measurement**: Ordinal Counting Probe

Source:
Jacob, S. N., & Nieder, A. (2007). *The ABC of cardinal and ordinal number. representations.* Tubingen, Germany: Primate NeuroCognition Laboratory.

Number Sense—5:
Deciphering Ciphers—Breaking the Code

What it is: A technique for developing recognition and understanding of numerals and eight basic math operation symbols.

When to use it: When students require extended assistance in comprehending numerals and math vocabulary.

⚠️ Prerequisites are the ability to count to 20, to identify the cardinal number for a group or set, and to identify when two sets have the same, more than, or less than quantities.

Benefit: Students become competent in identifying numerals and discerning math symbols.

Materials:
- Blank cardstock of various sizes
- Markers, paper, pencils, pens
- Stopwatch
- Overhead projector and/or easel with large paper
- Samples of addition, subtraction, multiplication and division word problems
- Teacher Key Planning Form, Appendix B, p. 250
- Tracking Progress Form, Appendix B, p. 251
- Numbers and Symbols Identification Probe, Appendix A, pp. 217-219, **OR** Quantity Discrimination—Line Probe, Appendix A, pp. 220-222, **OR** Quantity Discrimination—Numbers Probe, Appendix A, pp. 223-226

Implementation Steps:
Part A: Numerals—Reading & Writing Numbers

1. Explain to students that they are going to learn to read and write math language. Compare it to learning to write their names. Explain that letters are used to write words, such as a name that belongs to a person, and numerals are used to write numbers that belong to a quantity of elements. Engage in discourse about this notion of names belonging to a person. Sample questions and comments might be:
    - If I say, "Sharon," who do I mean?
    - Close your eyes. Can you picture Sharon in your mind?
    - What about having two students with the same name?

Note: Point out that one word/numeral never refers to two different things in math (e.g., in math language 3 always means ●●● elements or things).

2. Explain that in math language numerals are the names of quantities. Demonstrate this by showing some of the ways to write how many (quantity) of something. For example, select two objects, e.g., ☆☆. On the overhead or easel pad, write/read/ say the following:
   - I have (draw the star shapes) ☆☆
   - I have *two* stars.
   - I have *2* stars.

   Engage in classroom discourse comparing these different ways of communicating how many or quantity. For example, discuss how "☆☆" is the same as "*two stars*" and is the same as "*2 stars.*" Say, "In math language, instead of writing the word or drawing the number of things that tells "how many." For instance, *two*, we use the numeral *2*.

Note: This is an excellent opportunity to connect learning math language with learning other languages, especially if you have English Language Learners in your classroom.

3. Explain that there is also a way to write and read the words *same as* in math language. Using your easel pad or overhead write and say, "*Same as* in math language looks like this: =. = means *same as*. = has a name. It is called an **equal sign**. Equal means same as." Proceed to write and read the following math sentences, demonstrating the use of the equal sign to indicate same:
   - ☆☆ = ☆☆
   - ☆☆ = 2
   - 2 = ☆☆
   - 2 = 2

   Have students read in unison with you as you point and read the math language. Explain that these math sentences are called **equations**. When you write a math sentence using the = sign it means that whatever is on the left side of the = sign is the same as or equal to whatever is on the right side of the equation. This is known as reciprocity.

4. Repeat Step #2 above for the remaining numerals, 0,1,3,4,5,6,7,8,9.

Note: When you write and read about the numeral,1, be sure you address the written and verbal ways of representing singular versus plural, e.g., "star" versus "stars."

5. Now it is time for students to write and read numerals. Have each student select ten blank cards for their personal use. Designate a space where a student can sit or stand. Ask one student to go to that space. As the students observe, write the numeral *1* on an 8" x 10" piece of cardstock and give it to the student in the designated space to hold. Point to the numeral *1* and say, "One student." Write and review the math sentences as described in Step #3 (e.g., *1* = 🧍).

6. Ask students to close their eyes and visualize the numeral that their classmate is holding. Ask them to write the numeral *1* in the air with their pointer fingers. Next, have them write the numeral *1* on one of their personal blank cards. Have the students point to their numeral *1* and read/say in unison, "One."

Note: Some students may need to trace over numerals before they can write them independently.

7. Have students select ten manipulatives each, such as blocks or stickies. Explain that when they place one thing on their numeral cards, the numeral becomes a number that tells how many. Have students place one thing on their personal numeral *1* card. Have them take turns explaining what their number *1* means.

8. Repeat Steps #5-7 for the remaining nine numerals.

9. Reinforce to students that they now know a lot about writing and reading math language. Explain that now that they know ten numerals, they will be able to write all the other numbers. Demonstrate by asking ten students to go to the designated space and write the numeral 10 on number cards, as described above. Engage in discourse about using the numerals 1 and 0 to create the numeral *10*, and that means ten things, such as ten people:

ŤŤŤŤŤŤŤŤŤŤ . Emphasize that numeral is *"ten,"* not *"one zero."* Repeat writing and reading math sentences as describe in Step #3.

10. Using manipulatives, repeat Steps #1-9 as you create class size and personal numeral cards for numerals *11–20*. Emphasize how to say each of the double digit numbers.

11. Continue this technique with numerals *21 – 100* as needed.

12. Tell students that it is time to write numerals on paper. Demonstrate by writing and reading math sentences using dots or dashes; for example: *1 =* ● and ● *= 1*, etc.

Variation #1: Once students are able to write the numerals, have some students take turns reading the numerals as other students flash the numeral cards.

Variation #2: Read one numeral at a time and have students write the numerals. Have them read their numerals aloud.

Planning:
• Use the Teacher Key to create your plans for this activity. For example:

Teacher Key: Writing and Reading Numerals
Technique #5: Deciphering Ciphers— **Matching a Numeral to its Quantity**
Sample A: 1. *1 means* ● _____   2. write numeral *1*_____   3. identify/read/say *1*_____   4. write = _____   5. = means "same as"_____   6. write/read *1 =* ● _____   7. *2 means* ●● _____   8. write numeral *2*_____   9. identify/read/say *2*_____   10. write/read *2 =* ●● _____

Part B: Operation Symbols—Reading and Processing Math Symbols that define relationships between numbers

1. Tell students that they will be learning three key symbols that explain relationships between numbers. These symbols are part of the code of mathematics that they are learning to decipher.

2. Explain that they already know about the symbol that tells us about two things being equal, = (the equal sign). Draw an equal sign on an overhead or easel paper. Then, write examples of simple equations relating to numerals and quantities as described in Step #12.

3. Next, write the following math sentence:

     ●●● = 2

   Engage in classroom discourse about what is incorrect about this equation. Sample statements include:
     • ●●● is not the same as 2.
     • ●●● does not mean the same as 2.
     • ●●● does not equal 2.

   When students use the words "not equal," draw the math symbol, ≠. Write,

     ●●● ≠ 2

4. Explain that they will now learn to write a math sentence that explains the relationship between two quantities that are not the same, or not equal. This math sentence tells if a quantity is more than or less than another quantity. Demonstrate and describe:
     • ●●● is more than ●●
     • Say, "The symbol or code that means 'more than' is >."
     • Write:  ●●● > ●●
     • Read and say, "three is more than two" (you may want to tell students that another way to say "more than" is "greater than"), then
     • Read and say, "three is greater than two."

Repeat the previous demonstration for the symbol <, which means less than:

●● < ●●●

Engage in classroom discourse about what changed.

5. Challenge students to write and read math sentences using > and < as you say "greater than" and "less than."

Planning:
• Use the Teacher Key to create your plans for this activity.

Teacher Key: Writing and Reading Numerals
Technique #5: Deciphering Ciphers—Writing > math sentences
Sample A: 1. 2 > 1 _____ 2. 3 > 1 _____ 3. 3 > 2 _____ 4. 4 > 3 _____ 5. 4 > 2 _____ 6. 4 > 1 _____ 7. 5 > 4 _____ 8. 5 > 3 _____ 9. 5 > 2 _____ 10. 5 > 1 _____

Part C: Operation Symbols—Reading and Processing Math Symbols that define math operations

1. Explain to students that they will now learn how to write and read the symbols that tell them what action to take, or what to do with numbers when they are asked to solve math problems. This is also part of the code of math. Explain further that what one does with numbers is called **operations** or **calculations**. Explain that math operations are:
    • adding or putting things together; the symbol used to show that you **add** is **+**
    • subtracting or taking things away; the symbol used to show that you **subtract** is **-**
    • dividing or separating things into equal quantities; the symbol used to show that you **divide** is **÷**

- multiplying, a quick way of adding (when things are separated into equal quantities); the symbol used to show that you **multiply** is **X**.

2. Let students know that the tricky part of knowing what operation symbol to write and what action to perform is understanding what the problem is asking for. Explain that it is necessary to learn the words that call for addition. Read sample addition problems with students and create a list of words from those problems that call for the operation of addition, or +. The list will include:
   - sum
   - all, in all
   - together, all together
   - join
   - total
   - and
   - plus
   - add
   - increase
   - more than

3. Repeat Step #2 looking for words that mean the operation of subtraction, or -. The list will include:
   - take away
   - decrease
   - subtract
   - have left, have left over
   - minus
   - less than
   - separate

4. Repeat Step #2 looking for words that call for the operation of multiplication or X. The list will include:
   - times
   - increase by
   - more than
   - product
   - all together

Note: Emphasize with students that multiplication words are similar to addition words because multiplying is a quick way of adding things that are of equal quantity.

5. Repeat Step #2, looking for words that call for the operation of division or ÷. The list will include:
   - separate equally
   - equal groups
   - each

6. Create a Symbol Challenges worksheet for your students. Make a list of words that indicate a math operation and challenge students to write the matching symbol. A sample Symbol Challenge might look like this:

Word(s)	Symbol
Add	
Sum	
All together	
Decrease	
Subtract	
Less than	
Equal amounts	
Separate equally	
Total	
Have left	

Progress Tracking:
- Use the Tracking Progress Form to record students' daily progress each time the technique is used. For example:

Tracking Progress for Student: Tom Smith

Technique #5: Deciphering Ciphers—Writing and/or Reading Math Sentences

Date: _____

	Writes	Reads
Sample: A		
1. 2 > 1	_____	_____
2. 3 > 1	_____	_____
3. 3 > 2	_____	_____
4. 4 > 3	_____	_____
5. 4 > 2	_____	_____
6. 4 > 1	_____	_____
7. 5 > 4	_____	_____
8. 5 > 3	_____	_____
9. 5 > 2	_____	_____
10. 5 > 1	_____	_____

• **Curriculum Based Measurement**: Numbers and Symbols Identification Probe, *OR* Quantity Discrimination—Line Probe, *OR* Quantity Discrimination—Numbers Probe

Sources:
Falkner, K.P., Levi, L., & Carpenter, T.P. (1999). Children's understanding of equality: A foundation for algebra. *Teaching Children Mathematics*, 6(4), 232-236.

Markovits, Z. & Sowder, J. (1994). Developing number sense: An intervention study in grade 7. *Journal for Research in Mathematics Education*, 25 (1), 4-29.

Suggested Resources

Baker, S., Gersten, R., & Lee, D-S. (2007). *Recent research in math interventions: Implications for practice.* Center on Instruction. Florida: RMC Research Corporation. Available: http:// www.centeroninstruction. org

Chard, D.J., Simmons, D.C., & Kameenui, E. J. (1998). *Word Recognition: National Center to Improve the Tools of Educators, Curricular and Instructional Implications for Diverse Learners.*

Dehaene, S. (1997). *The number sense: How the mind creates mathematics.* USA: Oxford University Press.

Griffin, S. (2004). *Teaching number sense.* Educational Leadership, 61(5), 39.

Minton, L. (2007). *What if your ABCs were your 123s?: Building connections between literacy and numeracy.* CA: Corwin Press.

Morsund, D. (2007). Improving Math Education in K-8 schools. Available from: http://uoregon.edu/~moursund/Books/ElMath/ElMath.html

Stein, M., Kinder, D., Silbert, J., & Carnine, D. (2005). *Designing effective mathematics instruction* (4th ed.). Saddle River, NJ: Prentice Hall.

Tuley, K. & Bell, N. (1997). *On cloud nine: Visualizing and verbalizing for math.* CA: Gander Publishing.

Witzel, B. S., Ferguson, C. J., & Brown, Dale, S. (2007). Developing early number sense for students with disabilities. Available from: www.ldonline.org/article/14618

Chapter 7
About Computational Fluency

"If you can't do the math, then get out of the equation."
—Hilary Duff, *The Math*

Fluency has generated a great deal of attention and debate from educators. What is its worth and usefulness in mathematics? Why? Fluency has often been regarded as the product of stand-alone "drill and kill" instruction in which students are required to memorize facts without understanding concepts or relevance. After years of research, it has been verified that to develop fluency in computation a student must strike a balance between proficiency in computing numbers and a full understanding of the concept behind the skills (Russell, 1999).

Conceptual understanding in mathematics means learners are thinking, generating and justifying their own ideas that connect numbers and symbols in the computation process (Carpenter et al., 2003). This kind of understanding does not occur if instruction emphasizes a singular way of doing something, in this case computation (Allsopp et al., 2007). When students do not understand the underlying concepts of number and operation sense, but simply memorize facts, it becomes extremely difficult for them to make meaningful connections or generalize other applications. In summary, for students to achieve a proficient level of computational fluency, sometimes referred to as procedural fluency, they must be able to solve number problems with efficiency, accuracy and flexibility.

A recent report from the National Mathematics Advisory Panel of 2008 urges teachers to target "quick and effortless" recall of arithmetic facts in the early grades. This means first getting students to the point of being on "friendly terms" with numbers (having a well-developed number sense) so they can recognize numbers, see their many purposes and understand the relationships of number concepts before asking them to fully focus on number operations and number connections (Wells, 1995 in Rothstein et al., 2007).

> ...number sense is essential if one is to be successful understanding patterns, operations, place value and sophisticated number relationships required for computational fluency (NCTM, 2000 in Rose et al., 2007).

As computational fluency is explored more fully, it is important to briefly address some basic information about the brain and mathematics. It should come as no surprise that the brain's architecture determines the sort of abilities that come naturally to each individual. A fundamental problem with learning math is that while some of the capacity for number sense may be genetic, the ability to perform exact calculations is dependent upon cultural tools such as symbols and algorithms. This becomes more complicated by the fact that the brain has to absorb these algorithms (procedures for calculations) in areas that were not originally set up for math. Therefore, learning math does not always harmonize with our built-in circuitry (Holt, 2008). As complex as this all sounds, the reality remains that it is possible to strengthen skills in number sense. In fact, it is essential to do so if one is to be successful in understanding patterns, operations, place value and sophisticated number relationships required for computational fluency (NCTM, 2000 in Rose et al., 2007).

Some research has indicated that difficulty with learning basic math facts is related to the development of phonological processing skills (Hecht, Torgesen, Wagner, & Rashotte, 2001 as cited in Allsopp et al., 2007). There is also speculation that trouble with math could be a result of how students are exposed to the subject. Educators must ask themselves the following question: Is the focus of math instruction on drill and memorization, or is it on building meaningful connections through multiple representations for the purpose of making sense of the concepts?

The National Math Advisory Panel concluded that mathematics curriculum should focus on the most critical skills in the early grades, and that instruction of these skills should be delivered through explicit, highly structured experiences in order to minimize errors. You may be thinking, what are these critical skills and how are they best taught? There are no easy answers, but educators can and should look to the syllabi of countries that have high math achievement at all levels for insight into effective instruction. In doing so, it is evident that math curriculums in countries with high math achievement levels have narrowed the number of concepts that are taught in the early years while focusing on the relationships between numbers and concepts. This purports that mathematics should not be taught as a set of disconnected rules, facts and procedures. Expecting students to remember procedures and memorize facts without giving them the foundational understanding of number sense and operation sense yields fertile ground for growing mathematical anxiety. How then does one go about successfully building computational fluency to avoid perpetrating the self-fulfilling prophecy of, "I'm not good at math?"

Computational fluency is built on a three-part mathematical foundation:

> . . . classroom experiences cannot be taught as a set of disconnected rules, facts and procedures.

1. Understanding the meaning of the four basic operations of addition, subtraction, multiplication and division, what they do and their relationship to one another;
2. A working knowledge of number facts and realization of their relationships;
3. A thorough understanding of the base ten number system, how numbers are structured in the system and how the place value of those numbers behaves (Russel, 2007 & Booker G. et al., 1997 as cited in Siemon, D., 2007).

As you can see, knowledge of number facts is one part of computational fluency and a necessary component of every instructional mathematics block. Furthermore, it is important for students to attain a certain level of fact fluency to solve number problems because the brain has a limited capacity to process information. If too much energy goes into figuring what 4 plus 8 equals, then little is left over to understand the concepts underlying the complex multi-digit number problems (Gersten &

> . . . it is important for students to attain a certain level of fact fluency to solve number problems.

Chard, D., 2001). This is similar to the principle of reading fluency related to comprehension of text. If a student spends more time and energy on decoding while reading, then passage comprehension is difficult or non-existent. Keep in mind that students' fluency varies in both reading and mathematics. Therefore, the amount of practice required to attain a high level of fluency will vary. In addition, different approaches are required to teach the other components of computational fluency (understanding operations and their relationships) in order for all students to be successful with concept acquisition.

One of the authors experienced this first hand when her son was learning about multiplication. The child's teacher introduced this concept through skip counting and he was having a difficult time recalling the facts and making sense of the relationship between the concept of skip counting and multiplying. It was clear that he required a different approach for skill acquisition. Providing him with visual charts and additional instruction about the relationship between addition and multiplication helped him make the connection between these two operations and this strengthened his mathematical repertoire. Had he been pressured to rely on one single procedure to learn facts, his ability to solve problems might well have been inhibited.

As mentioned earlier, computational fluency does not occur as a by-product of mathematic instruction and cannot be taught solely through worksheets or memorization. It is important to remember the stages of counting discussed in Chapter 6 and bear in mind that students must move through the counting stages before they are ready to use that knowledge to solve addition and subtraction problems with numerals (Ben Hur, 2004). Only when children can count consistently to figure out how many objects there are, are they ready to use counting to solve number problems (National Research Council, 2001).

> **Computational fluency does not occur as a by-product of mathematic instruction and cannot be taught solely through worksheets or memorization.**

For computational fluency to occur, students must first engage in activities that include multiple exposures to counting procedures so that they internalize the meaning of the basic facts for later automatic recall. Second, they must learn about the structure of the base ten system, the operations, as well as the relationship between numbers (NCTM, 2005). Again, educators must keep in mind that mathematics does not consist of isolated rules, but rather of connected ideas. Structured discourse and interaction provide opportunities for students to make connections between the language, mental images, and the numbers and underlying principles of mathematics. Engagement with teachers and peers (cognitive) as well as with self (meta-cognitive) enhances one's ability to apply and generalize facts and concepts. To bring students to the level of proficiency required for the conceptual understanding of computational fluency, instruction must be an interactive, reflective and meaningful process.

An effective mathematics curriculum includes computational fluency. The techniques found in this chapter address the understanding of number-fact relationships, place value, and operations using manipulatives, mental imaging and numerals. To develop computational fluency, a student must first have a thorough understanding of number sense. If you still have questions about number sense and the stages of counting, we suggest you review this information in the previous chapter.

During math instruction, a discerning teacher will recognize when a student is not demonstrating computational fluency and will pursue assessment. To assist, we offer the Cardinal Questions as they relate to fluency:

1. **What does the student know** about computational fluency?
    - What does the student know about basic facts and other number relationships?
    - What does the student know about the structure of the base ten system and place value?
    - What does the student know about relationships between operations?

2. **What does the student do** when asked to solve computation problems?
    - Does the student compute the basic facts of addition, subtraction, multiplication and division?
    - Does the student have a working knowledge of number facts?
    - Does the student compute these facts fluently?
    - Does the student know the underlying concepts of math operations?
    - Does the student know how the math operations relate to each other?
    - Does the student skip count?
    - Does the student understand reciprocity?

- Does the student represent math problems using math language and symbols?
- Does the student understand the base ten system?
- Does the student understand place value?
- Does the student know different approaches for solving number operations?
- Can the student explain the steps he/she has taken to solve a number problem?
- Can the student explain why the steps used to solve number problems work?

Once you have assessed the student's fluency of math facts and computation ability and you are ready to begin preparing an intervention, think about the remaining three Cardinal Questions:

3. **How does the student learn?** (see Chapter Two)

4. **How does the student approach or react to an unfamiliar task?** (see Chapter Two)

5. **What will you do with the knowledge gained from answering the previous four questions?**

Armed with this information, the following five techniques will assist you in the instruction of computational fluency:

1. Frame It
2. Sequence Counts
3. Amazing Arrays
4. Chips and Columns
5. It's All In The Timing

"By holding on a little longer....
We find the fire makes us stronger,
and through it all we learn
endurance is the key to our proficiency."
—Mercury Rising, *A Narrow Door*

Comptational Fluency—1:
Frame It

What it is: A technique for understanding and rapidly recalling basic addition and subtraction facts.

When to use it: When students do not understand the concept of each of these operations.

⚠️ Prerequisites include the ability to say, read and write numbers up to 20 and count quantities up to 100 (rational counting).

Benefit: Students will gain a conceptual understanding of the operations of addition and subtraction when they solve complex number problems.

Materials:
- Twenty items to use as counters for each student
- One 11" x 14" sheet of unlined paper and one pencil for each student for Part III
- Small white board and marker for each student (optional)
- Overhead projector and clear colored counters or whiteboard/chalkboard/large flip chart with stick-on counters
- Two Ten Frame Templates for each student, Appendix B, pp. 255-258
- Tracking Progress Form, Appendix B, p. 251
- Partner Practice Form, Appendix B, p. 260
- Computation Probe, Appendix A, pp. 227-230

Implementation Steps:

Part 1 A—Counting
1. To begin, distribute one ten-frame template and a set of ten counters (they should all be the same color) to each student. Pair up the students so they can engage in discourse and obtain feedback from a partner.

Ten-Frame

2. Explain to students that they will be using counters on a ten- frame to develop recognition of quantities and numbers from 1-10 and 1-20. They will later add and subtract those quantities up to 20.

3. Demonstrate and explain that when building a number on the ten-frame, they must fill in the top row from left to right first before filling in the bottom row.

4. Call out a number between one and ten and have the students build the frame on their own by placing a counter in each square until they have reached the number you called out.

5. When both students in the pair have the frame filled in, tell them to check whether their partner's frame matches their own. Partners can keep track of their own progress by scoring a point each time their frames match. If there is no match, no point is awarded. Pairs then discuss why there is not a match and revise their frames so they align. Continue calling out numbers until a set of ten is reached. After each set, have the pairs total their score and record it on the Partner Practice Form.

Progress Tracking:
• Use the Partner Practice Form to record the students' daily progress each time the technique is used. For example:

Partner Names: *Joe and Sally*		
Score 1 for each match, 0 if no match		
?	**Match**	**Topic:** *counting from 1-10*
1. 6	1	**Total points: 9**
2. 7	0	
3. 4	1	**What problems did we have?**
4. 3	1	
5. 8	1	**One of us did not know number 7**
6. 9	1	
7. 2	1	
8. 1	1	
9. 1	1	
10. 5	1	

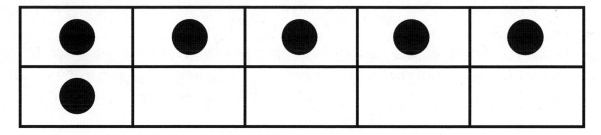

Variation: Give each student a set of ten-frames already filled in with dots and use them for flashcards; or, develop your own set of large ten-frame cards for group instruction. Flash each card and have student(s) respond by naming the number represented by the frame. Challenge students to develop rapid response of quantity recognition by decreasing wait time.

6. Once students can quickly and correctly respond to the counting phase with the counters, move to imaging with the use of a blank frame. Have students remove all the counters from their frames. Tell them to close their eyes and imagine what the frame would like with 4 dots, 10 dots, etc.

Part 1 B—Adding and Subtracting Counters

7. Tell students that they are going to use the frames to add quantities together to find the total or sum of all the counters. Call out a number and have students place that number of counters on the frame. Call out the second number and have students add that many more counters. Ask students, "How many counters are there all together?" or, "What is the total or sum of the two numbers?" Use these terms interchangeably so that students understand that they both mean to add. Students can respond aloud individually or as a group.

Variation: Have students write the answer on a small white board and hold it up when they are done. This allows for individual think time and monitoring by the teacher. Once everyone has held up the white board, proceed to the next problem.

8. As students become proficient with adding numbers from 1-10, move to subtraction by starting out with a larger number and removing or taking away another number using the counters. Again, use words

that convey what is left after subtracting one number from another. Don't forget to use zero and an entity for adding and subtracting.

9. Use the ten-frame to practice both addition and subtraction facts up to ten until students can move quickly back and forth between the processes. First, allow them to use counters, then practice visualizing the counters on the ten-frame to come up with the correct answer.

Note: Before students can write simple number problems they must be introduced to the words and symbols that indicate addition, subtraction and equal. Be sure to complete that lesson before moving on to the next step of this technique.

Part B—Solving Number Problems

1. Solve simple addition and subtraction problems by having students write numbers on paper or a white board as you say them. Tell students what type of problem you will be giving them (e.g., this will be an addition problem), then give them the first number (7) to write. Next, have them insert the correct sign (+ or -) depending on your next direction (add, subtract). Practice writing the number problems both in a vertical and horizontal format. Use the ten-frame if needed but fade to mental imagery to build fluency.

2. Once students are proficient with the activities in Parts 1A and 1B using the numbers 1-10, they are ready to use numbers 11-20 with the same activities.

3. Distribute two of the ten-frame templates to each student along with 20 counters. Proceed through Steps 1-9 again, first using the numbers 11-20, then using numbers between 1 and 20. Fade the frames as students become proficient with the addition and subtraction facts.

4. To determine students' level of proficiency, challenge them to come up with their own equations by writing all the number facts that add up to 6, 8, 10, 12, up to 20.

- **Curriculum Based Measurement**: Computation Probe

Sources:
Gilmore, C. K., & Spelke, E. S. (2008). Children's understanding of the relationship between addition and subtraction. *Cognition*, 107(3), 932-945.

Gilmore, C. K. & Bryant, P. (2006). Individual differences in children's understanding of inversion and arithmetical skill, *British Journal of Educational Psychology*, 76, 309-31.

Computational Fluency—2: Sequence Counts

What it is: A technique to identify and recall numbers, their patterns and relationships using skip counting and number charts.

When to use it: When students need to understand that successive counting of numbers yields the total number of a group of objects.

⚠ Prerequisites include the ability to create patterns, say, read and write numbers up to 100, and count quantities up to 100.

Benefit: Students will learn to solve equal group problems by skip counting, which is a prerequisite to addition and multiplication.

Materials:
- 100 beads of five different colors for each student and a string long enough to string 100 or more beads, or an 11" x 14" sheet of unlined paper and five different colored markers or crayons per student—Part I
- Overhead projector and transparent colored counters or whiteboard, chalkboard, or large flip chart with stick-on counters for Parts A and C
- A copy of a Traditional Hundreds Chart (Appendix B, p. 261) for each pair of students
- A transparency of the traditional number chart or large copy with stick-on counters
- Teacher Key Planning Form, Appendix B, p. 250
- Group Tracking Progress Form, Appendix B, pp. 252-253
- Computation Probe, Appendix A, pp. 227-230

Implementation Steps:
Part A—Count by Numbers

1. Provide each student with a string and beads. Break the students into groups of three.

2. Explain that each person in the group will use his/her beads to create a pattern. Using an overhead projector and counters or a string with beads, demonstrate the activity. Say, "We will be creating bead

patterns using twos. Place two beads of the same color on the string to represent the first sequence of twos. Then use another color to represent the next sequence of twos. Continue changing colors by twos until 50 beads have been thread. Each student in the group can choose his or her own color pattern, as long as it is representative of the number two."

3. Allow students enough time to string all the beads and check for accuracy as you observe the activity.

4. Next, demonstrate the sequence of twos by counting each bead aloud and asking the students to say the number representing the bead at the end of a color break. 1,2,**3**,4,**5**,6,**7**,8,**9**,10….50 (the student says the number in bold). As they identify the number at each color break, record the number on the board so they will see the sequence of counting by twos—2,4,6,8,10,12,14,16, etc.

5. In the groups of three students, have students take turns counting each string of beads. One student can count each bead and then all three can say the number at the color break. Next, have the students use their beads to count by twos.

6. Once students are able to count the beads using the color breaks, have them close their eyes and count the beads two at a time while imagining the color breaks as they are counting by twos. To check understanding, conduct this activity individually with students.

7. Repeat Steps #2 - 6 using sequences of threes, fours, fives, sixes, sevens, eights, nines and tens to teach counting by 2,3,4,5,6,7,8,9,10.

Note: Counting by fives and tens is easier than other sequences, so you may want to teach these sequences after introducing counting by twos.

Part B—Counting Groups

1. Provide students with at least 100 counters of different colors and unlined paper. Tell them they will use the counters to make groups and find out how many are in the total group. Demonstrate on the

overhead or flip chart with counters that stick. Say, "Arrange your counters in three groups of two and tell me how to find the answer." Students may tell you they found the answer by counting all the counters by individually (by ones), adding 2+2+2, or counting by twos to arrive at the correct answer: six. Explain that all these processes are correct but the fastest way to find the answer is to count each group or set using skip counting/counting by. Ask, "How many groups of two are there? To find the answer the fastest way, we will count by twos until we count the three groups." Show students how to do this by pointing to each group as you count, or by using three fingers to represent the three groups as you count 2, 4, 6.

2. Practice grouping and counting numbers this way until students understand the idea of counting by groups.

Planning:
• Use the Teacher Key to create your plans for this activity. For example:

Teacher Key for *Sequence Counts*	
Computational Fluency **Technique #2—Part II: Counting Groups**	
	Count by 2's
1. Two groups of two	Count by 3's
2. Four groups of three	Count by 3's
3. Two groups of three	Count by 2's
4. Five groups of two	Count by 5's
5. Three groups of five	Count by 7's
6. Six groups of seven	Count by 4's
7. Eight groups of four	Count by 2's

Part C—Sequencing with Number Charts

1. Pair up the students. Hand out one copy of the Traditional Hundreds Chart to each pair of students, along with transparent counters. Tell them to first watch as you demonstrate how to look for patterns that are made by skip counting sequences of numbers on the chart. Let the students know the first sequence they will count by will be threes, up to 30. Tell the students to say each number in the sequence aloud

while you place the counters on the overhead chart. After all the counters are placed on the chart, ask questions such as: "What kind of pattern do you see?" "Will 41 be in the pattern?" "How do you know?" "What other numbers fit the pattern?"

1	2	3	4	5	6	7	8	9	10
11	12	13	14	15	16	17	18	19	20
21	22	23	24	25	26	27	28	29	30
31	32	33	34	35	36	37	38	39	40
41	42	43	44	45	46	47	48	49	50
51	52	53	54	55	56	57	58	59	60
61	62	63	64	65	66	67	68	69	70
71	72	73	74	75	76	77	78	79	80
81	82	83	84	85	86	87	88	89	90
91	92	93	94	95	96	97	98	99	100

2. Have students work as partners to fill in their chart using the sequence of counting by threes.

3. Using the overhead or large chart, show students that the first shaded number in the sequence is 1 three, the next shaded number is 2 threes, etc. Point to different numbers in the sequence of 30 or less and ask, "How many threes are in that number?"

4. Continue having partners ask each other questions while you monitor students' understanding.

5. Use the chart to count by other numbers and the counters. Follow up by asking the students questions similar to the ones in Steps #1 and 2.

6. Challenge the student pairs to come up with their own questions about the chart and number sequences and allow the questions to be posed to the rest of the class.

7. Once students understand the sequence of numbers and skip counting, they are ready to move to arrays for mulitiplication and division (see Technique #3, Amazing Arrays, in Chapter 7).

Progress Tracking:

• Use the Group Tracking Progress Form to record the students' progress each time the technique is used. For example:

Name: *Sequence Counts*	KK	ME	SP	JT	BN			
Count by's	✓	✓	✓	✓				
Counting groups	✓	✓		✓				
Sequence charts		✓		✓				

• **<u>Curriculum Based Measurement</u>**: Computation Probe

<u>Sources</u>:

Fuson, K. C. & Fuson, A. M. (1992). Instruction supporting children's counting on for addition and counting up for subtraction. *Journal for Research in Mathematics Education*, 23, 1.

Heirdsfield, A. M., Cooper, T. J., Mulligan, J., & Irons, C. J. (1999). Children's mental multiplication and division strategies. In Zaslavsky, Orit, Eds. *Proceedings of the 23rd Psychology of Mathematics Education Conference*, pages 89-96.

Computational Fluency—3: Amazing Arrays

What it is: A technique for understanding and rapidly recalling basic multiplication and division facts.

When to use it: When students do not understand the concept of each of these operations.

⚠ Prerequisites include the ability to say, read and write numbers, count quantities up to 100 and skip count.

Benefit: Students will understand the concepts behind multiplication and division and see their relationship.

Materials:
- Fifty counters of different colors for each student
- One 11" x 14" sheet of unlined paper and a pencil for each student
- Overhead projector and transparent colored counters or whiteboard, chalkboard, or large flip chart with stick-on counters
- Number Strip, up to the number 20 for each child, Appendix B, p. 262
- Small whiteboard and marker for each student (optional)
- Teacher Key Planning Form, Appendix B, p. 250
- Computation Probes, Appendix A, pp. 227-230

Implementation Steps:
Part 1 A—Multiplication with Manipulatives

1. Explain to students that they will be using the operation of multiplication. Multiplication of numbers is similar to addition because each calls for adding numbers by groups. Multiplication is a much quicker way of adding large numbers.

2. Using the overhead, tell the students you will be making arrays (groups of counters that create patterns). Arrays are one way to represent multiplication by grouping numbers together.

3. Show them how to arrange six counters in two groups of three. Point out Group 1 and 2 and then the three items in each group. Tell them to look carefully at the pattern or array created by the grouping. Ask, "How many counters are in the array?"

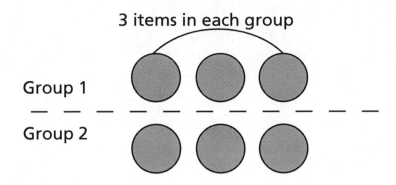

3 items in each group

Group 1

Group 2

4. Rearrange the array to show three groups of two. This time, point out the three groups and the two items in each group. Have students explain how the pattern differs from the first array. Ask students to determine the total number of counters in this array. Discuss why the number remains the same even though the arrangement changed.

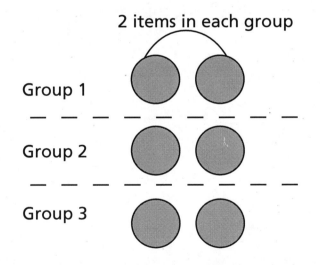

2 items in each group

Group 1

Group 2

Group 3

5. Demonstrate a few more examples, then have the students make their own arrays as they follow your directions (e.g., make an array with three groups of four, then four groups of three). If students have not discovered that they can skip count each group to arrive at the answer, show them this process.

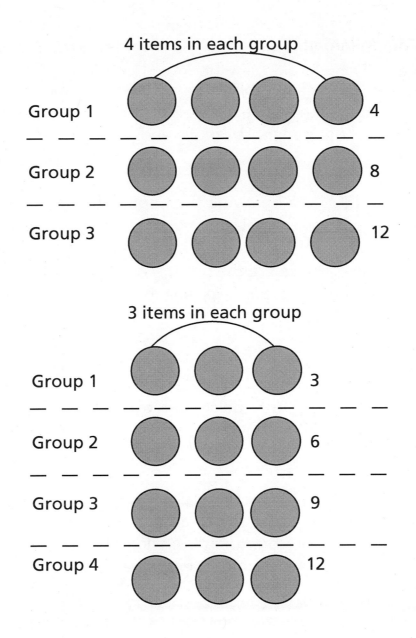

4 items in each group

Group 1   ⬤ ⬤ ⬤ ⬤   4

Group 2   ⬤ ⬤ ⬤ ⬤   8

Group 3   ⬤ ⬤ ⬤ ⬤   12

3 items in each group

Group 1   ⬤ ⬤ ⬤   3

Group 2   ⬤ ⬤ ⬤   6

Group 3   ⬤ ⬤ ⬤   9

Group 4   ⬤ ⬤ ⬤   12

6. Have students complete several more arrays as you check for understanding. Encourage students to picture the equal groups and how many items in each group as a way to develop mental math images.

7. Once students can arrange and count arrays, they are ready to use them with number strips to deepen their understanding of number relationships using the operation of multiplication.

8. Give each student a number strip, a piece of unlined paper and 20 counters (four each of five different colors). Have the students place the paper on the desk horizontally and position the number strip above it.

9. Tell students you will be giving them some simple number problems to solve. They will use the counters to make arrays and the number strip to help find the answer. Start with an array that is familiar. Say, "There are three desks (these are the groups) and two pencils (these are the number of items in each group) on each desk. How many pencils are there all together?"

10. Using an overhead projector or other large board, demonstrate the following procedure:
    - Say, "First, I'll use the colored counters to represent the three desks and the two pencils by making an array of three groups of two."

    - Say, "Next, I'll put the counters on the number strip one group at a time." When all the counters have been placed, point to the counter at the end of each color break and ask the students to count the numbers, 2, 4, 6.

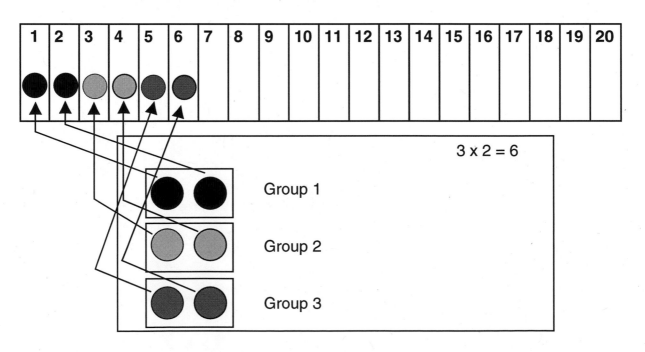

- Next, have students write the number problem 3 x 2 = 6 on the right side of the paper while saying, "Three groups of two equals six. This tells us that three groups/sets of two are six."

- Change the problem to show that 3 x 2 is the same as 2 x 3 by saying, "This time there are two desks with three pencils on each desk." Have students represent the problem in an array and with the number strip before they write the problem on the paper.

- Continue with similar problems until students can quickly count the groups to solve the problems.

- Ask predictive follow-up questions to determine students' understanding, such as, "I have three sets of two, how many counters will I have if I put on another set of two?" and "I have three sets of two, how many counters will I have if I take off a set of two?" Write the corresponding number problems on the paper (4 x 2 = 8, 2 x 2 = 4) as students provide the answers.

Planning:
• Use the Teacher Key to create your plans for this activity. For example:

Teacher Key for *Arrays*

Technique #3—Amazing Arrays

Sample A:
Multiplication problems:
1. Five sets of four (5x4)
2. Two sets of five (2x5)
3. Four sets of two (4x2)
4. Three sets of six (3x6)
5. Six sets of three (6x3)
6. Four sets of three (4x3)

Part 1 C—Multiplication with Imaging

1. Ask students to flip over the number strip so that only blank squares are showing.

2. Say, "If there are five people in each car and there are three cars, how many people are there in all?" Use the counters and arrange them to show your groups of people and cars. Some students will be able to use the array and skip counting to solve the problem.

   If additional assistance is needed, continue using the number strip and say, "Picture where the numbers are on the strip." Continue to follow the procedures outlined in Step #10 of Part I.

3. Encourage students to imagine or visualize the last number counted on the strip as they move the counters and skip count to solve the number problem.

4. Have students explain how they arrived at the answer and the different processes that were used. Continue practice using imagery until students can quickly solve the problems presented.

Part 1 D—Multiplication with Numbers

1. Have students use paper and pencil to solve number problems involving groups and sets (multiplication). They may need to use their fingers to skip count the groups until they become fluent with recalling the facts.

2. Tell students to think about the process they used with the number lines and counters as you give them new number problems to solve. Present the problems by saying, "Three sets of five is the same as what?" Have them write the problem $3 \times 5 = \Box$, and then solve it. Other examples are: $7 \times 5 = \Box$, $8 \times 2 = \Box$, $5 \times 10 = \Box$, $6 \times 3 = \Box$.

3. Challenge students by shortening the think time between each problem. Problems can be presented orally and the students can write the answers on whiteboards or respond aloud as a group.

Note: Writing number problems this way shifts the focus from counting the number in a group to seeing the number of groups. If students are having difficulty, go back and provide more practice with Part I or Part II activities.

Part 2 A—Division with Manipulatives

1. Use the counters to introduce the concept of division. Explain that when dividing numbers one must start with the total number in the group and then divide the total number of items into smaller groups. Division is the opposite or inverse of multiplication where groups of numbers are added together.

2. Place 15 counters on the overhead (see example below) and say, "If I have 15 pieces of candy and each friend gets three pieces of candy, how many friends are there?" Show students how to group the counters into equal groups of three to represent the candy pieces. Once the counters are equally distributed, ask, "How many groups of three are in 15?" Answer, "Five, which means there are five friends sharing the candy."

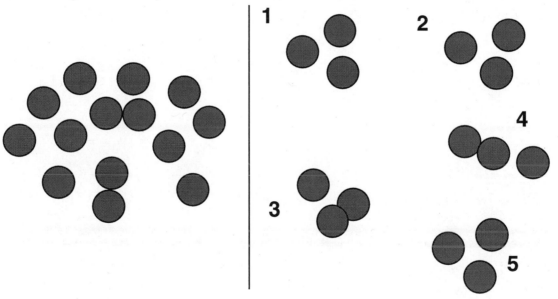

3. Continue with problems that give the total and number in each group to solve how many groups, using this repeated addition strategy. Example: "There are 24 tennis balls that need to be packed into cans that hold four tennis balls each. How many cans will be needed? Or how many groups of four?"

4. Next, make an array on the overhead. Ask students to identify how many are in the array. Explain that when working with division of whole numbers one can picture an array of the total and the number

of groups known to determine the number in each group? This is the "think of multiplication" strategy. For example, if there are 15 counters in an array, and we want to break the array into five groups, how many items would be in each group, or five whats are 15?

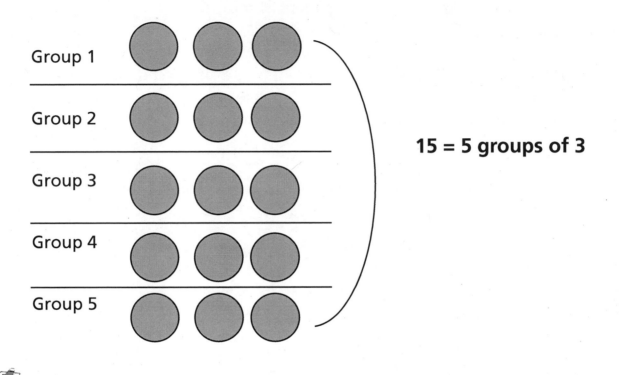

15 = 5 groups of 3

Note: Sharing (or partition) is a more powerful notion of division, which relates arrays to multiplication and extends to fractions and algebra.

5. Have students continue to make arrays and solve similar problems. For example: 49 tennis balls are shared equally among players. How many tennis balls does each player get? Incorporate imagery by telling students to think: 7 whats are 49?

Part 2 B—Division with Imagery

1. Tell students they will be solving division problems by using mental images of the arrays. Write the problem
    $$28 \div 7 =$$
    Have students visualize an array of 28 counters. Explain that they have the total of 28 and need to ask themselves, "If I have seven shares of 28, how many counters are in each share? Or, seven whats are 28?"

Note: Having students think about division in this way will support the concepts of fractions and ratios.

2. Continue with problems that are similar, encouraging students to use mental math by asking themselves questions as they look at the problem (e.g., 56 ÷ 7, think: 7 whats are 56?).

Variation: Use fact families to help students arrive at an answer. For example, 56 ÷ 7 = ☐. If students aren't fluent with all the sevens, have them ask themselves what they do know (e.g., "I know that 7 fours are 28 and if I double 28 I get 56, then I know that 7 eights are 56.").

Part 2 C—Division with Numbers

1. Have students use paper and pencil to solve number problems involving total and groups (division). They may need to draw arrays if they are not yet fluent with the basic facts of multiplication.

2. Remind students to think about the process they used with the counters as you give them number problems to solve. Present the problems by saying: "36 divided by 4 equals what?" Have them write the problem 36 ÷ 4 = c, and then say, "Four whats is 36?" Continue with other examples until students are fluent with these basic facts.

3. Challenge students by shortening the think time between each problem. Problems can be presented orally and students can write the answers on whiteboards or respond aloud as a group.

• **Curriculum Based Measurement**: Computation Probe

Source:
Siemon, D. & Virgona, J. (2001). *Roadmaps to numeracy—Reflections on the middle years numeracy research project paper presented to Australian Association for Research in Education Conference*, Fremantle, Perth. Retrieved June 1, 2008 from www.aare.ed.au.

Computational Fluency—4:
Chips and Columns Champions

What it is: A technique for understanding the concept of place value, which is necessary for rapid recall of numbers and number exchanges.

When to use it: When students are not grasping the how and why of place value columns and their relationship to spoken and written numbers.

⚠️ Prerequisites include the ability to say, read and write number names up to the number 20, count quantities and solve simple addition and subtraction problems, count by groups (ones, tens, hundreds) and represent them with numbers.

Benefit: Students will see the relationships between number positions and place value in a base ten system.

Materials:
- A set of 30 chips or other counters, ten each of three different colors for each student (stackable poker chips work especially well)
- A copy of the Restructured Numbers Chart for each student, Appendix B, p. 265
- Transparency of a blank Restructured Hundreds Chart or a large blank version of the chart on a white board or poster board.
- Chip Color Value Chart, Appendix B, p. 263, to identify the number value of each color chip
- Hundreds, Tens & Ones Chart, Appendix B, p. 264, to compare the chips with place value
- Computation Probe, Appendix A, p.227-230

Implementation Steps:
Part A—Chip Count

1. Hand out a set of chips, paper, and a pencil to each student in the group.

2. Explain to students that they are about to become "Chip Champions" by counting and grouping chips to represent numbers up to 100.

3. To begin the activity, explain the number value for each chip according to color using a key similar to the one below.

Chip color	Chip Value
Red	100
Blue	10
White	1

4. Tell students that they will first practice making the numbers from 20-99 using the representative chips, then they will name the numbers and find them on the hundreds chart shown below.

Note: For this activity, students should be able to represent and name the numbers from one to nineteen. If they cannot, review this skill before proceeding, then have the students find these numbers along with zero on the hundreds chart.

Restructured Hundreds Chart

	99	89	79	69	59	49	39	29	19	9
	98	88	78	68	58	48	38	28	18	8
	97	87	77	67	57	47	37	27	17	7
	96	86	76	66	56	46	36	26	16	6
	95	85	75	65	55	45	35	25	15	5
	94	84	74	64	54	44	34	24	14	4
	93	83	73	63	53	43	33	23	13	3
	92	82	72	62	52	42	32	22	12	2
	91	81	71	61	51	41	31	21	11	1
100	90	80	70	60	50	40	30	20	10	0

Developed by Kemp, Eaton & Poole, 2008, adapted from Nesbitt Vacc, 1997

Note: The restructured chart goes from right to left starting in the bottom right corner with zero and counts up (this can provide students with a perspective of the relationship between ones and tens, going from right to left, as well as smaller and larger numbers going from bottom to top). This chart differs from traditional number charts that begin with one in the upper left corner and end at 100 in the bottom right, which are used primarily for counting in sequence, counting by multiples and identifying numbers.

5. Have the students make up their own numbers using the chips (e.g., 6 tens and 3 ones), then have the other group members count the stacks of chips, first blue then white, to determine the number. Ask each student to find that number on their hundreds chart while you write the number on the blank class restructured hundreds chart. Continue with several examples to fill in the class hundreds chart and check that students understand how to count the chips.

6. Next, use the chart to follow up with questions such as, "Which number is bigger 63 or 80?" Or, "Which number comes first in the number sequence, 90 or 55?" Continue with different numbers until students can compare and order the numbers with fluency. Engage in discourse to find out how they arrived at each answer before moving on to Part II.

Part B—Place Value Challenge

1. Demonstrate and explain that ten white chips is the same as one blue chip, ten blue chips is the same as one red chip, and one hundred white chips is the same as or equal to one red chip. Tell students that ten white chips can be exchanged for a single blue chip, and vice versa. If students do not understand that ten blue chips is equal to one red chip, show them how to count by ones and exchange, then by tens, up to 100.

2. Next, show examples. For instance, put down eleven white chips and ask students, "If we exchange one blue chip for ten white chips, what will we have?" Explain that ten and one still makes eleven, and therefore one blue chip and one white chip yield the same quantity as

eleven white chips. Continue with these examples using white, blue and red chips until students are able to group chips correctly.

3. Once students are able to group and exchange chips, introduce simple addition and subtraction problems without regrouping (e.g., 2 + 3, 9 - 5, 4 + 4, etc.).

4. As they become fluent with these problems, move on to addition with regrouping, using numbers up to 20. Follow this procedure:
   - Ask, "How many chips do you have if you count seven white chips and then add five more?"
   - Tell them to exchange one blue chip (10) for ten white ones and determine the answer. If necessary, explain the process of exchanging one blue chip for ten white chips again.
   - Continue with similar types of problems and exchanges using larger numbers.

5. Next, show students easy subtraction problems with regrouping. Start with the number twelve, represented by one blue chip and two white chips. Ask students how they could take away three from the twelve. Wait for a student to suggest they can exchange the blue chip for ten white chips and take three away.

6. Practice additional subtraction problems with regrouping until students are fluent with problems with and without regrouping.

Note: Fluency at this step means a student is using the colors both representationally and quantitatively. This representation is necessary for students to understand the concept of place value.

7. Continue to use the chips for double-digit addition and subtraction; first without regrouping (23 + 46, 33 + 45, 44 - 21, 56 - 34, etc.) and then with regrouping (25 + 25, 35 + 28, 24 - 6, 44 - 15, 56 – 47, etc.). While students are manipulating the chips, check for understanding.

8. Once students reach this point, more difficult double-digit problems can be introduced and practiced. If students require re-teaching, return to the previous steps.

9. When students are accurately and fluently manipulating the double-digit numbers, give them a red chip (100) and have them subtract a double-digit number such as 42. A student who understands how to represent this quantity will use the blue and white chips to arrive at the answer. Provide additional practice for problems that involve the red chips. If a student is unable to make this transition, engage in discourse with the student to determine where the breakdown is occurring and return to that step in the process.

Part C—Connecting the Chips and the Columns

1. Explain to students that when numbers are written numerically, they are written in columns that start from the left and progress to the right. The value of the number columns is like the different colored chips: the column on the right is like the white chips, indicating how many ones there are in the number; the column to the left of the ones is like the blue chips, indicating how many tens (or chips worth 10) are in the number; and the column to the left of the tens column indicates how many hundreds you have like the red chips. Let them know that the columns have the same names as the chips: ones, tens and hundreds. Explain that when writing numbers, the number names coincide with the column names. Once this activity is mastered, students reach the level of Chips and Columns Champion.

Hundreds	Tens	Ones
100s	10s	1s
Red chip	Blue chip	White chip

2. If students do not understand the number, chip and column relationship, use the chart and chips to demonstrate by writing a number in the corresponding column and counting out chips to represent the number.

Hundreds	Tens	Ones
100s	10s	1s
4 Red chips	2 Blue chips	7 White chips

3. Show the students how adding and subtracting double-digit numbers (without regrouping) on paper is the same as adding and subtracting with the colored chips. Provide students with a sheet similar to the one below. Demonstrate how to solve the problems (e.g., when subtracting 52 from 67, taking 5 tens from 6 tens and 2 ones from 7 ones is the same on paper as it is with the blue and white chips), then have students use the colored chips by placing them in the boxes above the numerals to check their answers. Again, provide plenty of practice opportunities before moving on to regrouping.

6 7 - 5 2	2 3 + 3 4	4 3 - 2 1	1 6 + 4 3	8 8 - 7 3

4 Demonstrate how adding and subtracting numbers that require regrouping on paper is the same as using the chips that required exchanging. Now may be a good time to introduce the concept of borrowing/carrying numbers. Show the students how to use the chips on their papers as a concrete representation while you stick the chips on the chalkboard in their representative column or use colored chips on an overhead projector. This is a critical step that helps make the transition from concrete representation using manipulatives to numbers on paper.

5. Begin with a problem such as 34 + 19. Have the students use the chips to represent 3 tens and 4 ones and then do the same for 19. Have

them count all the white (ones) chips and then exchange for a blue ten chip, putting the ten white or one blue chip in the proper columns. Ask them how many white chips are left (3) and show them where these belong in the column representation. Then have them count the number of blue chips or tens (5). Show them how they can place a one over the tens column to remind them of how many they exchanged, then count the numbers in the tens place and write that number in the correct columns.

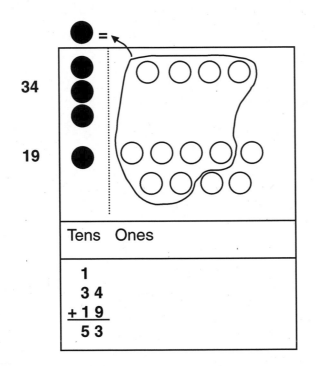

6. Once students are fluent with the addition problems, it is time to introduce subtraction in the same way. When borrowing, make sure that students don't get the substituted numbers and the cross outs confused. Remind them that this process is the same as exchanging the colored chips or regrouping the chips and that crossing out and putting in new numbers serves to remind them of what numerals they have exchanged, borrowed from, or added to when they are regrouping the numbers in the problem.

Step 1   **Step 2**   **Step 3**   5

● = ○○○○○
    ○○○○○

Tens	Ones	Tens	Ones	Tens	Ones
		1 1		1 1	
2 2		2 2		2 2	
- 7		- 7		- 7	
				1 5	

7. Begin with a problem such as, 22 - 7. Have students represent the problem with colored chips above the problem. Ask them how they can take seven white chips away from two white chips by exchanging (borrowing) from the blue chips/tens column. Most students should be able to figure this out. Make the transition to the numbers by showing them how this is represented by crossing out the two tens, leaving one ten in that column and adding the borrowed ten (blue chip) to the white chips/ones column. Continue practicing double-digit subtraction with regrouping until students can solve problems without the chips.

8. Practice writing double- and triple-digit numbers in the columns identified with hundreds, tens and ones so students can make the connection between the written numerals and place value. For more detailed information on writing numbers in represented groupings, refer to the article below on place value by Garlikov.

9. Once students can solve double-digit problems, including being able to calculate and explain how they arrived at the answer, move on to bigger numbers. If necessary, use chips at the beginning then fade as students become proficient.

• **Curriculum Based Measurement**: Computation Probe

Sources:
Garlikov. R. *The concept of teaching place value in math.* Retrieved from: www.garlikov.com/place value.html on 5/12/08.

Vacc, N. N., (1995). Gaining number sense through a restructured hundreds chart. *Teaching Exceptional Children*, Fall Issue.

Yang, M.T.L. & Cobb, P., (1995). A cross-cultural investigation into the development of place-value concepts of children in Taiwan and the United States. *Educational Studies in Mathematics,* 28(1). Retrieved from www.springerlink.com on 5/27/08.

Computational Fluency—5: It's All in the Timing

What it is: A technique for rapidly recalling basic facts of addition, subtraction, multiplication and division to develop fluency.

When to use it: After students can accurately solve basic fact problems using the four operations and need to focus on rapid recall.

⚠️ Prerequisites are the ability to write and accurately solve number facts in addition and subtraction up to the number 20, and multiplication and division through the tens.

Benefit: Students will build fluency in basic computation problems in order to focus on comprehension of a word problem.

Materials:
- Answer keys for each practice sheet
- A sheet protector for each sheet
- Transparency markers and pencils for each student
- Transparency of a practice sheet and overhead projector
- Timer
- Prepared Practice Sheets Template, Appendix B, p. 266, or prepared sheets from publishers
- Tracking Progress Form, Appendix B, p. 251
- Computation Probe, Appendix A, pp. 227-230

Implementation Steps:
1. Using the template, prepare practice sheets of basic facts (addition, subtraction, multiplication, division) and answer sheets at students' appropriate levels or determine the appropriate prepared sheet for each student.

Note: There should always be more problems on a practice sheet than can be completed during the established time frame. If it is a one-minute timing of basic facts, the sheets should contain at least 50 to 60 problems. This is important because the goal of practice timings is to complete as many problems as possible during the allocated time (in this case, one minute) and not the entire sheet. Keep in mind that students may be working on different sheets at the same time. Some may be on addition facts 1-10, while others may be on facts 11-20 or even subtraction. It is best not to mix facts on the sheet in the beginning so students can develop rapid recall one operation at a time.

2. Introduce this technique by explaining the importance of math fluency which is solving computation problems quickly and accurately. It provides the best picture of what a person knows about basic facts. It is important to emphasize that a practice timing is not a test, nor is it graded. The practice timings should be viewed more like a strategic video or computer game where the student is competing against himself and the clock.

3. Hand out practice sheets, answer sheets and a sheet protector to each student. For ease of checking and scoring, answer sheets are best copied in a different color than the practice sheet and placed behind the practice sheet in the protector. Explain to students that they may have different sheets depending on the facts they are practicing, and that as they make progress they will be given a new sheet.

4. Point out the blank boxes at the top of the practice sheet. Tell students these boxes are "write-ins" and can be used at their discretion to write in up to ten hard to remember facts of their choice from their practice sheet.

Note: If students take the time to use the write-in facts at the top of the page, they will not have time to answer as many problems. But, with enough practice, they should be able to fade the use of these prompts and solve the problems without them.

Example of math practice sheet with 'write ins' (Addition 1-10)

2	7	3	4	5	4	2	6		
+7	+2	+4	+3	+4	+5	+6	+8		
9	9	7	7	9	9	8	8		

```
   4      5      2      1      3      2      2
  +2     +5     +7     +2     +7     +1     +4


   1      7      4      3      5      1      9
  +1     +2     +1     +4     +3     +1     +1


   6      2      3      2      2      4      8
  +2     +7     +3     +6     +3     +2     +1


   3      4      2      5      3      5      4
  +4     +5     +2     +4     +1     +1     +4
```

5. Have students look at their respective sheets and to fill in the boxes at the top with any facts that they feel might be "hard" to recall during the practice timing. Have them fill in at least one or two boxes. Remind them that they do not have to use the boxes during the practice unless they get stuck. Once students have filled in the boxes, have them place their practice sheet in the sheet protector.

6. Using an overhead projector, demonstrate how to complete the practice sheet. Start with the problem in the top left and move across the first row to the last problem at the end or the row, then return to the left and down to the second row. Tell students to check the write-in boxes at the top of their sheet if necessary, or to skip the problem they cannot solve and move to the next.

7. Explain the procedure for conducting the practice timing. Tell students that when they hear you say, "Ready, pencils up, get set, begin," they will first hold up their pencils, then turn the paper over and begin the task. Let them know that you will start the timer when you say the word "begin." At the end of the timing, you will say, "pencils down, stop working, turn your paper over and thank you." Practice the

directions several times so students become accustomed to the procedures and understand what they are to do.

8. Next, hand out a marker to each student and set the timer for one minute. Remind students that they should complete as many problems as they can correctly within the specified time and not think they must finish the entire sheet. Emphasize that practice timings are similar to a strategic video and computer game and should be considered a competition with one's self to achieve one's personal best each time.

9. Conduct the practice timing. Once completed, instruct students to take out the answer sheet, place it on top of the practice sheet and line up the problems. This way, students can easily correct and score their own sheets.

Example of answer sheet (Addition 1-10)

4 +2 6	5 +5 10	2 +7 9	1 +2 3	3 +7 10	2 +1 3	2 +4 6
1 +1 2	7 +2 9	4 +1 5	3 +4 7	5 +3 8	1 +1 2	9 +1 10
6 +2 8	2 +7 9	3 +3 6	2 +6 8	2 +3 5	4 +2 6	8 +1 9
3 +4 7	4 +5 9	2 +2 4	5 +4 9	3 +1 4	5 +1 6	4 +4 8

10. Show students how to check their answers and score their practice sheets. Count one point for each correct digit written (i.e. if the answer is 6 and the student writes 6, he scores 1 point, if he writes 8, he scores 0 points; if the answer is 10 and the student writes 10, he scores 2 points, but if the student writes 12, he receives 1 point for the one digit that is correct …see scoring example below).

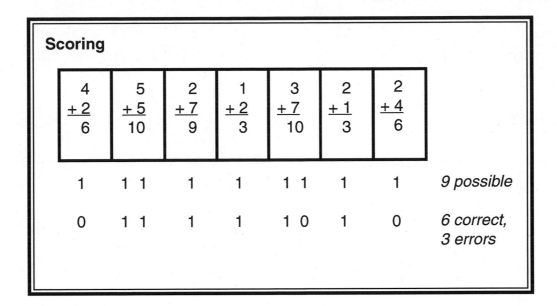

11. Have students score their own sheets by counting the total number of correct and incorrect digits. Explain that they will monitor their own progress by keeping track of their scores each time they practice. If they have more correct answers than the previous practice, then they are to check the up arrow box. If they do not increase the number of correct answers or the number of incorrect answers increases, then they are to check the down arrow.

Progress Tracking:
• Use the Tracking Progress Form to record the students' daily progress each time the technique is used. For example:

Name: Jane				
Date	# Correct	# Incorrect	↑ Progress ↓	
9/25	12	6		
10/4	15	4	✓	
10/12	17	4	✓	
10/18	17	5		✓
10/30	19	4	✓	

12. After recording the results of at least three practice timings, have students review their overall progress. If they are making progress, have them indicate so on their form. If they are not making progress, discuss with them what needs to change so they will be successful the next time.

• **Curriculum Based Measuremen**t: Computation Probe

Sources:
Delazer, M., Domahs, F., Bartha, L., Brenneis, C., Locky, A., Trieb, T. & Benke, T., (2003). Learning complex arithmetic—an fMRI study. *Cognitive Brain Research* 18, 76–88.

Garnett, K. (1992). Developing fluency with basic number facts: Intervention for students with learning disabilities. *Learning Disabilities Research & Practice* 7:210–216.

Rohrbeck , C.A. et al. (2003). Peer-assisted learning interventions with elementary school students: a meta-analytic review. *Journal of Educational Psychology,* 95(2), 240-257.

Suggested Resources

Bresser,R. (2003). Helping English-Language Learners Develop Computational Fluency. *Teaching Children Mathematics*, Vol. 9.

Focus On: Number Sense and Computational Fluency, K-4, San Mateo County Office of Education. Available from: www.smcoe.k12.ca.us/

Gersten,R., Baker, S., & Chard, D. (2006). *Effective Instructional Practices for Students with Difficulties in Mathematics: Findings from a Research Synthesis.* Center on Instruction.

Griffin, S. (2003). Laying the Foundation for Computational Fluency in Early Childhood. *Teaching Children Mathematics.* Vol. 9, 6; p. 306

Multiplicative Thinking: Situations for Multiplication and Division Powerpoint. www.nzmaths.co.nz/

New Zealand Maths website—www.nzmaths.co.nz

Trafton, P. R. & Thiessen, D. (1999). *Learning Through Problems: Number Sense and Computational Strategies/A Resource for Primary Teachers.* Plymouth, NH: Heinemann

Chapter 8
About Problem Solving

"People ask me questions, lost in confusion.
Well, I tell them there's no problem, only solutions."
—John Lennon, *Watching the Wheels*

Since you are now studying geometry and trigonometry, I will give you a problem. A ship sails the ocean. It left Boston with a cargo of wool. It grosses 200 tons. It is bound for Le Havre. The mainmast is broken, the cabin boy is on deck, there are 12 passengers aboard, the wind is blowing East-North-East, the clock points to a quarter past three in the afternoon. It is the month of May. How old is the captain? (Gustav Flaubert)

Flaubert's satirical example above may conjure up memories of the deer-in-the-headlights-look you had when you were first faced with word problems—or, perhaps you simply stopped reading at the point where the ship left Boston. Satire aside, if we accept the notion that math is a language and a science of ideas, and if we believe that computation and problem solving do not exist in isolation, then we must recognize the value of problem-solving skills.

Many teachers and researchers also agree that the point of mathematics instruction is to help students learn how to use math as a language and as a tool to represent and to resolve problem situations across all disciplines (Moursand, 2003). It is common knowledge that mathematics requires the manipulation of math symbols in order to calculate solutions; however, these skills are only meaningful if students understand the thinking and reasoning of problem posing, problem solving, computation and proof. This parallels the acquisition of reading whereby students are required to manipulate sounds and letters of the language before they can read words and apply strategies to comprehend and make meaning of text. "Problem solving forms the base for application and comprehension of mathematics and is the process by which meaningful learning takes place (NCTM, 2005)."

With carefully planned combinations of explicit instruction and strategic techniques (presented in the correct sequence and at the right pace), students learn to use the language of mathematics to think, reason and problem solve. As mentioned in the previous chapters, even very young students can make sense of relationships of quantity or size and situations, and can learn to apply these strategies to problem solving. Students often learn concepts more readily when working with word problems or "math stories," as opposed to pure computation tasks that do not include a context that relates to their learning (National Research Council, 2006). Once students have acquired number sense from 1-10, they can solve simply-worded problems using physical counters or role play to represent a story problem. As the numbers get larger, students learn more efficient ways to approach word problems such as expanding their use of mental imaging to internalize and generalize beyond their immediate, physical experience or personal familiarity.

It bears repeating that the vocabulary of mathematics, which is different from "ordinary" or everyday language, is a critical skill that must be addressed as new mathematical concepts are introduced (NCTM, 2005). In order for students to make connections between the meaning of words they already know and use, and the specialized meaning of those same words when they talk and write about math computation and problem solving, their vocabulary must evolve as problems become more complex (Rothstein et al. 2007). As discussed in Chapter 5, the effective teaching of mathematical vocabulary cannot be a random process, but rather must be an organized approach that puts the mathematical vocabulary into the appropriate context.

Mathematical problem-solving is a complex cognitive activity. Problem solving has two stages: problem representation and problem execution. It is not possible to derive a solution to a problem without being able to represent it appropriately. In order to accurately represent the problem, the solver must understand the context and concepts that underlie it. This process is similar to deciphering the main idea and supporting details of a reading passage. Students who have difficulty with reading comprehension will most likely have similar difficulty representing a problem in order to execute a solution (Montague, 2006). Albert Einstein, whose theories of relativity are well known, used imagery as the base for his mental processing and problem-solving, and summarized the importance of imagery for him by saying, "If I can't picture it, I can't understand it" (Bell and Tuley, 2003).

In the book, *Comprehending Math, Adapting Reading Strategies to Teach Mathematics, K-6,* Hyde discusses how to help students become successful problem solvers and thinkers by "braiding" together reading comprehension, cognitive processes and mathematics. Successful word problem solvers, just like successful readers, learn to read math problems for meaning (comprehension), using cognitive and meta-cognitive (thinking about your own thinking) processes. When problem solving happens efficiently, it incorporates reading, writing, speaking and listening. Students who use all these skills ask themselves the following questions each time they solve a word problem:

- What is this about? (main idea)
- How can I relate to this problem? (making connections)
- How can I put it in my own words? (paraphrasing)
- What do I see? (visualization)
- What do I know? (facts and inferences)
- What do I need to find? (essential information)
- What do I need to do? (representation and operations)
- What steps do I need to take in order to do it? (strategies and algorithm)
- Does my answer make sense? (reviewing)

So what's a teacher to do to help students develop these skills? An effective mathematics curriculum includes problem solving. The techniques found in this chapter address visualization, making representations and connections, questioning and using strategies to solve word problems. To develop problem-solving skills, a student must first have a thorough understanding of the language of math, number sense and computational fluency. If you still have questions about any of these topics, go to the previous chapters to review this information.

During math instruction a discerning teacher will recognize when a student is not demonstrating successful problem-solving skills and will pursue assessment. To assist, we offer the Cardinal Questions as they relate to word problem solving:

1. **What does the student know** about the purpose of word problems and how to approach a solution?

2. **What does the student do** when asked to solve a word problem?
    - Does the student read or listen to the entire problem before trying to solve it?
    - Does the student visualize and verbalize the main idea?
    - Does the student list the facts that are known?
    - Does the student identify the problem type?
    - Does the student identify the unknown in the problem?
    - Does the student paraphrase the problem in sentence form?
    - Does the student convert the problem into numbers and functions (math language)?
    - Does the student know what steps to take to solve the problem?
    - Does the student check the answer to see if it makes sense?
    - Does the student check his/her calculations?
    - Does the student explain and monitor the steps he/she took to solve the problem?

3. **How does the student learn?** (See Chapter Two)

4. **How does the student approach or react to an unfamiliar task?** (See Chapter Two)

5. **What will you do with the knowledge gained from answering the previous four questions?**

Armed with this information, the following five techniques will assist you in the instruction of good problem-solving skills:
    1. Math Heads
    2. See the Story
    3. What's Your Problem?
    4. Think Aloud
    5. I Can Explain That!

"Take a deep breath and a step back, enough to see that everything's working out fine, its only a matter of time."
—Tristan Prettyman, *Get Away*

Problem Solving – 1:
Math Heads

What it is: A technique to keep track of math vocabulary words and then reinforce the vocabulary in a cooperative learning format.

When to use it: When students need to remember key vocabulary terms so they can read about, think about, talk about and apply math terminology to number and word problems at all levels.

⚠ Prerequisites include prior introduction to and explanation of mathematic words/terms and the ability to read the words/terms and definitions.

Benefit: Students will build vocabulary knowledge needed to comprehend word problems.

Materials:
- Chart paper for a classroom size taxonomy
- One set of teacher cards with vocabulary word and its corresponding definition or term on each card (Start with at least 20 different words and add to the set as vocabulary is introduced)
- Four or more sets (one set per group of students) of cards that contain only the definition, description or picture for each word in the teacher's vocabulary set.
- A die or spinner with numbers 1-6. A die or spinner with the letters A,B,C,D,E
- A blank piece of paper or the Math Head Alphabet Template, Appendix B, p. 267, for each student
- Teacher Key Planning Form, Appendix B, p. 250
- Math Head Scoring Sheet, Appendix B, p. 268
- Concepts and Applications Probe, Appendix A, pp. 231-232

📝 *Note: See the end of this chapter for resources on math vocabulary. Don't forget that the vocabulary must be introduced before students engage in the activity.*

Implementation Steps:

Part A—Vocabulary Development

1. Provide each student with a prepared taxonomy sheet, such as the Math Head Alphabet Template, or have students create their own "math taxonomy" in a notebook. The term taxonomy is used because it organizes and classifies vocabulary words by topic or subject (Rothstein et al., 2007).

2. Create a classroom taxonomy (see below) using a sheet of chart paper. This will show students how to develop a taxonomy themselves, as well as serve as a reference. Instruct students to write the letters alphabetically down the left hand side of the paper, and then discuss a title for the taxonomy, such as "Math Head Words" and write it at the top of the paper.

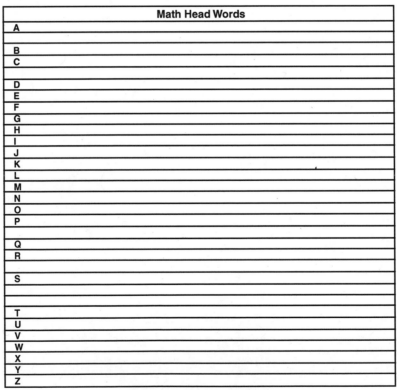

Taxonomy for Math

3. Explain to students that a taxonomy is used to keep track of math words they know and words they will get to know. As the words accumulate and students learn the word meanings, they will become

mathematicians or Math Heads. Let students know that the words they write on this sheet will not only be useful for remembering new math words, but that they will also be used in the Math Heads game.

4. Demonstrate how to use the taxonomy by writing a math word (i.e., subtraction) on the chart. The first time you use the taxonomy, use any word that is related to math as long as students can explain the relationship. Write the word next to the corresponding beginning letter on the chart and have students do the same on their sheet. As you introduce and explore each math unit, you can develop taxonomies specific to the topic (e.g., measurement, time, geometry, etc.).

5. You can build a taxonomy list together as a class for each unit or students can add words to their own lists as they encounter them. The individual lists can then be shared with the class for further discourse. Either way, the taxonomy becomes a tool for communicating about math, as well as vocabulary development for later word problem solving.

Part B—Math Heads Together

1. This activity is adapted from "Numbered Heads Together" (Maheady, 2001). Prior to using this activity, you will need a predetermined vocabulary list or words from the classroom taxonomy in order to create:

   ✓ One large set of cards (8" x 10") for the teacher with the vocabulary word/term on one side of each card and the definition on the other.

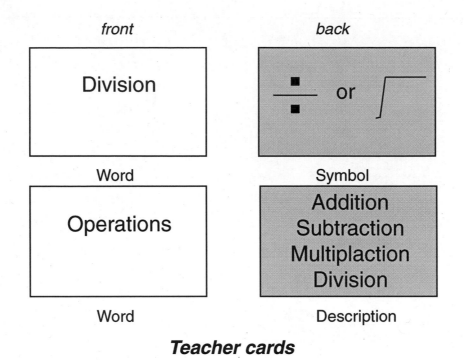

Teacher cards

✓ Four or five sets of cards for students (4" x 6" or 5" x 8") with only the definition/description/picture of each word on each card.

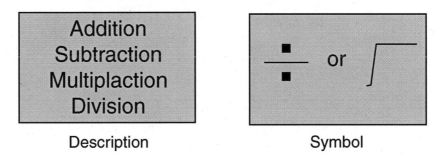

Student cards

Note: These sets of cards can be created with the students to obtain their input for the best possible student-friendly definitions, description or picture to depict each vocabulary word.

Planning:
• Use the Teacher Planning Key to create your plans for this activity. For example:

Teacher Key for *Math Heads*

Problem Solving
Technique #1—Part B: Numbered Heads

Vocabulary Words—Unit 2
1. Operations
2. Addition
3. Sum
4. Take away
5. Array
6. Put together
7. Subtraction
8. Left over
9. Quantity
10. Difference

---

2. Provide specific instruction related to cooperative learning if students have not engaged in this type of activity before. Be sure to remind students that cooperative learning is about the team and not just the individual.

3. Divide the class evenly into groups of four or five (four is more manageable). If there is an uneven number, have the extra student(s) act as judge(s) and/or score keeper(s). Within each group, have students count off by ones to the highest number in the group. For example, if you have 24 students in your class, and you have six groups of four students, then there will be six students in the room, each assigned to numbers 1, 2, 3 and 4. Tell students they must remember their assigned number for this activity.

4. Explain the activity to the students. Say: "We will be reviewing vocabulary from our class taxonomy, using a game called Math Heads. To be successful at this game, you must work as a team. The students in your group are your team." If this is the first time using this activity, identify each group/team with the letters A,B,C,D, or let the groups pick team names.

5. Say: "Each group has an identical set of cards containing definitions, description or pictures of math words/terms that are familiar. All

teams will use these cards to match the vocabulary word that I present to everyone at the same time."

6. Explain the rules and the process for matching the terms to the vocabulary word cards. Say: "Each student in your group has a number from 1-4, it is important to remember your number as this is how I will call for answers and how you will score points for your team."

7. Demonstrate the game by choosing a card (e.g., operations) from the teacher set. Show the side of the card with the vocabulary word to all of the teams. Check to make sure every person on all teams can see the card.

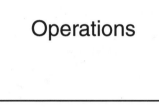

Operations

8. Tell the teams to look through their set of cards and discuss possible matches for this vocabulary word. Allow about 20-30 seconds for the search. Once the team thinks they have the correct match, tell them to check with each member to be sure that all are in agreement with the choice.

Say: "It is important for the team members to work together and agree, so that no matter what number I call (1,2,3 or 4), any member of the team can answer the question correctly and be able to explain why that answer is the best choice." Allow enough time for students to discuss their choice and come to agreement (one minute is recommended). You may want to use some type of signal to obtain the group's attention before the next step.

9. Once you have everyone's attention, use a die or spinner to identify a number between one and four. If a three is rolled, say, "All number three's stand with your answer card and hold it up for me (and/or the judges) to see." Every team that is showing the correct answer scores a point. Have the scorekeeper write down points awarded to each respective team.

Math Heads: Together Scoring Sheet						
Teams						
Vocabulary Word/Team	A	B	C	D	E	F
parallel						
quotient						
product						
horizontal						
regroup						
double						
less than						
greater than						
all together						
Team Totals						

10. To play the game, set a time limit of 20-30 minutes, or choose a set number of cards to present. Follow the process outlined in Steps #7-10. The team with the most points at the end earns the "Math Head" title for the day/week.

Variation: Make the game more challenging by randomly (roll a die or use a spinner with team names) choosing one person to stand and ask this student to defend his/her choice or use the word in a sentence. This follow-up can be part of the one point score or you can give a bonus point if the response warrants.

• **Curriculum Based Measurement**: Concepts and Applications Probe

Sources:
Gifford, M. & Gore, S. (2008). *The effects of focused academic vocabulary instruction on underperforming math students,* ASCD report. Alexandria, VA: Association for Supervision and Curriculum Development.

Maheady, L. (1991). Heads Together: A peer mediated option for improving the academic achievement of heterogeneous group. *Remedial and Special Education,* 12(2), 25-33.

Problem Solving—2
See the Story

What it is: A technique to represent word problems with pictures or symbols.

When to use it: When students are unable to represent a word problem after reading it.

⚠️ Prerequisites are the ability to visualize while listening or reading (grades two and up) word problems, and understand the vocabulary and the operations in the problem.

Benefit: Students comprehend word problems by using visuals to make accurate representations as they develop schema.

Materials:
- A variety of manipulatives such as counters, small blocks, tiles (optional)
- Overhead projector or chalkboard
- Transparency of the See the Story Template
- Transparency markers
- Colored highlighters or pencils for students
- Short Story Problem Samples, Appendix B, pp. 271-274 (provide copies of the story problems for the students if they can read)
- Blank paper or See the Story Template, Appendix B, p. 270
- Copy of the See the Story Poster, Appendix B, p. 269
- Concepts and Applications Probe, Appendix A, pp. 231-232

Implementation Steps:
Part A—1. Picture Visualization

1. Explain to students that you are going to draw pictures to represent a story.

2. Remind them that visualization is making pictures in your mind. Visualizing is a planful way to understand a word problem so you can solve it correctly.

3. Have a See the Story/Visualize poster in the room, or a small bookmark to remind students of the technique.

4. Explain that you will be reading a simple story passage aloud. Tell students that while you are reading they are to close their eyes and listen. As they are listening they should picture in their minds what is happening in the story.

5. Show students the See the Story Template using the overhead, or draw a large version on the board. Let students know they will use this template when they draw their own representation of the story.

6. Model how to use the See the Story technique. Tell students to close their eyes, listen to the story and make pictures in their mind based on what they are hearing.

    1st Sample story: One day two big dogs were running in the park chasing a ball. Then 2 little dogs ran over and started chasing the ball. A man came and took one of the big dogs away. How many dogs were left chasing the ball?

7. You may want to have several students share what they pictured when you were reading.

Note: If students are unable to picture the story, we encourage you to teach them how to visualize. Ideas for this can be found in Kemp & Eaton, RTI: The Classroom Connection for Literacy, page 154.

8. Tell students you will read the story again, sentence by sentence, and they will draw a representation of what they are picturing. Emphasize that it is not necessary to draw well. The most important part of this activity is to understand what is happening in the story.

Read:

One day, two big dogs were running in the park chasing a ball.

9. Say and draw: "When I read this sentence, I picture two big (great danes) dogs chasing a ball in a park. To represent the park I'll draw a big circle. Then I'll make a big triangle for each of the dogs and put a D in both of them to remind me they are dogs. Finally, I need to draw a ball just in case that detail is important later on. I now have two dogs and a ball represented from my story."

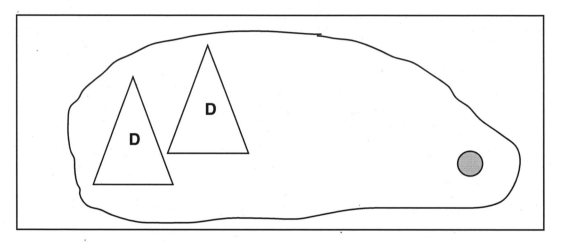

Now, read the next sentence:

"Then, two little dogs ran over and started chasing the ball."

10. Say and draw: "In my mind, I saw two more little dogs (chihuahuas). I think I'll represent them as a small hotdog shape, and I'll put a little *d* in each of them to remind me they are little dogs."

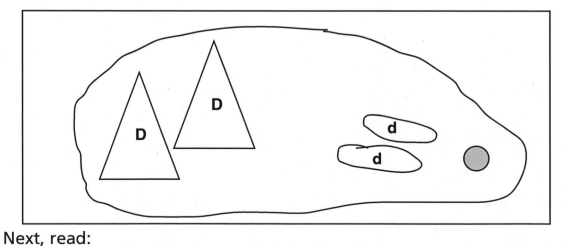

Next, read:

"A man came and took one of the big dogs away."

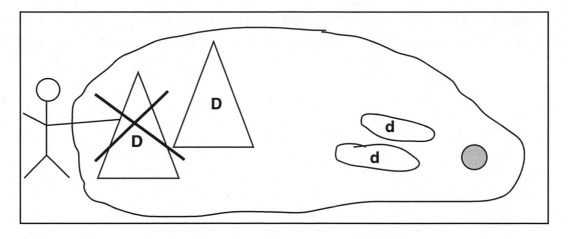

11. Say and draw: "In my mind I see a man, so I'll add him to my picture but draw him off to the side. I have to do something to my picture to show that the man came to take the dog. This part is a little harder because I have to show that one of the big dogs has left the park. I can either draw another picture showing one less big dog, I can erase a dog, or I can put a big X (similar to crossing something out when writing) on the dog that is connected to the man to show it is not there anymore."

12. Say and draw: "The last sentence asks: 'how many dogs are left chasing the ball?' Now I look at my picture and count all the shapes with D in them that are still in the park. I count 1,2,3, because I don't count the dog that is crossed out. Remember, the last number I count tells me how many are left, which means the answer to the question 'How many dogs were left chasing the ball' is three."

13. The last step of See the Story is to check the picture frame to see if it matches the sentences from the story. Do this by asking: "Does the drawing fit the sentence and does it make sense?" If the answer to these questions is yes, then there is a greater chance of correctly solving the word problem.

Variation: Instead of drawing, have students use manipulatives such as counters or other objects and place them on the See the Story template to represent the dogs they are visualizing. As you read the story, have them add the counters and then remove one to represent the dog that gets taken away. Eventually, fade the manipulatives and encourage students to draw what they see in their mind before you move them on to schemas or diagrams.

Note: If students still do not grasp the visualization strategy, try acting out the story. Have the entire class watch one group of students or split the class into groups of six and have each group physically act out the word problem. One student can read the story and the others role play what is happening. Once they have completed the role play, have them draw a picture of what they did.

14. Hand out a See the Story template to each student. Tell the class that they will practice picturing the story again, but this time they will be drawing along with you after they listen to the story. Have them close their eyes as you read and remind them to make pictures in their minds based on what they hear. Refer to the See the Story poster.

    Sample story: *Sammy has four Hot Wheel cars. He saved the money he got for his birthday and bought two new Hot Wheel cars. His big brother gave him three more cars that he didn't want any more. How many cars does Sammy have now?*

15. Repeat Steps #1-13, while you and the students engage in discourse about the process. Read each sentence and add to the picture each time until you have a complete story. Encourage students to tell you what they "see" and draw what they say. As students complete the story picture, tell them that their pictures do not have to look exactly like yours, but they need to tell the same story.

16. Repeat Steps#1-13 , this time reading the story aloud or allowing students to read independently and have them draw their picture stories independently. Remind them again that it is okay to have different representations or drawings, because each person may visualize or see things differently.

Variation: Have students work in pairs or small groups as they use the technique. The students can take turns writing a story and then having their partner draw the representation. Have the groups share their completed stories to demonstrate similarities and differences in the representations.

Part B—Schemas
1. Explain to students that visualizing or picturing a story and then planning it out in a diagram called a schema. A schema is a diagram

or a plan of how to represent on paper a story that we pictured in our minds. The plan or diagram can be pictures, but often shapes or lines represent the objects in the story. The See the Story technique is still used, but the schema might look different. Use a story the students are familiar with and show them how to develop a schema.

Sample Story: *One day, two big dogs were running in the park chasing a ball. Then 2 little dogs ran over and started chasing the ball. A man came and took one of the big dogs away. How many dogs were left chasing the ball?*

2. Use the See the Story Template and have students show a schema for the story. If students can make the schema without having to write each sentence, allow them to do so. Remind students again that a schema can be represented in different ways, but it is still a visual representation of the story.

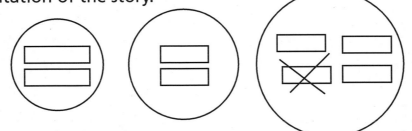

![speaker icon] <u>Variation</u>: Group student in pairs and have each student develop a schema individually and then tell a story to the partner using the representation they have drawn. The partners can also develop a schema together, trade the drawings and then take turns telling a story based on the others schema.

• **<u>Curriculum Based Measurement</u>**: Concepts and Applications Probe

<u>Sources</u>:
Bell, N. & Tuley, K. (2003). Imagery: *The sensory-cognitive connection for math.* Internet Special Education Resources (ISER).

Jitendra, A. (2002). Teaching students math problem-solving through graphic representations. *Teaching Exceptional Children,* 34(4), 34-38.

Wheatley, G.H. (1998). Imagery and mathematics learning. *Focus on Learning Problems in Mathematics,* 20(2/3), 65-77.

Problem Solving—3
What's Your Problem?

What it is: A technique to identify the word problem type in order to determine the operation and solve the problem.

When to use it: When students do not understand the types of word problems and/or steps of word problem solving.

⚠️ Prerequisites are knowledge of the basic operations, word problem types and the ability to work with others cooperatively.

Benefit: Students become competent at communicating math processes needed to solve word problems.

Materials:
• Copies of the Problem Type Reference Sheet, Appendix B, p. 275
• Copies of the What's Your Problem? Worksheet, Appendix B, p. 277
• Copies of the What's Your Problem? Team Checklist, Appendix B, p. 276
• Selection of word problems or Story Problem Samples 1 and 2, Appendix B, pp. 271-274, to suit level of instruction
• Concepts and Applications Probe, Appendix A, pp. 231-232

Implementation Steps:
Part 1
1. Hand out a Types of Problem reference sheet to each student. Review each of the problem types, using the chart and check for student understanding.

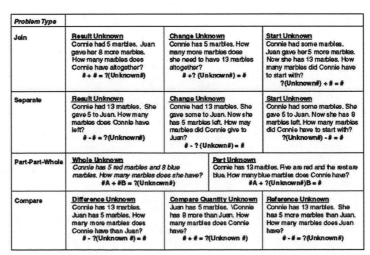

Problem Type			
Join	**Result Unknown** Connie had 5 marbles. Juan gave her 8 more marbles. How many marbles does Connie have altogether? # + # = ?(Unknown#)	**Change Unknown** Connie has 5 marbles. How many more marbles does she need to have 13 marbles altogether? # +? (Unknown#) = #	**Start Unknown** Connie had some marbles. Juan gave her 5 more marbles. Now she has 13 marbles. How many marbles did Connie have to start with? ?(Unknown#) + # = #
Separate	**Result Unknown** Connie had 13 marbles. She gave 5 to Juan. How many marbles does Connie have left? # - # = ?(Unknown#)	**Change Unknown** Connie had 13 marbles. She gave some to Juan. Now she has 5 marbles left. How may marbles did Connie give to Juan? # - ? (Unknown#) = #	**Start Unknown** Connie had some marbles. She gave 5 to Juan. Now she has 8 marbles left. How many marbles did Connie have to start with? ?(Unknown#) - # = #
Part-Part-Whole	**Whole Unknown** *Connie has 5 red marbles and 8 blue marbles. How many marbles does she have?* #A + #B = ?(Unknown#)		**Part Unknown** Connie has 13 marbles. Five are red and the rest are blue. How many blue marbles does Connie have? #A + ?(Unknown#)B = #
Compare	**Difference Unknown** Connie has 13 marbles. Juan has 5 marbles. How many more marbles does Connie have than Juan? # - ?(Unknown #) = #	**Compare Quantity Unknown** Juan has 5 marbles. \Connie has 8 more than Juan. How many marbles does Connie have? # + # = ?(Unknown #)	**Reference Unknown** Connie has 13 marbles. She has 5 more marbles than Juan. How many marbles does Juan have? # - # = ?(Unknown#)

2. Explain to students that they will be reading the word problems and identifying each problem type. They will use the chart to decide on one of the following types: join problem, separate problem, part-part-whole problem, or compare problem.

3. Use an overhead projector to show students the What's Your Problem? Worksheet. Let them know that for the first activity they will only need to fill in the first two columns.

What's Your Problem? Worksheet			
Team Members			
Problem Type: (J) Join (PPW) Part-Part- Whole (S) Separate (C) Compare		**Agreement Initials**	
Problem #	**Type**	**Math Symbol Sentence**	**Answer**

4. Explain further that students will be working in teams of four, each team will receive one worksheet and all members of the team will be responsible for the information on that worksheet.

   Tell students that, as members of a team, they are expected to:
   - Work as a group
   - Encourage each other
   - Come to agreement

   Assign each person on the team one of the following roles: reader, scribe, checker and timekeeper. The reader will read each of the word problems aloud to the team. The scribe will write the group's answers on the worksheet. The checker will make sure everyone is in agreement after each group decision. The timekeeper will keep track of the time allotted for the activity in order to complete the problems and do a final check.

5. Having grouped students into teams of four, arrange the teams around the classroom and then assign roles by handing out or having students select role cards.

6. Once teams are established, give the scribe the What's Your Problem? Worksheet. Give a sheet containing a pre-determined number of word problems to the reader. Instruct the scribe to fill in the team member names at the top of the sheet. Let the team timekeepers know how much time teams have to complete the first two columns of the worksheet. Write the end time where everyone can see it so teams can budget their time accordingly. Finally, let the checkers know that part of their role is to make sure all team members are in agreement on the answers. They do this by witnessing each team member write his/her initials in the box located on the worksheet. Check for any last minute questions or clarifications.

7. You may review the answers with the teams or have teams exchange worksheets and then review the answers. Teams are expected to clarify and correct any problems they did not identify correctly.

Note: If at any time during the activity students have difficulty reading the word problem, recognizing vocabulary, or understanding the text, instruct them to first check with their team members for clarification before bringing the teacher over for help.

Part 2—Solving the problems

1. Using the same word problem sheet and worksheet, have the teams complete the remaining columns (this can be done one at a time or all at once). Explain to the teams that now that they know the type of problem they are working on, they are expected to solve it. Hand out a What's Your Problem? Checklist to each team and tell them to follow the steps below (also on the checklist).

a. Highlight, underline or circle the numbers you know from the problem.
b. Determine what you need to do to answer the question: count or add, subtract, multiply or divide. Make a plan.
c. Write each step in math language (symbols) and perform the calculations you need to find the solution.

What's Your Problem?
Team Checklist

Team member names:

> **Steps:**
> 1. Highlight the numbers that you know
> 2. Determine what operation(s) will answer the question.
> 3. Write a math sentence to perform the calculations.

Check (✓) each task as you complete it for problem #_____.

_____ We read the problem.
_____ We agree that the problem question is this:
(Write the question in the space below)

_____ We showed the steps to find the solution using the steps above.

_____ We solved the problem and came up with this answer.

Note: You may choose to differentiate the complexity of problems in order to meet the varied levels of your students. Code the problems with A, B, C or other symbols according to level of complexity. Students may choose the level of complexity they feel comfortable with at first, and earn more points as they challenge themselves with higher-level word problems.

<u>Variation</u>: Have students or teams develop their own word problems (make sure they can also answer them). Exchange the word problems with other teams and follow the steps in Part 1 and 2.

- **Curriculum Based Measurement**: Concepts and Applications Probe

Sources:

Hardy, S. (2005). *Researched-based math interventions for middle school students with disabilities.* Available: http://www.k8accesscenter.org/

Maccini, P. & Gagnon, J. (2006). *Mathematics strategy instruction (SI) for middle school students with learning disabilities.* LD OnLine. Available: http://www.ldonline. org/article/14919.

Montague, M. (2003). *Solve it! A practical approach to teaching mathematical problem-solving skills.* Reston, VA: Exceptional Innovations.

Teaching shapes using read alouds, visualization, and sketch to stretch. Read Write Think. International Reading Association. NCTE. Available: http://www.readwritethink.org

Problem Solving—4
Think Aloud

What it is: A technique to teach students a thinking process for reading and setting up math word problems.

When to use it: When students need assistance setting up and reading word problems.

⚠ Prerequisite: Understanding the vocabulary, operations and the questions being asked in the word problem.

Benefit: Students become competent in using meta-cognitive strategies to think through the process of solving word problems.

Materials:
- Overhead Projector
- Copies of the Think It, Write It Worksheet (use whichever of the two Worksheets are most appropriate for your students), Appendix B, pp. 278-279
- Transparency of the structured Think It, Write It Worksheet
- Word problems appropriate to student ability
- Concepts and Applications Probe, Appendix A, pp. 231-232

Implementation Steps:
Part A

1. Explain to students that you are going to teach them how to "think aloud" as they read math word problems. Tell them you will demonstrate how to go about thinking about each part of a math word problem in order to solve it accurately. Explain that you will think aloud as you work and that to help you remember the steps to thinking aloud, you will use a structured worksheet. Have the students listen and watch as you demonstrate how to think aloud while completing the worksheet.

2. Display the worksheet on an overhead so you can complete it as you think aloud and work through the entire problem. Fill in the information at the top of the worksheet.

Think It~Write It
Addition and Subtraction

Name:	Date:
Problem:	_____ Alone _____ and Me

What is this about? (in my own words – paraphrasing <10 words) Who? What happened?	I can solve it this way:(make a plan—math representation and operations) _____received means add (+) _____left means take away (-) _____more than (compare) (+) _____less than (compare) (-)
What do I know? (facts stated in the problem) Known: _____ has/had _____ What changed? Someone... _____received _____(has more or add) _____gave _____(separated or subtract)	What steps do I need to take? (compute: show all steps and symbols)
What do I need to find? (problem question/direction = the unknown) Unknown: How many or Find _____ _____Altogether (Add) _____Left (Subtract) _____More than_____(Compare) _____Less than_____(Compare) _____Part/Part/Whole _____	New Vocabulary: Connections to Life:
What do I see? (visualize – schema – tally marks)	Check: Does my answer make sense? (answers the question or follows the direction)

3. Tell students the first thing to do is to read the whole problem to find out what it is about. Say, "Here is the math problem I want to solve (read):

   Charlie has seven goldfish and five angel fish in his fish tank. His cousin gives him two more gold fish and one more angel fish. How many fish does Charlie have in all?"

4. Now, say aloud whatever you are thinking as you complete the structured worksheet. For example, you may say: "What is this about (in my own words)? This is about a boy, who has some fish and gets more fish." Write, "boy has fish and gets more fish."

5. "What do I need to find out?" Say: "Usually, the part of the problem that tells me what I have to find has a question mark, in this case, 'How many fish does Charlie have in all?' I know the words mean altogether. I have to join the numbers or put the numbers together."

6. Once you have determined the question, show students where to write it on the Think It, Write It Worksheet.

7. Say, "Okay. Now I need to think: what do I have to do to figure this out? What information do I need? Do I need to know what angel fish are? I don't think so, but I'll write it here in the Vocabulary section to remind me, just in." (Demonstrate)

Continue: "Let's see. I have to find out how many fish Charlie has altogether. It seems that I can figure this out with the information I have, even if I don't know what angel fish are."

Say: "Can I see this problem in my mind? Here is what I see: (Draw on the worksheet in the designated space.)"

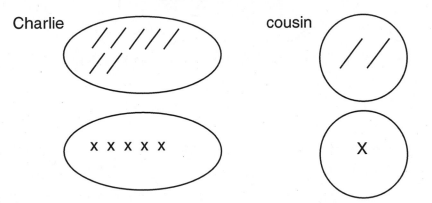

8. Say, "Okay. What steps do I need to take to find out how many fish Charlie has altogether? I can count all the marks: one, two, three, four, five, six, seven eight, nine, ten. eleven, twelve. Twelve fish. Then I can keep counting up with the marks I made for the fish his cousin gave him. Twelve, thirteen, fourteen, fifteen. So now I see that Charlie has fifteen fish all together.

What is another way I could figure this out? I could use the number symbols, 7, 5, 2, and 1. If I start with seven and count up five more. That makes twelve. And if I count up with the 2 and the 1, I still see that Charlie has fifteen fish."

There is still another way I can represent this story! I can use the numbers and the math symbol that means *altogether* or *adding on* or *counting up*.

7 fish + 5 fish are 12 fish altogether.

12 fish + 2 fish is 14 fish altogether.

14 fish + 1 fish is 15 fish altogether.

So I just thought of 3 different ways I could solve this math problem."

9. Explain to students that on their first try, they will not need to solve the problems, they are just going to think through the process aloud alone or with a partner. Say, "If I was going to solve this problem for the answer, the final step would be to check my answer to see if it makes sense. This step is important in order to know if my answer is correct."

10. Say: "Before I finish the sheet, I want to go back to the vocabulary section. I have written *angel fish*. I don't know this type of fish but that didn't keep me from thinking through the problem. Still, I want to look it. I don't think it is a math word, but let's see."

Note: Teaching someone to think means teaching a sensory system to process information. Think-alouds combined with written information teach students how to use the meta-cognitive processes: reading problems for understanding, paraphrasing, visualizing, hypothesizing, sometimes estimating, computing and checking. It helps them understand that not all information presented in a problem is always necessary to arrive at the solution. It shows them that they can use language and prior knowledge in conjunction with math and new knowledge to solve problems.

11. Repeat Steps #1–7 with a new problem. Have students think aloud while you complete the structured worksheet. Then have the students complete a worksheet along with you. Repeat the process with another problem.

12. Have students create their own word problems, then switch with other students to complete the think-aloud process using the structured worksheet.

• **Curriculum Based Measurement**: Concepts and Applications Probe

Source:
Swanson, H.L. (1999). Instructional components that predict treatment outcomes for students with learning disabilities: Support for a combined strategy and direct instruction model. *Learning Disabilities & Research*, (14), 129-140.

Problem Solving—5
I Can Explain That!

What it is: A self-monitoring technique to assist students in becoming independent word problem solvers.

When to use it: When students are unable to explain the process of solving a word problem.

Prerequisites: Understand vocabulary, operations and process of solving word problems. Ability to work independently.

Benefit: Assists students in remembering the meta-cognitive or think-aloud process to explain and solve word problems.

Materials:
- An overhead projector
- Copies of the Think It, Write It Checklist, Appendix B, p. 280
- Copies of the Think It Write Bookmark, Appendix B, p. 281
- An overhead transparency of the Checklist.
- A selection of word problems at various instructional levels
- Concepts and Applications Probe, Appendix A, pp. 231-232

Implementation Steps:

1. Explain to students that you are going to show them how to become independent problem solvers by using a checklist to self-monitor the steps they use when solving word problems. Let them know that using the checklist will help them organize their thinking, explain the process used and ensure that they do not miss important steps in the problem solving process.

2. Show students the checklist on the overhead.

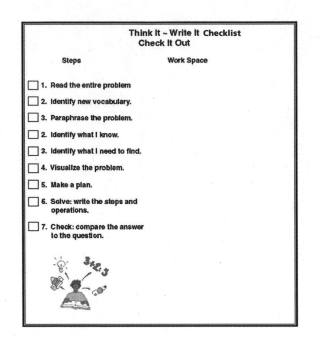

Think It ~ Write It Checklist
Check It Out

Steps   Work Space

☐ 1. Read the entire problem
☐ 2. Identify new vocabulary.
☐ 3. Paraphrase the problem.
☐ 2. Identify what I know.
☐ 3. Identify what I need to find.
☐ 4. Visualize the problem.
☐ 5. Make a plan.
☐ 6. Solve: write the steps and operations.
☐ 7. Check: compare the answer to the question.

3. Tell students that when using the checklist, they will follow the same process as for the Think It, Write It Worksheet, only this time the steps are listed down the left side of the page (without the information from the structured worksheet) and the work space is on the right.

4. Provide students with a copy of a word problem and read it together prior to solving it.

5. Proceed with the think-aloud process described in Technique #4 in this chapter, this time checking off each step on the checklist as it is completed in the workspace.

Note: Some students may need to write out each step, while others just need to think it through and check off the step. Work with students individually to determine their level of proficiency with the process.

6. Remind students that when they check off each step, they are self-monitoring. The checklist serves as a framework to help them explain their work and eventually solve the problem. Using this checklist will help them commit the steps of the process to memory for future use and will help them pinpoint difficulties they may encounter while thinking through the process.

7. Check for understanding by having students describe how and when they can use the checklist to explain and then solve word problems.

8. If students do not remember what each step means, review the steps again using the information from Technique #4, Think Aloud.

9. Once students are comfortable using the checklist, provide them with additional word problems at the appropriate level. Have them use the checklist to explain problem-solving process and then solve by showing the steps in the work space.

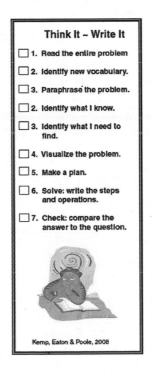 Variation: Have students choose a partner. Each partner solves a problem, then the partners exchange papers to check if the other followed the steps of the checklist to arrive at the correct answer.

10. When students no longer need to be reminded to show all their work, give each student a bookmark of the Think It, Write It steps. Remind them again that this is to be used to self-monitor the steps for explaining and solving word problems so they can accurately represent the words and correctly solve the problems.

Think It ~ Write It

☐ 1. Read the entire problem
☐ 2. Identify new vocabulary.
☐ 3. Paraphrase the problem.
☐ 2. Identify what I know.
☐ 3. Identify what I need to find.
☐ 4. Visualize the problem.
☐ 5. Make a plan.
☐ 6. Solve: write the steps and operations.
☐ 7. Check: compare the answer to the question.

Kemp, Eaton & Poole, 2008

- **Curriculum Based Measurement**: Concepts and Applications Probe

Sources:
Jitendra and DiPipi. (2003). *An Exploratory Study of Schema-Based Word-Problem-Solving Instruction for Middle School Students with Learning Disabilities: An Emphasis on Conceptual and Procedural Understanding.* www.ldonline.org

Smith, Constance Ridley. (2002). *When Does Learning Occur? Cognitive Approaches to Teaching and Learning.*

Suggested Resources

Abramson, M.F. (2001). *Painless Word Problems.* Hauppage, NY: Barron's Educational Series, Inc.

Baker, S., Gersten, R., & Lee, D. S. (2007). *Recent Research in Math Interventions: Implications for Practice.* Center on Instruction. Florida: RMC Research Corporation. Available: www.centeroninstruction.org.

Bender, W.N. (2005). *Differentiating math instruction: Strategies that work for K-8 Classrooms.* Thousand Oaks, CA: Crown Press.

Franco, B. (1998). *Adding Alligators and Other Easy-to-Read Math Stories.* Teaching Resources/Scholastic.

Harvey, S. & Goudvis. (2007). *Strategies That Work: Teaching Comprehension for Understanding and Engagement.* Portland, ME: Stenhouse Publishers.

Hyde, A. (2006). *Comprehending Math: Adapting Reading Strategies to Teach Mathematics, K-6.* Portsmouth, NH: Heinemann

Jefferson County website, http://jc-schools.net for math vocabulary

Maheady, L. (2001). Peer-mediated instruction and interventions and students with mild disabilities. *Remedial & Special Education*, 22(1), 4-15.

Montague, M. (2003). *Solve It! A practical approach to teaching mathematical problem-solving skills.* Reston, VA: Exceptional Innovations.

Read Write Think. International Reading Association. NCTE. Teaching Shapes Using Read Alouds, Vizualization, and Sketch to Stretch. Available: http://www.readwritethink.

Rothstein, A., Rothstein, E., & Lauber, G. (2007). *Write for mathematics, second edition.* CA: Corwin Press.

Sabean & Bavaria. (2005). *Closing the Achievement Gap: Best Practices in Teaching Mathematics.* Charleston, WV: The Education Alliance. Available: www.educationalliance.org/Downloads/Research/Teachingmathematics.pdf.

Slavin, R., & Lake. (2006). *Effective Programs in Elementary Mathematics: A Best Evidence Synthesis. The Best Evidence Encyclopedia.* Baltimore, MD: Johns Hopkins University. Available: www.bestevidence.org/

Smith, C., R. (2002). *When does learning occur? Cognitive approaches to teaching and learning.* Available: http://perweb.bercol.bm?idrc/resources/ cognitive_ approaches.ppt.

Steen, L., A.. (2007). How mathematics counts. *Educational Leadership*, 65(3), 9-14.

Westwood, P. (2006). *Teaching and learning difficulties: cross- curricular perspectives.* Camberwell, Vic, Australia: ACER Press.

Winograd, M. Math Think Alouds. Hot Chalks Lesson PlansPage.Com Available: www.lessonplanspage.com

Chapter 9
About Motivation

"They take the challenge to their hearts.
Challenging preconceived ideas,
saying goodbye to long standing fears.
Don't crack up, bend your brain, see both sides."
—Howard Jones, *New Song*

The depth of math literature and the breadth of student learning needs make clear the daily challenges that classroom teachers face as they attempt to convince students that they do have math abilities and potential. If students are not motivated, implementation of best practices will be in vain.

Most children enter school with an intrinsic motivation to learn math. Yet according to the National Math Advisory Panel's 2008 report, 62 percent of teachers said their most difficult challenge in teaching mathematics is working with unmotivated students. It then becomes the educator's responsibility to inspire students who were once motivated to stay the course (persistence) and to believe in themselves (self-efficacy).

> **Persistence is a common denominator for both struggling readers and the educators teaching them.**

Persistence is a common issue for both students who struggle with mathematics and the educators who teach them. Studies cited by the National Math Advisory Panel indicate that shifting the focus from ability to effort increases student engagement, which in turn improves math outcomes. Simply put, "When children believe that their efforts to learn make them 'smarter,' they show a greater persistence in learning" (National Math Advisory Panel, 2008). How then can educators instill persistence, self-efficacy and a love of math? In other words, how can educators motivate students who struggle with math?

A most interesting study, reported by the American Mathematical Society and mentioned in Chapter 1 of this book, talks to the rare identification of girls talented in math and ascribes this to the fact that American culture does not highly value such talent. Beyond this issue of females, however, a New York Times article about this study reviewed data from the most difficult math competitions for young people. This revealed that many students from the United States who succeed best in these competitions are immigrants or children of immigrants who come from countries where math education is prized and math talent consider to be cultivated through hard work and persistence. One can speculate that it is difficult to motivate students to work hard at something when its success is not considered special, unique or outstanding.

It is said that there are only two true motivators in the world: love and fear. Love and fear are the energies that fuel every human thought, word or action. They are the intrinsic motivators driving human beings. "Fear is the energy which contracts, closes down, draws in, runs, hides, hoards, and harms. Love is the energy which expands, opens up, sends out, stays, reveals, shares, and heals." (Walsch, 1996) Some people identify these two motivators as the carrot and the stick. If you contemplate the carrot and the stick, you realize they are external motivators associated with survival, which leads to the question, is mathematics necessary for survival??

Society provides many extrinsic (external) motivators (rewards), such as money, food, etc. Lamentably, educators often rely entirely on extrinsic reinforcement to inspire students to learn. While these are useful some of the time, ultimately students must be taught to appreciate the internal feelings that come with success and confidence.

Neuroscientists have determined that the brain's center, the hypothalamus, produces chemicals that result in a natural high similar to that induced by opiates (drugs used to regulate stress and pain) (Nakamura, 1993 cited in Jensen, 1998). The brain can be considered a pleasure-seeking system that wants to enjoy positive sensations and repeat the behaviors that produce them. Students who are successful usually feel good and often that's reward enough to keep going. In other words, success breeds success. Thus, in order to motivate students and

. . . "success breeds success."

keep them excited about math, it is important to pay attention to what is happening in their brains when they are learning or what conditions foster their success so they intrinsically (internally) develop the drive to learn.

Csikszentmihalyi (1990) talks about the concept of flow, the psychology of optimal experience. He defines flow as "the way people describe their state of mind when consciousness is harmoniously ordered, and they want to pursue whatever they are doing for its own sake." When we attain flow in our endeavors, we emerge with a sense of accomplishment, growth, satisfaction and the desire to continue or repeat the experience. To assist students in achieving this flow in their learning, it is helpful for educators to consider why they teach. To do this, ask yourself:

- Am I teaching because I love to learn myself?
- Am I teaching because I love the idea of expanding the minds of youth?
- Am I passionate about what I am teaching?
- Do I love to keep searching for new ways to reach students when they do not grasp a concept?
- Do I fear for my students when I realize they are not learning?
- Do I fear for myself if I am not able to teach students in a way that they learn?

Remember the Cardinal Questions? Know thyself. Know what motivates you to do the things you do.

The way in which teachers fill students' days with learning opportunities has a lasting effect on these students and their motivation to return the next day ready to learn. Consider the questions: Are students learning something they want to learn? Do they enter the classroom with a love of learning or a fear of what will happen if they do not? Do they arrive with apathy or with a sense of wonder? Do you tap into that sense of wonder or squelch it? And do you inspire in them a reason for learning math?

> **... do you inspire in them a reason for learning math?**

Let's consider the reasons why students need to learn math. There are "superficial" reasons (e.g., to achieve better grades, future employment, pleasing others, to get a high school diploma). These may be considered superficial because there are many productive members of society who have compensated for their mathematic deficits and are still thriving.

Consequently, it would appear that mathematics is not necessary for survival. With the use of calculators, computers, electronic measurement devices and laser transits, who needs to be proficient in basic math skills? With all of the new assistive technology (which can be used for basic and complex problems), it sometimes seems that it is not necessary to know math, because technology will take care of it for you. Consequently, consumers may believe that they have no reason to fear mathematic inability. Fear, therefore, no longer acts as a motivator.

The other, often overlooked challenge educators face is anxiety. As mentioned in Chapter 1, math anxiety is real and can quickly lead students to believe that they are just not good with numbers and can't possibly learn the skills needed to complete higher levels of mathematics (Wigfield & Meece, 1988).

Math anxiety is not a new issue, nor is it easy to address. Once students lose confidence that effort will yield success (usually by age nine), unfavorable beliefs take over and impede learning. Anxiety related to their own perceived inability directs their attention away from focusing on the task to focusing on ability (Boekaerts, 2002). Teachers must coach for effort so that students can see that effort, not just ability, is related to achievement (National Advisory Mathematics Panel. 2008). With this recognition, students can confront the learning process positively and understand that they are responsible for their own learning.

Continue to search for ways to motivate students so they will want to persist in learning math. Calvin Coolidge believed, "Nothing in the world takes the place of persistence. Talent will not; nothing is more common than unsuccessful men with great talent. Genius will not; unrewarded genius is almost a proverb. Education will not; the world is full of educated derelicts. Persistence, determination alone is omnipotent. The slogan 'Press On' has solved and always will solve the problems of the human race."

> **"Nothing in the world takes the place of persistence. "**

"Chug, chug, chug. Puff, puff, puff. Cling-clang, cling-clang.
The little train rumbled over the tracks...
I think I can, I think I can, I think I can."
—The Little Engine That Could

The Little Engine That Could by Watty Piper (Platt & Munk Publishing, 1930) is the story classic about believing in oneself (self-efficacy). Teach your students to emulate the little engine and press on: "I will persist, I will persist, I will persist. I can do math!"

There are no easy, clear-cut answers to the question of how to motivate students. However considering the Cardinal Questions as they relate to motivation is a helpful place to begin. Educators should ask themselves:

1. **What do I know** about motivation, about motivating myself, and about motivating others? It is critical to reflect on the question, **what do I know,** and, **what motivated me** to learn this?

2. **What do I do** for work and why? What do I do for fun and why?

3. **How do I learn?**
   - (See Chapter 2)

4. **How do I approach or react to an unfamiliar task?** In addition to what is presented in relation to this question in Chapter 4, consider the following:
   - What inspires me to approach an unfamiliar task?
   - How do I react when I am presented with an unfamiliar task or challenge that is not my choice?

5. **What will I do with the information I gain from answering the first four questions?** What will motivate me to use the information I have gained from answering the previous four questions to do something new or different?

A discerning teacher will recognize when a student is not motivated to read and will identify what motivates the student. The following Cardinal Questions help identify what motivates/how to motivate students.
   1. **What does the student know** about motivation?
      - Does the student know about external motivation?
      - What external motivators work for the student?
      - Does the student know about internal motivation?
      - Does the student understand the relationship between internal and external motivation?

- Does the student know how anxiety effects motivation?

What does the student know and why did they learn it? (A student knows more about things they want to learn or are motivated to learn.)

2. **What does the student do?**
   - What does the student do (hobbies, extracurricular activities, etc.) outside of school and why?

3. **How does the student learn?** (See Chapter Two)

4. **How does the student approach or react to an unfamiliar task?** (See Chapter Two)
   - Does the student approach or react to an unfamiliar task differently when he or she is given a choice?

5. **What will you do with the knowledge gained from answering the previous four questions?**
   - Will you consider linking students' interests with what they are working on in mathematics?
   - Will you take into consideration the role of anxiety related to students' performance?

Here are five techniques that will assist in assessing what motivates students:

1. How I See Myself
2. It's Okay Not To Know
3. My OOPS! List
4. Grade My Understanding
5. Topic Tattler

"Leave aside anxiety and just enjoy the ride.
I can't be sure of where we'll go,
the beat can be our guide.
Making music, making music,
sweet music by the numbers."
—Sophie Ellis Bextor, *Making Music*

Motivation #1:
How I See Myself...

What it is: A technique for developing an understanding of students' confidence levels and feelings.

When to use it: When students are unable to express their anxieties and feelings about math or other subjects.

⚠ **Prerequisites**: Students need to feel safe in the classroom and feel comfortable sharing their personal thoughts, perceptions and feelings.

Benefit: Students are able to develop confidence and thus improve motivation.

Materials:
- Assorted pens, colored pencils, markers and crayons
- Assorted magazines and newspapers
- Scissors
- Glue sticks
- Copies of the How I See Myself Template, Appendix B, pp. 282-283
- How Persistent Am I?, Appendix A, pp. 233-234

Implementation Steps:

1. Arrange students in small groups so that they may share magazines and newspapers.

2. Select one student in each group and ask him/her to describe one thing that another student in the group is good at doing in school. Then ask the student who was described if he/she agrees. Allow time for each student in the group to describe someone else and check for agreement.

3. Discuss how everyone has something they do well and other things they do not do as well. Engage students in discourse about how they sometimes react when they find things difficult to do. Possible answers may include:

- We avoid doing those things
- We get frustrated
- We feel bad about ourselves
- We think we can't do anything well
- We pretend we understand when we really don't
- We are afraid we will look like we are not smart
- We think we will never learn the task

4. Explain to students that when they have these feelings they lack self-confidence and may become frustrated or anxious. Discuss the importance of realizing that everybody has different skills and/or talents and different levels of confidence when engaging in various activities. Explain that it is also possible to get better at many things through effort and practice, and that you want them all to be confident learners.

5. Hand out a How I See Myself Template to each student. Tell students that you want them to complete the sentences on their papers by writing the answers, drawing pictures, or cutting out words or cartoons from the magazines and newspapers you have provided. Give students a variety of colored pencils and pens and/or markers.

How I See Myself...	
Name: Date: Page 2	
When I read I...	When I do math I...
Some of the things I want to learn about are...	Things I think I can do better now than before are ...

How I See Myself...	
Name: Date: Page 1	
When I am at school I...	The things I like about school are...
Things I am good at in school are...	Things I wish I could do better at school are...

6. Read through each item on the worksheet to ensure students understand what each sentence stem is asking. Then let the students work on creating their own sheets.

7. Allow ample time. Once everyone is finished, engage students in a discussion about what thoughts came to mind as they completed the sentences.

8. Have students discuss their responses in their respective groups or with the entire class.

9. This activity can be completed again after several months to discuss individual or group changes in self-perception.

Variation: Pick one question and ask each student in turn to share responses while making a list of these responses. If time allows, continue with the all the questions or explain to students that you will ask one question a day for the next several days until all responses have been recorded.

Monitoring:
- How Am I Persistent?

Motivation—2
It's Okay Not to Know

What it is: A communication survey related to learning.

When to use it: When students are not communicating that they do not understand.

⚠ Prerequisites for teachers are the skill of self-reflection and the willingness to address communication skills in the classroom and potentially make changes.

Benefit: Students will become self-advocates in learning.

Materials:
- A variety of sizes of blank cardstock (optional)
- Age-appropriate writing utensils
- Copies of It's Okay Not to Know Survey, Appendix B, p. 284
- Copies of How Persistent Am I?, Appendix A, pp. 233-234

Implementation Steps:

1. Explain to students that you are interested in understanding more about communication in the classroom. Tell them you need their feedback on how comfortable they feel in the classroom. Say something like this: "Here is how you can help me learn about our classroom. I am going to give you a survey with questions about school. Please answer the questions and tell me how you feel about being in this classroom. I really need everyone's help with this. I am going to ask you to do this anonymously, which means you do not have to put your name on the survey. Once I have the surveys I will read them and then we will talk about the results."

Note: You should only engage in this activity with your students if you are committed to making changes.

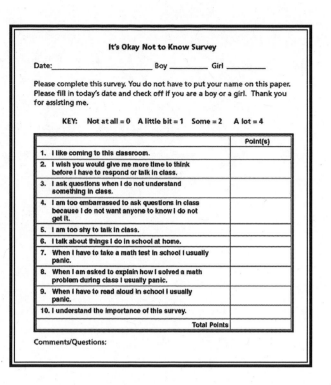

It's Okay Not to Know Survey

Date:_____ Boy _____ Girl _____

Please complete this survey. You do not have to put your name on this paper. Please fill in today's date and check off if you are a boy or a girl. Thank you for assisting me.

KEY: Not at all = 0   A little bit = 1   Some = 2   A lot = 4

	Point(s)
1. I like coming to this classroom.	
2. I wish you would give me more time to think before I have to respond or talk in class.	
3. I ask questions when I do not understand something in class.	
4. I am too embarrassed to ask questions in class because I do not want anyone to know I do not get it.	
5. I am too shy to talk in class.	
6. I talk about things I do in school at home.	
7. When I have to take a math test in school I usually panic.	
8. When I am asked to explain how I solved a math problem during class I usually panic.	
9. When I have to read aloud in school I usually panic.	
10. I understand the importance of this survey.	
Total Points	

Comments/Questions:

2. Provide class time for students to complete the survey. Present them with the survey, review the directions and tell students you will be reading it aloud. Read each statement and clarify vocabulary. Have students respond to each statement after you read it.

3. Collect the completed surveys. Review the students' feedback and record the responses in some sort of chart form for ease of understanding.

4. Provide class time to review the results and engage in discourse about the knowledge you gained from their responses.

5. Ask students for input. Tell them you would like to make changes based on the information provided. Say, "Let's brainstorm ways to improve our classroom." Record all suggestions and then determine what changes can occur and how to implement them.

6. Determine a date to review the plan and the effect of the changes.

7. On the selected date, repeat Steps #2 – 6.

8. Repeat as often as needed.

Variation: For students not yet reading and writing, use blank cards and have them draw happy or sad faces to represent how they feel about school.

Note: Ask students to complete this survey at least three times during the school year.

Monitoring:

- How Persistant Am I?

Motivation 3:
My OOPS! List

What it is: A technique to develop students' awareness of areas in which they have difficulty when engaged in math.

When to use it: When students demonstrate frustration and anxiety when engaged in math due to chronic mistakes.

 Prerequisites are the ability to recognize and discuss math mistakes.

Benefit: Students develop confidence in their ability to perform math.

Materials:
- Stickers, labels, colored folders and/or other items of particular interest
- Copies of My Oops List Template, Appendix B, p. 285
- Transparency of My Oops List
- Copies of How Persistent Am I?, Appendix A pp. 233-234

Implementation Steps:

1. Start by asking students what they think when they hear someone say, "Oops!" Once you have established that this indicates that someone has made a mistake of some kind, engage students in discourse about how we may benefit from our mistakes. Discuss how making mistakes is part of learning. Give examples of how people make mistakes in playing sports, learning to play a musical instrument or learning to how to cook. Discuss how we learn from mistakes and improve our skills. Have students discuss personal examples of making mistakes and how they corrected or changed what they did.

2. Say, "I am going to help you make an Oops List for particular areas of difficulty you may have in math. The purpose of this list is to help you correct any mistakes that are preventing you from being successful. It will also help you feel more confident about your math skills. Keeping an Oops List of your difficulties keeps you from making the same mistakes over and over again. Changing what you do may

also alleviate anxiety when you come to concepts that have proven difficult in the past."

3. Explain to students that they will be able to refer to these lists when they are working on class assignments or homework. The lists will be their own personal study guides for math.

4. Show students a copy of the sheet.

My **OOPS!** List		
Name:		
Topic	**Difficult Concept**	**Solution**
1.		
2.		
3.		
4.		
5.		

5. Using examples of common errors made by students, demonstrate how to fill out the Oops List.

6. Say, "Let's pretend these are some math mistakes that keep me from being successful. First, I write the topic area in the first box, and then I write the concept, skill or operation that gives me trouble in the next box."

7. Continue, "In the third box I write how to correct the problem for the future." Engage the students in discourse on the variety of ways of correcting the problem (e.g., ask for help from teacher, peers, refer

to math book, internet etc.) and how they might best represent this so that they understand the concept next time they look at the list.

8. Ask students to choose a personal concept, skill or operation that causes them to make mistakes and write it in the second box. Have them go back and identify what topic the difficulty comes under (problem solving, graphing, finding averages, etc.).

9. Give students about three minutes to find the best way to change or correct the mistake. They can ask other classmates, the teacher or consult their math book.

10. Finally, have students place their list in a notebook or binder so they can use it whenever they need a reminder on a concept or skill with which they continue to have difficulty.

Note: When giving students feedback on homework, quizzes or tests, remind them to record any mistakes that are problematic on their OOPS! List.

Monitoring:
*   How Persistent Am I?

Motivation # 4
Grade My Understanding

What it is: An activity for students to summarize what they learned in a class and provide the teacher with feedback on how much they understand.

When to use it: At the end of a lesson for students to process their understanding and to find out what help they still need.

⚠ A prerequisite for the teacher is the willingness to modify lessons based on students' feedback.

Benefit: Teachers learn about students' ability to summarize what they understand and about the impact of the lesson; students take responsibility for their learning.

Materials:
- Copies for students of Grade My Understanding Template, Appendix B, p. 286
- Copies of How Persistent Am I?, Appendix A, pp. 233-234

Implementation Steps:

1. Tell students that you are interested in having a conversation about school—both teaching and learning. Explain that you want students to tell you what they are learning during class time, what they understand about the concept/topic and what they still need in order to completely understand.

2. Introduce and talk about feedback. There are two ways to give feedback. The first is positive, which is when a person compliments or acknowledges something another person has done. The second is negative, which is when a person has a concern about something a person has done and makes a suggestion to that person to do it differently the next time. Positive feedback maintains behavior; if someone does something you like, let them know so they will do it again. Negative feedback changes behavior; if someone does

something that you don't like, let them know what they can do differently next time.

3. Give each student a copy of "Grade My Understanding." Demonstrate how to complete it.
    - First, they summarize what the lesson was about and whether or not it was interesting. They brainstorm together and create a word bank of vocabulary that can be used to describe degrees of interest (i.e., outstanding, superb, brilliant, boring, repetitive, confusing, etc.);
    - Second, they assign themselves a grade and explain why they gave themselves that grade;
    - Third, they explain what parts of the lesson they understood;
    - Fourth, they determine and explain what more they need to better understand the topic.

4. When you decide to use the form, inform students at the beginning of a lesson that you will be asking them to grade their understanding. Allow time at the end of class for them to complete the form.

5. From time to time, discuss the students' responses, especially when it involves a change being made as a result of the feedback.

Monitoring:
   - How Persistent Am I?

Motivation #5:
Topic Tattler

What it is: A technique to help students make personal connections and alleviate anxiety about a math topic or concept.

When to use it: Prior to introducing a new topic and when students are unsure about the relevance and purpose of what they are learning.

⚠ Prerequisites are the ability to attend to and participate in a discussion, and to provide responses in oral and written from.

Benefit: Students are motivated to learn unknown information as they make connections and gain deeper understanding of a topic.

Materials:
- Student copies of Topic Tattle Template, Appendix B, p. 287
- Transparency of Topic Tattle Template
- Pencils and/or pens
- Overhead projector and/or easel with large paper
- How Persistent Am I?, Appendix A, pp. 233-234

Implementation Steps:

1. Invite students to talk about the math topic they will be learning. Say, "As we discuss _____, I will model (show you) a way to organize your questions and thoughts related to the topic. This will help you make personal connections to the topic by determining a purpose for learning the information. This can lead to a newfound interest in the topic."

2. Explain to the students that taking the time to think about the learning they are about to undertake can stimulate new thoughts, alleviate anxiety and perhaps make the learning more enjoyable.

3. Hand out the Topic Tattler Template and display the template on the overhead. Demonstrate how to use the sheet by completing it for the topic you are about to introduce.

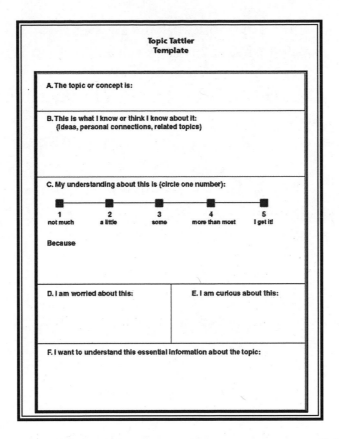

**Topic Tattler
Template**

A. The topic or concept is:

B. This is what I know or think I know about it:
   (ideas, personal connections, related topics)

C. My understanding about this is (circle one number):

1	2	3	4	5
not much	a little	some	more than most	I get it!

Because

D. I am worried about this:

E. I am curious about this:

F. I want to understand this essential information about the topic:

4. Tell students to fill in Box A with the topic you will be discussing.

5. Say, "Let's talk about this topic in more detail and find out what you know and how you feel about the topic. In Box B, write what you already know or think you know about this topic. Don't be afraid to write something even if you are unsure about it."

6. Continue, "Next, I want you to think about your current level of understanding about this topic. After you decide whether you know a little or a lot about the topic, write about why you feel this way in Box C. In other words, do you know something about the topic because you have learned about it before? If so, where? Or perhaps you have never heard of it and are totally lost. There is no right or wrong answers, so please write down what you think or feel." If students are comfortable they may share about their level of understanding and talk about it with the class.

7. Tell students that the next two boxes on the form are very personal and will reveal their individual concerns about the topic. Explain that

this information will help you determine what might peak students' interest so that you can focus on these areas during lessons.

8. Once students are at this point, stop and introduce the topic by providing them with the key ideas or the essential questions of the topic and a brief explanation of what each question or idea involves.

9. After you have completed the introduction and explained the key ideas or essential questions, go back to the Topic Tattler and ask students to complete Section F. Tell them that the information they write in this box will help them accomplish their learning goals for the topic.

10. Conclude by reviewing the purpose of the Topic Tattler. Remind the students that this information will:
    - Jump start their thinking about what they will be learning;
    - Allow them to consider their concerns and interests about the topic;
    - Identify what they think their present understanding is of the topic and what they want to understand by the end of instruction.

Monitoring:
- How Persistent Am I?

Chapter 10
Next Steps

"So walk with me through this city
We'll hold our hands up high
And we'll laugh, and we'll dance,
And we'll sing and we'll shout to the sky!"
—Thomas Bryan Eaton, *Turn, Slowly*

As you embark on the process of Response To Intervention and teaching all students the critical concepts of math, we hope this book has stimulated your desire to sing, shout and learn more about the exciting world of mathematics, including effective instruction, interventions and measurement of student learning. As mentioned in the introduction, this book is just the first movement of a symphony and there are many more movements to explore before we reach the final note. We encourage you to use the research and the resources mentioned to change your way of thinking about teaching math to all children.

One of the best ways to do this is through collaboration with others. Seek out individuals who share your passion. Spend time together brainstorming, discussing, laughing, shouting, and most importantly, challenging each other for the purpose of building new knowledge.

> **Seek out individuals who share your passion.**

Don't be surprised when you start saying things like, "That's a great idea! Why aren't others using it?" Or, "I'm not sure about this, let's keep talking." Or, "I don't understand, what does that mean?" And perhaps even, "We've got some great stuff here, maybe we should write a book or at the very least share our knowledge!" The realization that others share your interests, ideas and enthusiasm about a cause is the foundation for building powerful relationships which can lead to amazing results.

Keep in mind as you move forward with implementation that the heart of Response To Intervention is high-quality, culturally responsive instruction. With this form of instruction in place, an appropriate curriculum, interventions that work, and collaboration whenever possible, 85-90 percent of students will more than likely experience success. Students who require additional targeted or intensive interventions will benefit most if a planned approach is agreed upon by all team members and implemented with fidelity. This, of course, requires administrative support from inception.

> **Students who require additional.... interventions will benefit most if a planned approach is agreed to by all and implemented with fidelity.**

As students experience success at the secondary and tertiary levels of intervention they will either continue to receive this additional support, return to the core classroom program or will be considered for further intervention. The cohort of students who fail to respond to intensive levels of intervention is generally a very small number, about 5-10 percent. This population should receive full consideration for referral to special education.

When making a special education referral (if you are using RTI), supplying all the documentation collected throughout the interventions will make the process easier and faster. One possible format for gathering and assembling this information is the Intervention Tracking Form found in Appendix B, p. 247. This form, along with the data in chart form, will provide concise yet comprehensive information for the special education committee or multi-disciplinary team to review.

Prior to submitting a referral to special education, take time to review all the pertinent paperwork. Bear in mind that according to IDEA 2004, the reauthorized federal regulations governing students with disabilities, a student cannot be considered for special education if it has been determined that:
1. the student has not received appropriate reading and math instruction as set forth by NCLB, including the five precepts of reading;

2. the student is limited in English proficiency;
3. the student is culturally or economically disadvantaged.

Before making a referral, change these statements into questions and answer them honestly. Has the student received high-quality, scientifically-based math instruction since Kindergarten? Is the student an English language learner? Does the student have a cultural or economic disadvantage when it comes to learning? If you can answer "yes" to the first question and "no" to the last two, then it is appropriate to move forward with the referral, making certain to include documentation that satisfies the first question.

In most cases, the documentation of results obtained through progress monitoring at all tiers will provide the evaluation team with a wealth of information. With documentation in hand, a classroom observation, social history, physical examination and area-specific assessments may be all that is needed to complete a comprehensive evaluation.

> **It is important to note that progress monitoring does not stop once an IEP is developed.**

If a student is found eligible for academic or behavioral services, special education becomes the sustained, intensive intervention strategy employed to help the student access the general education curriculum. This degree of intervention often entails continuing intervention techniques that were provided at Tier III (if they have been effective). If the student has not responded to the intervention at this level, it is time to try something different! Remember, doing the same thing and expecting different results is Einstein's definition of insanity. The student's present ability level and his or her need for specially designed instruction should determine the Individualized Education Program (IEP). This IEP should not be designed on the basis of what is most readily available or what the teacher prefers to teach. It is also important to note that progress monitoring does not stop once an IEP is developed. Rather, monitoring continues on a daily, weekly or monthly basis using the present levels of performance as the baseline levels and the annual goals as performance benchmarks.

To get started with the process presented in this book, we recommend that you "think outside the fences that surround your mind" and…

Seek out a colleague in your building with whom you have not worked before.

Ask this person if he or she has read *RTI & Math: The Classroom Connection.*

If he or she has not, provide him or her with a copy or refer the person to National Professional Resources, Inc.

If the person has read the book, start by asking him or her the first Cardinal Question: "What do you know?"

Collaboration is key, but working outside the proverbial box of traditional roles is cutting edge. We can eliminate the ironclad concept of "your kids" and "my kids" by building professional learning communities that incorporate formative assessment, creative scheduling, dynamic student grouping and unconventional teaching arrangements. To establish collaboration with the authors of this book, please visit our web site at *www.schoolofsimilarities.com.* As you begin to break down the fences, both real and imaginary, bear in mind this final piece of advice from Karen Kaiser Clark: "Life is change, growth is optional!"

"Life is a journey
It can take you anywhere you choose to go.
As long as you're learning
You'll find all you'll ever need to know."
—Christina Aguilera, *A Voice Within*

Appendix A
Curriculum Based Measurement Probes, and their Directions

Each technique in Chapters 5-9 lists a suggested math probe for measuring student progress. Within this Appendix you will find both ready-to-use probes and examples of probes that require further development. We encourage the use of CBM probes as they provide useful information about an intervention's effectiveness quickly and reliability.

To administer the probes you will need the following materials:
1. an examiner's copy and student copy of the selected probe
2. timer or stopwatch
3. pencil, crayons
4. clipboard (optional).

The use of CBM probes for benchmark screenings and continuous progress monitoring requires a pool of at least 30 probes at the same skill or grade level. Again, you may develop your own or purchase them commercially. Refer to the Suggested Resources section of Chapter 4 and at the end of this Appendix for a list of commercially available curriculum based measurement probes.

Please note: If you develop your own pool of computation and/or concepts and application probes, you must first determine the specific math skills to be mastered by the end of the year. Probes should contain different problems at the same degree of difficulty and should represent the priority skills in the math curriculum for a particular grade level. Every identified skill is given equal representation on a completed probe with no more than 25 to 30 problems per probe (Hosp et al, 2007).

Appendix A

Kemp, Eaton & Poole, 2009

Language and Concepts
Directions

<u>Materials</u>: Math Language & Concepts Probe Sheet and Markers, Crayons, or Colored Pencils — 1 Red, 1 Blue, 1 Yellow, 1 Green, 1 Orange, 1 Purple, 1 Pencil

<u>Directions</u>: Give one probe sheet to each student. Ask them to follow the directions below as you read them.

Say:	*Score*
1. With your pencil, write your name on the line at the top of the paper. (Have the student show you where to put their name, if they can't write it independently.)	1 0
2. Draw a blue dot at the center of the line that you just wrote your name on.	1 0
3. Draw a purple dot on top of the block.	1 0
4. Draw a green dot on the front of the block.	1 0
5. Draw a yellow dot on the side of the block you can see.	1 0
6. With your pencil draw a few dots on the star that is behind the block.	1 0 1 0
7. Draw a red dot on every point of the star in front of the block.	1 0 1 0
8. Put a yellow x on the star that you can see only part of.	1 0
9. Find an arrow that is pointing up and color it red.	1 0
10. Find the arrow that matches the red arrow you just colored and color it red.	1 0
11. Color the arrow showing a direction going from left to right purple.	1 0
12. Use your markers to create a pattern of dots on the line at the bottom of the page.	1 0 1 0 1 0
13. With your pencil, circle the dot that is at the beginning of your pattern.	1 0
14. Mark an x on the dot at the end of your pattern.	1 0
15. Color every other Smiley face green.	1 0
16. Make a yellow x on the Smiley face in the middle of the row.	1 0

___/20

Use the results of this probe to guide your classroom instruction for receptive and expressive language concepts.

Kemp, Eaton & Poole, 2009

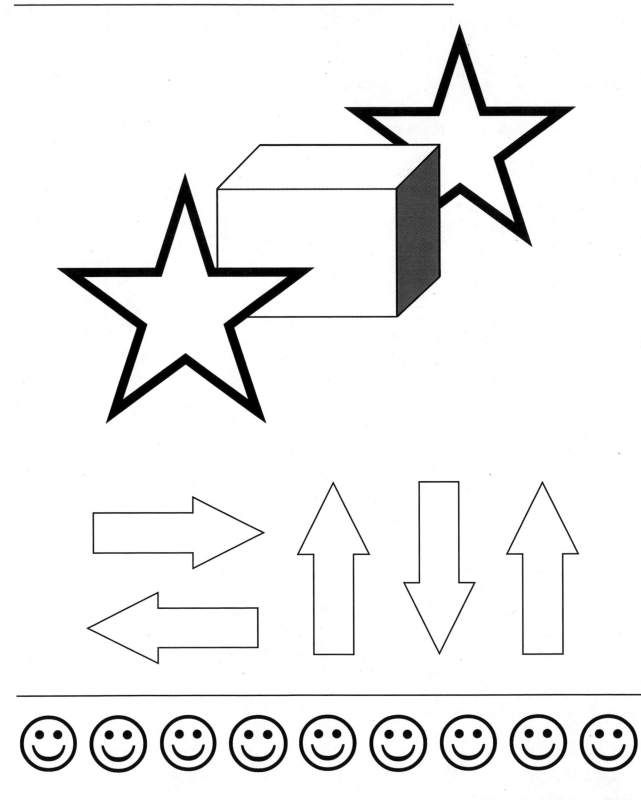

Kemp, Eaton & Poole, 2009

Counting in Sequence
Directions

Time: 1 minute

Directions:

1. Place probe on a clipboard or hard surface and position yourself so that student cannot see what you record. Say, "When I say begin, please start counting aloud starting with the number one like this: 1, 2, 3, until I tell you to stop. If you cannot remember a number, I will tell you what it is and you may continue. Are there any questions? Ready? Please begin".

2. Start timing. If the student does not say "1" after 3 seconds say "1" and continue. Follow along on the scoring sheet. Put a slash through any incorrect responses. Circle the last number stated at the end of one minute.

Scoring:

✓ Student receives one point for each correct response. Example: student says 6,7,8,9....the score is 4 points.

✓ If the student self-corrects, count it as a correct response.

✓ If a student hesitates beyond 3 seconds, provide the number, but count it as an incorrect response and continue.

✓ If a student repeats a sequence, count it as correct. Example: 5,6,5,6,7,8.

✓ If a student skips a number, count it as incorrect and continue testing.

✓ Do not provide more than one number during testing. If a student needs to be told a second number, discontinue the test.

Kemp, Eaton & Poole, 2009

Counting in Sequence
Sample Scoring

1	2	3	4	5	6	7	8	9	10
11	12	13	14	15	16	17	18	19	20
21	22	23	24	25	26	27	28	29	30
31	32	33	34	35	36	37	38	39	40
41	42	43	44	45	46	47	48	49	50
51	52	53	54	55	56	57	58	59	60
61	62	63	64	65	66	67	68	69	70
71	72	73	74	75	76	77	78	79	80
81	82	83	84	85	86	87	88	89	90
91	92	93	94	95	96	97	98	99	100
101	102	103	104	105	106	107	108	109	110
111	112	113	114	115	116	117	118	119	120
121	122	123	124	125	126	127	128	129	130
131	132	133	134	135	136	137	138	139	140
141	142	143	144	145	146	147	148	149	150

1. Count the number of responses: 38
2. Count the number of incorrects: 3
3. Subtract the incorrects from the total responses:
   Correct numbers counted in sequence = 35

Proficiency: 75-150 numbers per minute

Kemp, Eaton & Poole, 2009

Counting in Sequence Probe
Scoring Sheet

1	2	3	4	5	6	7	8	9	10
11	12	13	14	15	16	17	18	19	20
21	22	23	24	25	26	27	28	29	30
31	32	33	34	35	36	37	38	39	40
41	42	43	44	45	46	47	48	49	50
51	52	53	54	55	56	57	58	59	60
61	62	63	64	65	66	67	68	69	70
71	72	73	74	75	76	77	78	79	80
81	82	83	84	85	86	87	88	89	90
91	92	93	94	95	96	97	98	99	100
101	102	103	104	105	106	107	108	109	110
111	112	113	114	115	116	117	118	119	120
121	122	123	124	125	126	127	128	129	130
131	132	133	134	135	136	137	138	139	140
141	142	143	144	145	146	147	148	149	150

Student Name: _____   Date: _____

Notes:

Kemp, Eaton & Poole, 2009

Quantity Array - Dots
Directions

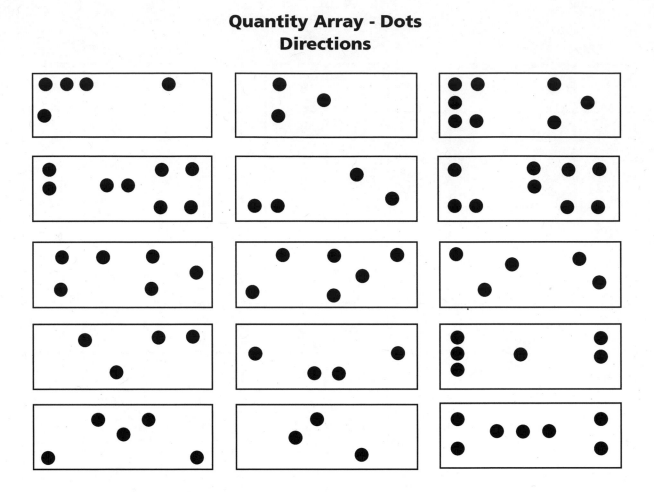

Directions:

1. Place the student copy of probe in front of the student. Say, "The paper in front of you has boxes with dots in them. Look at the first box" (point).

2. Say, "When I say begin, tell me the total number of dots in each box. Start here (point) and go across the page and then down to the next row". Demonstrate by dragging your finger across and down the rows. Say, "If you come to one you do not know, I'll tell you to try the next one. Do you have any questions? Ready? begin."

3. Start probe. If student does not respond within 5 seconds tell him to move on. You can prompt the student by saying, "Tell me how many dots." Record the number of correct and incorrect responses on the scoring sheet.

Kemp, Eaton & Poole, 2009

Quantity Array - Dots
Scoring Sheet

✓ If student correctly identifies the number, count the item as correct.

✓ If the student says the wrong number, count the item as incorrect.

✓ If student does not respond within 5 seconds, count as incorrect.

✓ If student skips an item, count the item as incorrect.

✓ If student skips an entire row, count each item in the row as incorrect.

Scoring sheet:

Write the number the student says in the blank. If the student skips an item, put a (-)) in the blank. If you have to tell the student to try the next one, put a (-) in the blank.

1. ( ) _____
2. ( ) _____
3. ( ) _____
4. ( ) _____
5. ( ) _____
6. ( ) _____
7. ( ) _____
8. ( ) _____
9. ( ) _____
10. ( ) _____
11. ( ) _____
12. ( ) _____
13. ( ) _____
14. ( ) _____
15. ( ) _____

Student Name: _____ Date: _____

Kemp, Eaton & Poole, 2009

Quantity Array - Dots
Probe

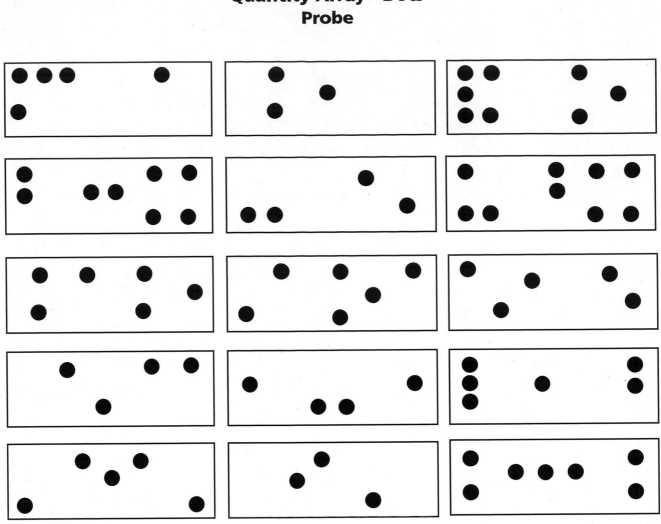

Missing Number
Directions

Time: 1 minute

Kindergarten—1-10
1st grade—1-20

Development: Go to Numberfly at www.interventioncentral.org/php/numberfly/numberfly.php for help in creating your probe.

Directions:

1. Place a copy of probe in front of the student. Place the examiner copy on your clipboard. Position yourself so that the student cannot see what you are recording. Say: "The paper in front of you has boxes. Each box has two numbers in it and a blank line. I would like you to tell me what number goes on the blank line. Let's try one. What number goes on this blank line?" Point to the first box and the blank line.

2. If the student correctly identifies the missing number, say "Good, 2 is the number that goes on the blank line." If the student does not correctly identify the missing number, say " The number that goes on this line is 2 because we count 1, 2. 3." Point to the numbers in the box as you say this. "Let's try the next one." Point to the blank line in the second box. "What number goes on this blank line?"

3. Say: "I want you to keep telling me what number goes in each blank space until I tell you to stop. Do you have any questions? Ready? Start."

4. Start timing. If student does not respond within 3 seconds ask him to try the next one. Follow along on your copy of the probe. Put a slash through incorrect responses. At the end of timing, circle the last identified number, and say "Stop".

Scoring :

✓ If student correctly identifies the missing number, count the item as correct.

✓ If student does not correctly identify any missing numbers in the first five boxes, discontinue assessment and record zero.

✓ If student incorrectly identifies the missing number put a slash through the blank on your copy.

✓ If the student hesitates in identifying the missing number for more than 3 seconds, count the item as incorrect and tell her to try the next box.

✓ If student skips an item, count the item as incorrect.

✓ If student skips an entire row, count each item in the row as incorrect.

✓ If student incorrectly identifies five boxes in a row, discontinue assessment.

Sample Scoring

7	8	___	6	___	8	16	17	/
___	12	13	0	1	___	15	/	17
5	___	7	13	14	___	1	___	3
9	10	___	17	18	___	___	11	12
___	13	14	4	___	6	/	1	2
18	___	20	/	15	(16)	7	8	___
4	5	___	3	4	___	6	___	8
0	___	2	11	___	13	18	19	___
8	9	___	13	___	15	___	4	5
16	17	___	2	3	___	18	___	20

Kemp, Eaton & Poole, 2009

1. Count number of items up to the circled item (total response): **17**

2. Count number of incorrects: **4**

3. Subtract incorrects from total responses:
Total Correct = **13**

Proficiency: (norms from www.aimsweb.com)

Grade	%ile	Fall	Winter	Spring
K	50	5	10	14
	25	1	6	10
1	50	12	17	19
	25	7	12	14

Kemp, Eaton & Poole, 2009

Missing Number
2 Samples

(3 numbers- by 1's, 2's, 5's to 20)

1	___	3	___	12	13	6	7	___	0	___	2
2	___	4	17	___	19	___	5	6	8	___	10
___	14	15	2	___	6	5	10	___	16	17	___
11	12	___	16	17	___	3	___	5	___	13	14
9	10	___	___	6	7	12	14	___	3	___	5
___	8	10	15	___	17	5	6	___	___	19	20

(4 numbers by 1's, 2's, 5's, 10's to 100)

7	8	9	___	20	___	40	50	16	17	18	___
10	___	12	13	0	1	___	3	25	___	35	40
2	___	6	8	13	14	___		1	2	___	4
9	10	___	12	11	12	___	14	___	20	30	40
___	33	34	35	3	4	___	6	___	10	15	20
28	29	___	31	___	15	16	17	6	7	8	___
4	8	10	___	43	44	___	46	56	___	58	59
0	___	2	3	61	___	63	64	17	18	19	___
7	8	9	___	12	13	___	15	70	80	90	___
96	97	___	99	82	83	___	85	16	18	___	22

Ordinal Counting
Directions/Scoring Sheet

Tell student to look at the probe and that you will ask him to point to the rods based on their place or position in the row. If the student correctly responds, reinforce the answer. If the student does not point to the correct rod, show him the correct rod. Ask the student the 10 different positions listed below.

Scoring sheet:

Write a (+) in the blank if the student identifies the correct rod. Write a (-) in the blank if they do not identify the correct the rod. If the student skips an item, put a (-)) in the blank. If you have to tell the student to try the next one, put a (-) in the blank.

1. (first) _____

2. (twentieth) _____

3. (second) _____

4. (fifth) _____

5. (third) _____

6. (tenth) _____

7. (sixth) _____

8. (twelfth) _____

9. (nineteenth) _____

10. (eleventh) _____

Student Name: _____ Date: _____

Alternate format: Have student count and point to the rods using ordinal numbers. Score 1 point for each correct response. 10/10

Proficiency: 100%

Kemp, Eaton & Poole, 2009

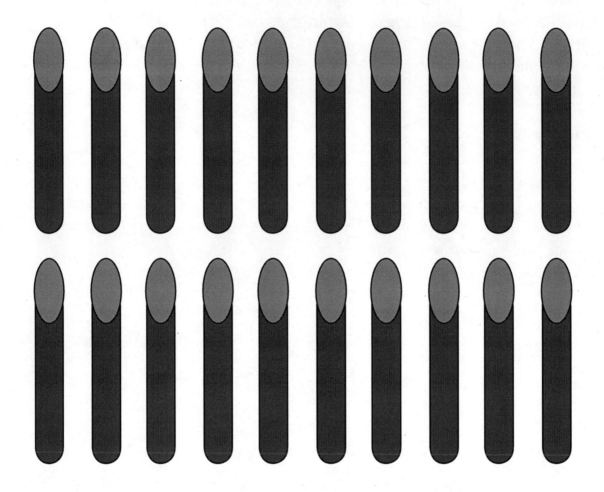

Kemp, Eaton & Poole, 2009

Number/Symbol Identification
Directions

Timing: 1 minute

Development: Go to Numberfly (for number identification only) at www. interventioncentral.org/php/numberfly/numberfly.php for help in creating your probe

Directions:

1. Place a copy of the probe in front of the student. Place the examiner copy on your clipboard. Position yourself so that the student cannot see what you are recording. Say; "The paper in front of you has numbers and symbols on it. I am going to ask you to tell me the name of each number and symbol." Point to the first item and ask, "What is this?"

2. If student correctly identifies the number/symbol say, "Good! Look at the next item. What is this?"

3. If student incorrectly identifies the number/symbol say, "This is - _____ .

4. Say, "When I say 'start', I would like you to tell me the name of each of the numbers or symbols. Start with the top row and read across the page and then go to the next row and read across again." Demonstrate by running your finger across and down the rows. "If you don't know the name, skip it and try the next one. Do you have any questions? Ready? Start."

5. Start timing. If the student does not identify the first number/symbol after 3 seconds, ask him to try the next. Follow along on your copy of the probe. Put a slash through any incorrect response. Circle the last item identified at the end of one minute and say, "Stop."

Kemp, Eaton & Poole, 2009

Scoring:

✓ Count one for each correct response.

✓ If student skips an item, count the item as incorrect.

✓ If student skips an entire row, count each item in the row as incorrect by putting a slash through the entire row.

✓ If student misses the first 5 items, discontinue testing and record zero.

✓ If the student misses any 5 items in a row, discontinue testing.

Sample Scoring

3	5	19	~~5~~	14	2	≠
+	16	~~13~~	6	20	=	5
12	18	2	-	(17)	20	0
1	8	15	4	>	3	+
9	=	10	11	7	-	16
<	4	13	20	12	6	1
≠	0	18	5	9	10	1
8	15	7	>	14	17	11

1. Count the total number of responses: **19**

2. Count the total number of incorrects: **2**

3. Total number correct is **17**

Proficiency: (norms from www.aimsweb.com)

Grade	%ile	Fall	Winter	Spring
K	50	32	47	50
	25	14	33	43
1	50	42	58	61
	25	27	46	51

Kemp, Eaton & Poole, 2009

Number/Symbol Identification
Probe/Template

3	5	19	<	14	2	≠
+	16	13	6	20	=	5
12	18	2	-	17	20	0
1	8	15	4	>	3	+
9	=	10	11	7	-	16
<	4	13	20	12	6	1
≠	0	18	5	9	10	1
8	15	7	>	14	17	11

Kemp, Eaton & Poole, 2009

Quantity Discrimination-Shapes/Lines
Directions

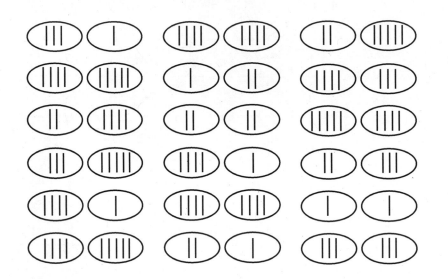

This probe can be used to identify more/less/same or equal/not equal. Before administering, determine which of these concepts you will assess.

Time: 1 minute

Directions (See and Say):

1. Place the student copy of probe in front of the student. Say, "The paper in front of you has ovals with lines inside. Look at the first two." Identify specifically for the student which concepts you are assessing: more/less/same or equal/not equal.

2. If the student correctly identifies the concept, say "Good," and proceed to the next set of ovals

3. If the student does not correctly identify the concept, give him appropriate prompts.

4. Show him where to start and go across the page to the right and then down to the next row." Demonstrate by dragging your finger across and down the rows. "Ready? Start here" (point).

Kemp, Eaton & Poole, 2009

5. Start probe. If student does not respond within 3 seconds provide answer and tell student to move on. Record the number of correct and incorrect responses on the scoring sheet.

Scoring:

✓ If student correctly identifies the concept, count the item as correct.

✓ If student does not respond within 3 seconds, count as incorrect.

✓ If student skips an item, count the item as incorrect.

✓ If student skips an entire row, count each item in the row as incorrect.

✓ If student makes 5 errors in a row, discontinue.

Alternate Format: See and Write Directions

1. Give student a copy of the probe. Say, "There are ovals with lines in them. Look at the first two and write the symbol for greater than/ less than or equal to/not equal depending on what you are assessing. If student writes the correct symbol for the first item, let him know he is correct. If they do not write the correct symbol, identify it for them and proceed.

Proficiency: no more than 1 error.

Kemp, Eaton & Poole, 2009

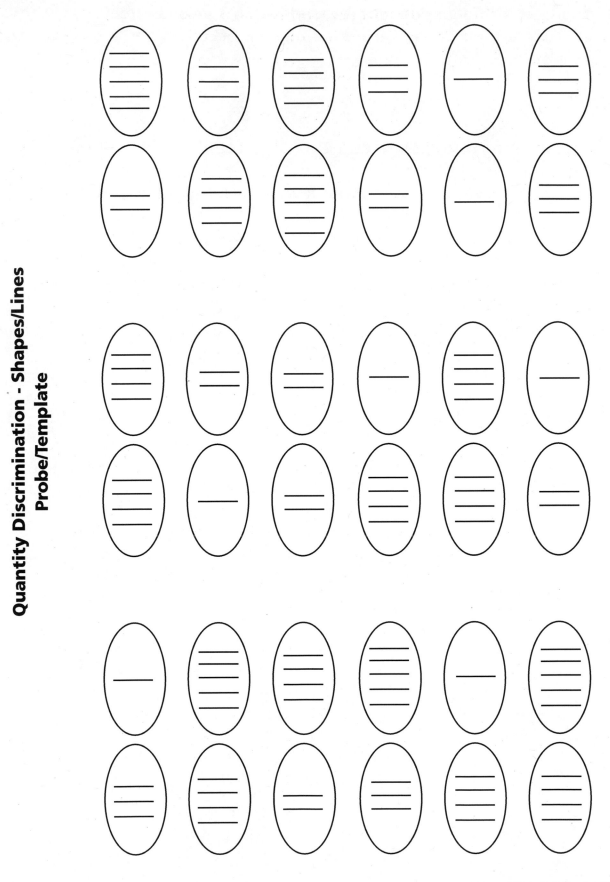

Kemp, Eaton & Poole, 2009

Quantity Discrimination - Numbers
Directions

7	18	12	20	1	11	10	14
8	15	13	17	5	14	16	15
0	3	6	8	2	9	19	4
20	13	6	11	12	5	2	10
16	7	14	3	8	19	1	9
18	17	11	6	7	15	2	13
5	9	1	14	16	4	8	0
10	18	17	20	3	7	12	13
4	8	14	6	1	9	5	15
11	7	8	17	19	11	2	4

Time: 1 minute

Development: Go to Numberfly at www.interventioncentral.org/php/numberfly/numberfly.php for help in creating your probe.

Directions (See to Say):
1. Place the student copy of the probe in front of the student. Say, "The paper in front of you has boxes with two numbers in each box. Look at the first box" (point) "Tell me the number that is bigger."

2. If the student correctly identifies the bigger number, say "Good, 18 is bigger than 7."

3. If the student does not correctly identify the bigger number say, "The bigger number is 18. You should have said 18 because 18 is bigger than 7. Look at this box (point). Which number is bigger?"

4. Say: "When I say 'start", I want you to tell me the number that is bigger in each box. Start here (point) and go across the page and then down to the next row". Demonstrate by dragging your finger across and down the rows. Say, "If you come to a box and do not know which number is bigger, say, 'skip' and move to the next box. Do you have any questions? Ready? Start here" (point).

Kemp, Eaton & Poole, 2009

5. Start timing. If student does not respond within 3 seconds, ask her to try the next one. Follow along on the examiner's copy of the probe. Put a slash through incorrect responses. At the end of one minute circle the last identified number. And say "Stop".

Scoring:

✓ If student correctly identifies the bigger number, count the item as correct.

✓ If the student states both numbers in the box, count the item as incorrect.

✓ If student states any number other than the bigger number of the pair in each box, count the item as incorrect.

✓ If student does not respond within 3 seconds, ask her to move on to the next box.

✓ If student skips an item, count the item as incorrect.

✓ If student skips an entire row, count each item in the row as incorrect.

✓ If student misses 5 in a row, discontinue probe.

Sample Scoring

7	18	12	20	1	11	10	14	4
8	15	13	1̸7̸	5	14	1̸6̸	15	8
0	3	6	8	2	9	19	4	12
20	13	6	11	12	5	2	10	16
16	7	14	3	8	19	1	9	20
1̸8̸	17	11	⑥	7	15	2	13	24
5	9	1	14	16	4	8	0	28
10	18	17	20	3	7	12	13	32
4	8	14	6	1	9	5	15	36
11	7	8	17	19	11	2	4	40

Kemp, Eaton & Poole, 2009

1. Count the total number of items up to the circled item (total responses): **21**

2. Count the number incorrect: **3**

3. Subtract the incorrect from the total responses:
   Total correct responses = **18**

Proficiency: (norms from www.aimsweb.com)

Grade	%ile	Fall	Winter	Spring
K	50	11	20	27
	25	6	11	19
1	50	22	32	33
	25	14	26	27

Alternate Format: See and Write Directions

1. Give student a copy of the probe. Say, " There are boxes with numbers in them. Look at the first two and write the symbol for greater than or less than based on the numbers you see. If student writes the correct symbol for the first item, let them know they are correct. If they do not write the correct symbol, identify it for them by saying, "you should have written this symbol because…"

Proficiency: no more than 1 error.

Kemp, Eaton & Poole, 2009

Quantity Discrimination - Numbers
Probe/Template

7	18	12	20	1	11	10	14
8	15	13	17	5	14	16	15
0	3	6	8	2	9	19	4
20	13	6	11	12	5	2	10
16	7	14	3	8	19	1	9
18	17	11	6	7	15	2	13
5	9	1	14	16	4	8	0
10	18	17	20	3	7	12	13
4	8	14	6	1	9	5	15
11	7	8	17	19	11	2	4

Student Name: _____ Date: _____

Kemp, Eaton & Poole, 2009

Computation
Directions

A 6 x 8 48	B 876 + 125 1001	C 213 - 23 190	D 167 + 32 199	E 87 - 85 2	13
F 542 - 222 320	G 3 x 0 0	H 370 + 430 800	I 946 - 257 689	J 352 + 241 593	26
K 801 + 110 911	L 230 - 130 100	M 9 x 7 63	N 360 + 148 508	O 40 - 25 15	39
P 854 - 235 619	Q 57 + 42 99	R 121 - 20 101	S 4 x 7 28	T 613 + 188 801	52
U 188 + 277 465	V 839 - 218 621	W 246 + 253 499	X 546 + 253 1799	Y 5 x 9 45	66

Time Allocation:

Grade 1	2 minutes
Grade 2	2 minutes
Grade 3	3 minutes
Grade 4	3 minutes
Grade 5	6 minutes
Grade 6	6 minutes

Directions for Group Administration:

1. Say: "The paper in front of you is a computation math probe. It has several different types of math problems that you will be working on all year. At first you may not be able to do all of the problems, but as you learn more throughout the year, you will be able to do more and you will see your score go up. I will give you_____minutes to do as many problems as you can. When I say 'start', begin with the first problem (point) and work across the row and then down to the next row and across. If you come to an easy problem do it right away. If you come to a harder problem, skip it and move on to the next one. Do as many problems as you can until I say 'stop'. If you finish before I say stop, go back to the harder problems and try again. You want to work quickly and accurately. Any questions? Ready? Start."

Kemp, Eaton & Poole, 2009

2. Start timing. At the end of the timing, say, "Pencils down, thank you.".

Scoring:

✓ Score each correct digit (CD) in the answer as one point. Note: in a complex answer, such as for multi-digit multiplication, each correct digit in the steps to arrive at the answer is counted.

In a problem like
```
    34
 + 46
    80
```
There are 2 possible correct digits in the answer. (2CD)

In a problem like
```
    1470
  x 182
    2940
  117600
  147000
  267540
```

There are 22 possible correct digits in the solution (22CD)

✓ If a student gets the correct answer, she receives full credit for the total number of digits, even if she does not show all of the steps.

✓ If a problem is crossed out or unfinished, the student receives points for each correct digit written.

✓ Reversed digits are scored as correct (backwards 3 for example). This does not apply to upside down 6's and 9's since it is not possible to tell what the student intended.

✓ Do not count numbers carried and written as correct digits

Note: The most useful math computation probes are not only designed to provide equal representation of problem types and aligned to the appropriate grade level curriculum but should also contain more problems than a student can complete in the allotted time.

Kemp, Eaton & Poole, 2009

Proficiency: Suggested norms

Grade level	End of year digits per minute
1	17 - 25
2	24-32
3	31-41
4	53-72
5	52-69
6	36-51

Kemp, Eaton & Poole, 2009

Computation Probe
Sample

Student Name:_____ Date: _____

A 6 x 8	**B** 876 + 125	**C** 213 - 23	**D** 167 + 32	**E** 87 - 85
F 542 - 222	**G** 3 x 0	**H** 370 + 430	**I** 946 - 257	**J** 352 + 241
K 801 + 110	**L** 230 - 130	**M** 9 x 7	**N** 360 + 148	**O** 40 - 25
P 854 - 235	**Q** 57 + 42	**R** 121 - 20	**S** 4 x 7	**T** 613 + 188
U 188 + 277	**V** 839 - 218	**W** 246 + 253	**X** 546 + 253	**Y** 5 x 9

Kemp, Eaton & Poole, 2009

Concepts and Applications
Directions

Time:

Grade	Time	# of Problems
2	8 minutes	18
3	6 minutes	24
4	6 minutes	24
5	7 minutes	23
6	7 minutes	24-25

Directions for Group Administration:

1. Say: "The paper in front of you is called a Concepts and Applications Probe. It has several different types of math problems that you will learn this year. At first you may not be able to do all of the problems, but as you learn more throughout the year, you will be able to do more and you will see your score go up. I will give you ___ minutes to do as many problems as you can. When I say 'start', begin with the first problem (point) and work across the row and then down to the next row and across. If you come to an easy problem do it right away. If you come to a harder problem, skip it and move on to the next one. Do as many problems as you can until I say 'stop'. If you finish before I say stop, go back to the harder problems and try again. You want to work quickly and accurately.

2. I will score these probes by giving you a point for each correct answer. Some of the problems have more than one answer. Remember, you get credit for each correct answer, so be sure to fill in as many as you can. Any questions? Ready? Start."

Scoring:

   ✓ Count one for each item answered correctly.

Proficiency: Suggested norms

Mid year	25th %ile	50th %ile
Grade 2	4 pts.	7 pts.
Grade 3	13 pts.	16 pts.
Grade 4	8 pts.	13 pts.
Grade 5	8 pts.	12 pts.

Kemp, Eaton & Poole, 2009

Concepts and Applications
Sample/Development

Here is a sample probe. You can develop your own, or one can be obtained from publishers to assess students' knowledge and understanding of math other than computation.

To develop the probes, first identify the domains (i.e. numbers sense, data analysis, patterns, algebra, geometry and measurement) within the grade level curriculum that you want to assess. The specific items generally include naming numbers, vocabulary, measurement, word problems, charts and graphs, area, perimeter, decimal and fractions. Alternate forms of the probe need to be constructed if it is to be used for progress monitoring.

Write a number in each blank. Use these numbers 3243 3493 3278 _____ is the largest _____ is the smallest	Write a number in the blank. Six hundred twenty-nine _____	Jorge buys 4 packages of soap with 7 bars in each package. How many bars of soap does he buy in all? _____
It took the movers 2 hours to unload the truck. They made 8 trips into the house, each time carrying 7 boxes. How many boxes did they bring into the house? _____	A B C D E F G H I J K L M N O P Q R S T U V W X Y Z Write the eleventh letter. _____	Write the number in each blank. 8 hundreds 8 tens 2 ones _____ 0 hundreds 2 tens 5 ones _____
Fill in the blanks. 20, 30, 40,___, ___ 83, 85, 87,___, ___	Sarah's family went fishing for 4 days. Each day they caught 6 fish. How many fish did they catch in all? _____	Write this number in words. 964 _____
Write the number in each blank. 1 hundreds 0 tens 3 ones _____ 7 hundreds 4 tens 8 ones _____	Fill in the blanks. 12, 24, 48,___, ___ 8, 16, 24,___, ___	Write a number in each blank. Look at this number: 6304 Which digit is in the tens place? _____ Which is in the thousands place? _____
There are 523 students at Smith Elementary. On Monday 38 were absent. How many students were present at school on Monday? _____	Rewrite $\dfrac{8}{6\,\overline{)42}}$ ____ ÷ ____ = ____	Write < , > or = in each blank. 2457 _____ 2347 6879 _____ 6807

Kemp, Eaton & Poole, 2009

How Persistent Am I?
Directions

Use this checklist at the end of a class as often as you would like to have students report their effort, understanding and anxiety related to the lesson and /or topic.

Directions:

Give each student a copy of How Persistent Am I? Checklist. Review the directions and demonstrate how to fill in the columns. Ask students to provide honest, open feedback.

Today's Date	6/9								
1. How hard did I try?	3								
2. How well did I follow the teacher's directions?	2								
3. How much did I like this topic?	0								
4. How much understanding of the topic did I gain?	2								
5. How often did I ask for help or clarification?	0								
6. How much anxiety do I have?	4								
Total Points									

Kemp, Eaton & Poole, 2009

How Persistent Am I?
Checklist/Template

Name: _____

Directions: Write the date in the appropriate column. Then answer the questions about your effort for today's class using the following point system: Not (none) at all = 0   little bit = 1   Some = 3   A lot = 4

Date								
1. How hard did I try?								
2. How well did I follow the teacher's directions?								
3. How much did I like this topic?								
4. How much understanding of the topic did I gain?								
5. How often did I ask for help or clarification?								
6. How much anxiety do I have?								
Total Points								

- -

Name: _____

Directions: Write the date in the appropriate column. Then answer the questions about your effort for today's class using the following point system: Not (none) at all = 0   little bit = 1   Some = 3   A lot = 4

Date								
1. How hard did I try?								
2. How well did I follow the teacher's directions?								
3. How much did I like this topic?								
4. How much understanding of the topic did I gain?								
5. How often did I ask for help or clarification?								
6. How much anxiety do I have?								
Total Points								

Kemp, Eaton & Poole, 2009

Blank Probe Sheet (10)

Blank Probe Sheet (28)

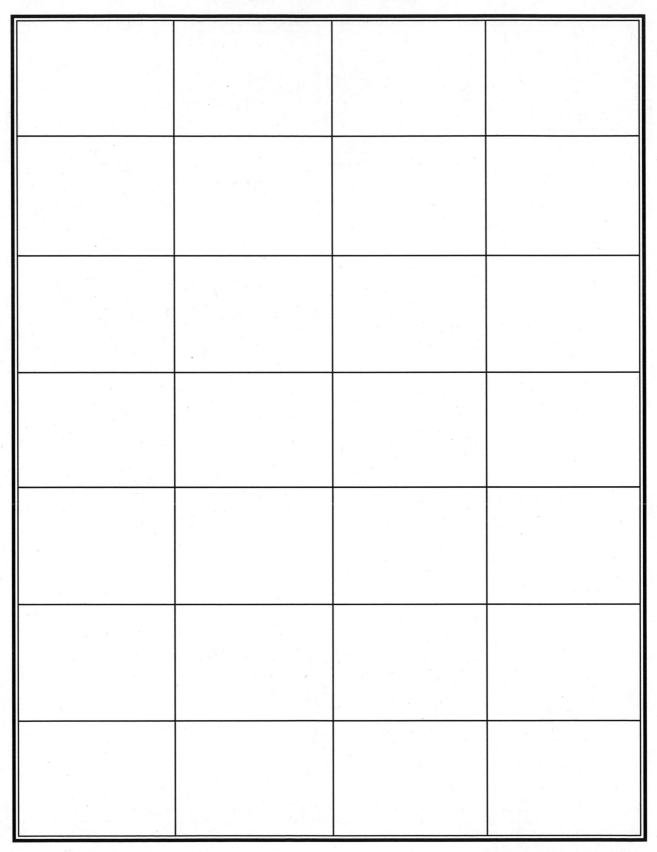

Kemp, Eaton & Poole, 2009

Blank Probe Sheet (40)

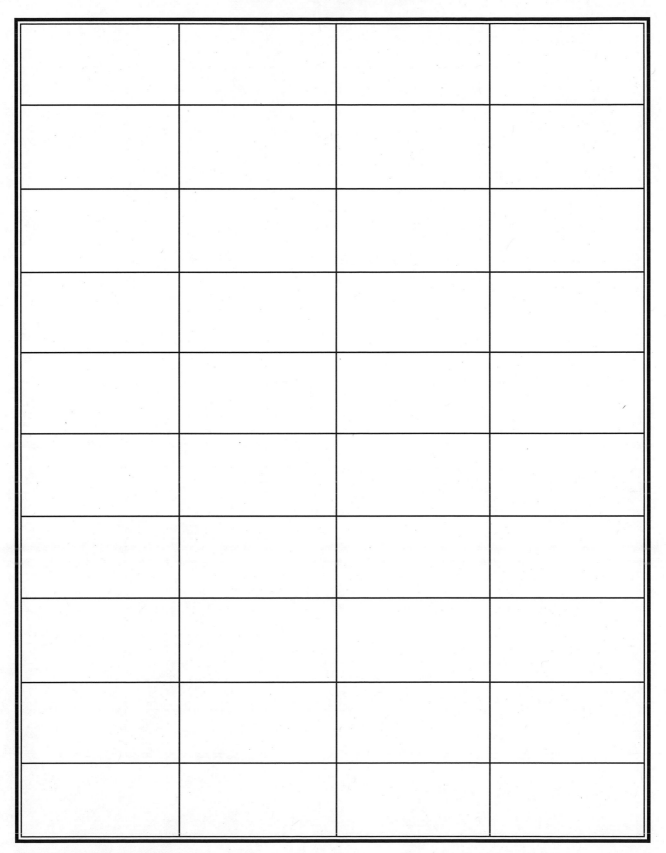

Data Collection Sheet
Template

Name:					
Date:					
Practice Sheet					
Score cdpm*					
Date:					
Practice Sheet					
Score cdpm					

Name:					
Date:					
Practice Sheet					
Score cdpm					
Date:					
Practice Sheet					
Score cdpm					

* cpdm = correct digits per minute

Kemp, Eaton & Poole, 2009

Sample Chart 1

Name _____ Grade _____ Content Area _____

Target Skill

Raw data

date & score

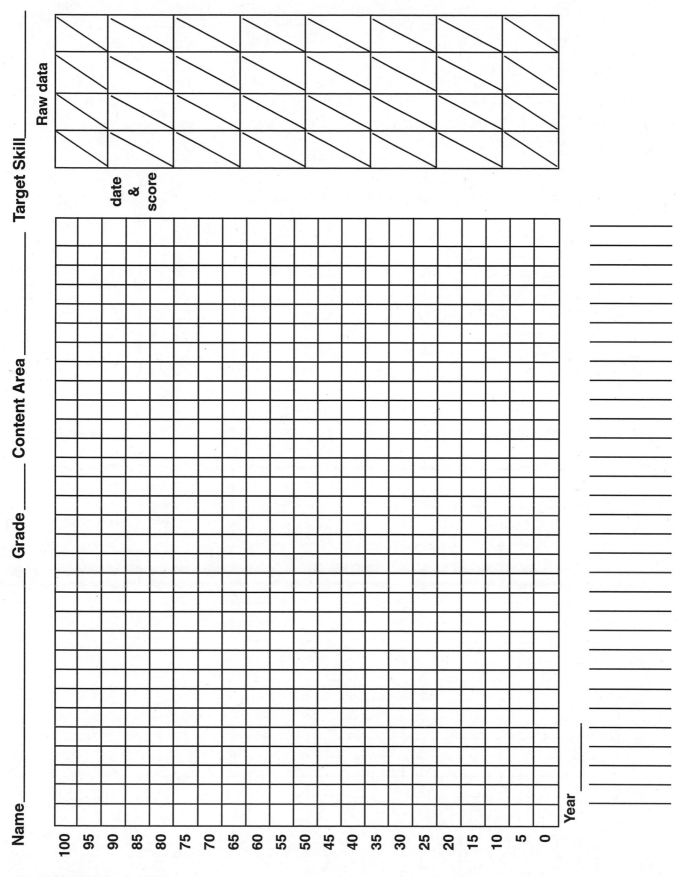

100
95
90
85
80
75
70
65
60
55
50
45
40
35
30
25
20
15
10
5
0

Year _____

Sample Chart 2

Name _____   **Grade** _____
Content Area _____   **Target Skill** _____

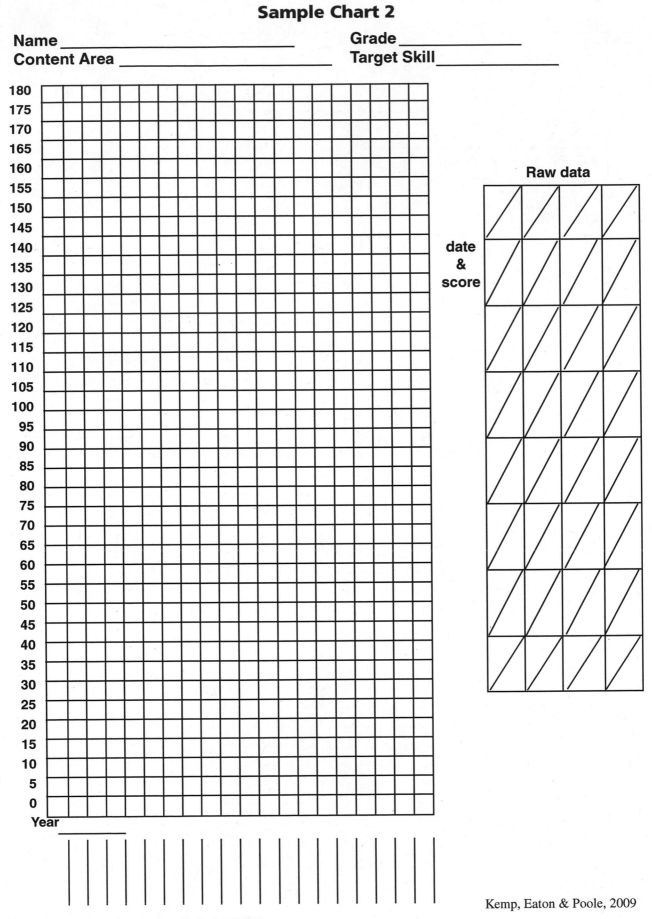

Raw data

date
&
score

Year _____

Kemp, Eaton & Poole, 2009

Sample Chart 3

Name _____   **Grade** _____

Content Area _____   **Target Skill** _____

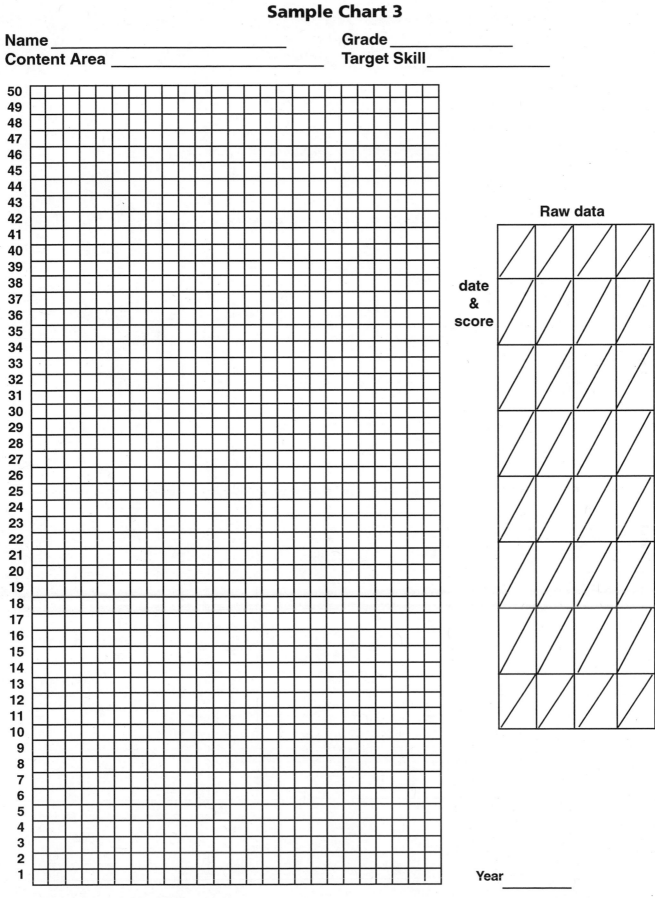

Raw data

date
&
score

Year _____

Kemp, Eaton & Poole, 2009

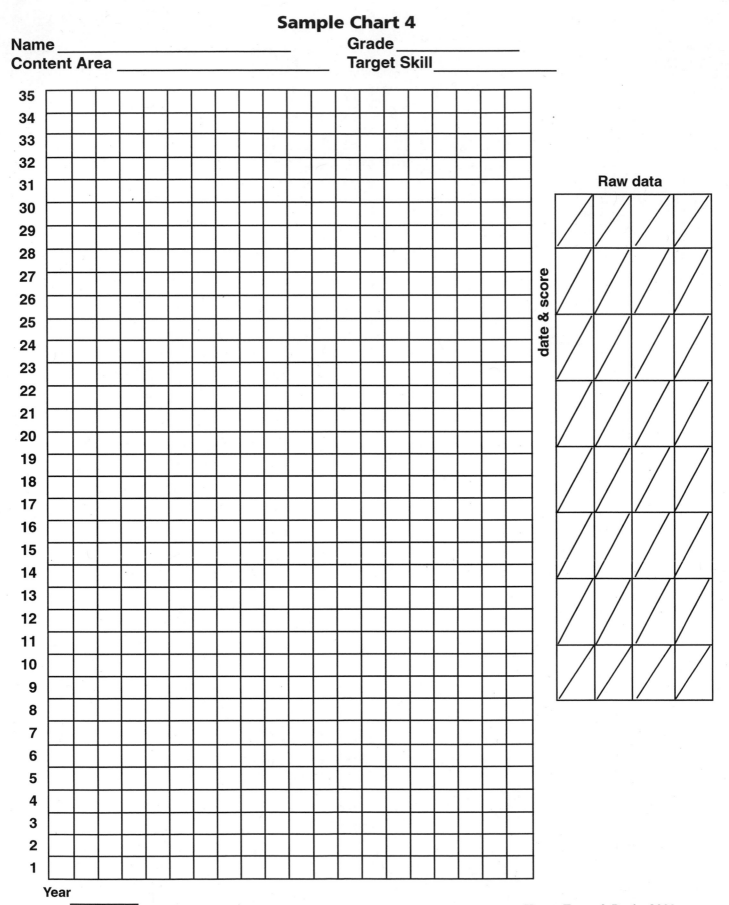

Suggested Resources for Appendix A

AIMSweb. (2004) The AIMSWeb, Early Numeracy Measures.

Allsopp, D., Kyger, M., Lovin, L., Gerretson, H., Carson, K., Ray,S. (2008). Mathematics dynamic assessment: Informal assessment that responds to the needs of struggling learners in mathematics. Teaching Exceptional Children, 40 (3)6-16.

Connell, J. E (2005). Constructing a math applications, curriculum-based assessment: An analysis of the relationship between applications problems, computation problems and criterion referenced assessments. Dissertation, Available from: http://etd.lsu.edu/docs/available/etd-07132005-110918/unrestricted/Connell_Jr_dis.pdf

Fuchs, L. S., Hamlett, B., & Fuchs, D. (1999). Monitoring basic skills progress (2nd ed.) [Computer software]. Austin, TX: Pro-Ed.

Hosp, Michele, K., Hosp, John L., and Howell, Kenneth W. (2007). The ABC's of CBM: A practical guide to curriculum-based measurement. New York:The Guilford Press.

Shapiro, E. S. (2004). Academic skills problems: Direction assessment and intervention (3rd ed.). New York: Guilford Press.

Vanderheyden, A. M., & Burns, M. K. (2005). Using curriculum-based assessment and curriculum-based measurement to guide elementary mathematics instruction: Effect on individual and group accountability scores. Assessment for Effective Intervention, 30, 15-31.

Wright, J. (2008). Intervention Central
Early Numeracy and Kindergarten math measures
www.interventioncentral.org

NumberFly—Probe generator for Discrimination, Missing Number and Number Identification: www.interventioncentral.org/php/numberfly/numberfly.php

Appendix B
Templates and Reproducibles

Appendix B includes reproducible templates for use in conjunction with the information and techniques in Chapters 3-8. There are three types of templates in this Appendix: Building Forms, Instructor Forms and Technique Forms.

- **Building Forms**:
  The Intervention Tracking Form and the RTI Planning Document are especially useful for school based support teams throughout the RTI process. We encourage you to share them accordingly.

- **Instructor Forms**:
  The Planning and Progress Tracking Forms may be used with all of the techniques. These forms assist with instructional preparation and collection of student data. We encourage you to modify these templates to meet your needs.

- **Technique Forms**:
  There are specific templates related to many of the interventions that are integral to implementation. Each technique includes a list of required materials with reproducible identified by tile and page number. The templates are included for your convenience. You may modify according to student level and instructional appropriateness.

Appendix B

Kemp, Eaton & Poole, 2009

Intervention Tracking Form - Page 1

Name: _____

Content	Universal Screening	Specific Skill Areas of Concern	Classroom Intervention
Core Program **Cardinal Questions—** ****Learning Strengths** _____Visual _____Auditory _____Motor- Kinesthetic **Kind of Smart:** _____ ****Executive Skill Strengths** ____Working Memory ____Meta-cognition ____Time Mangagment ____Sustained Attention ____Organization ____Persistence ____Flexibility ****Behavioral Mindset** ____Motivated ____Accepting ____Acts out ____Shuts down ____Diverts attention **UDL Strategies** 1. 2.	Date: Results Date: Results Date: Results	1. 2. 3.	Date: Target Area: Technique: Start date: Duration: Location Person(s) responsible Data to be collected Follow-up date Results:

Kemp, Eaton & Poole, 2009

Intervention Tracking Form - Page 2

Name: _____

Intervention Tier _____	Intervention Tier _____	Intervention Tier _____
Date:	Date:	Date:
Target Area:	Target Area:	Target Area:
Technique:	Technique:	Technique:
Start date:	Start date:	Start date:
Duration:	Duration:	Duration:
Location	Location	Location
Person(s) responsible	Person(s) responsible	Person(s) responsible
Data to be collected	Data to be collected	Data to be collected
Follow-up date	Follow-up date	Follow-up date
Results:	Results:	Results:

Kemp, Eaton & Poole, 2009

Response To Intervention Planning Document

Intensive Interventions	Provider	Monitoring how often?
1.		
2.		
3.		
4.		
5		

Targeted Interventions	Provider	Monitoring how often?
1.		
2.		
3.		
4.		
5		

Core Reading Program by Grade	Time - 90min
K	
1	
2	
3	
4	
5	

Universal Screening:

Benchmark dates: Fall	Winter	Spring

Tier III
60m/day
5-10%

Tier II
30 min/2x wk
10-15%

Tier I
Core Reading
and Classroom
Interventions

85-90% of students
benefit

Kemp, Eaton & Poole, 2009

Teacher Key Planning Form

Teacher Key for_____

Technique # _____	**Description:** _____

Directions:

Sample __:	Sample __:	Sample __:	Sample __:
1. _	1. _	1. _	1. _
2.	2.	2.	2.
3.	3.	3.	3.
4.	4.	4.	4.
5.	5.	5.	5.
6.	6.	6.	6.
7.	7.	7.	7.
8.	8.	8.	8.
9.	9.	9.	9.
10.	10.	10.	10.
Sample __:	**Sample __:**	**Sample __:**	**Sample __:**
1. _	1. _	1. _	1. _
2.	2.	2.	2.
3.	3.	3.	3.
4.	4.	4.	4.
5.	5.	5.	5.
6.	6.	6.	6.
7.	7.	7.	7.
8.	8.	8.	8.
9.	9.	9.	9.
10.	10.	10.	10.

Kemp, Eaton & Poole, 2009

Individual Tracking Progress Form

Student:

Activity:

Date:	Date:	Date:	Date:
1.	1.	1.	1.
2.	2.	2.	2.
3.	3.	3.	3.
4.	4.	4.	4.
5.	5.	5.	5.
6.	6.	6.	6.
7.	7.	7.	7.
8.	8.	8.	8.
9.	9.	9.	9.
10.	10.	10.	10.

Date:	Date:	Date:	Date:
1.	1.	1.	1.
2.	2.	2.	2.
3.	3.	3.	3.
4.	4.	4.	4.
5.	5.	5.	5.
6.	6.	6.	6.
7.	7.	7.	7.
8.	8.	8.	8.
9.	9.	9.	9.
10.	10.	10.	10.

Group Tracking Progress Form 1

	+	-	Comment					

Group Tracking Progress Form 2

Student Name	Skill								

Kemp, Eaton & Poole, 2009

Basic Language Concepts for Math

above	last
after	least
ahead	left
across from	less than
ahead	lower
alike	match
all	medium-sized
always	middle
another	more than
as many	most
away from	narrowest
backward	near
back	next to
before	never
behind	none
below	nothing
between	other
bottom	outside
center	over
corner	pair
different	part
each	right
end	row
equal	second
every	separated
except	several
farthest	side
fewest	skip
fifth	some, not many
first	starting
following	third
forward	through
fourth	together
front	top
half	under
identical	upper
inside	widest
large	whole

Ten Frames and Blanks

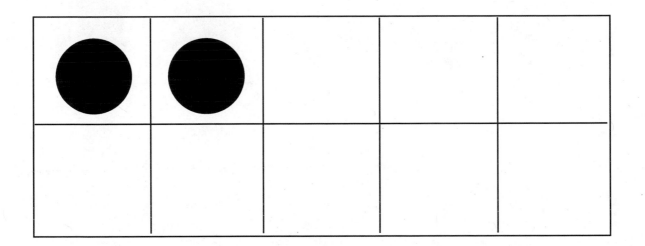

Kemp, Eaton & Poole, 2009

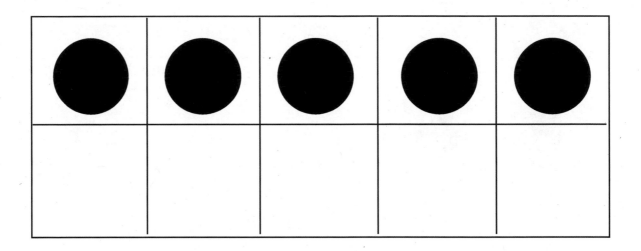

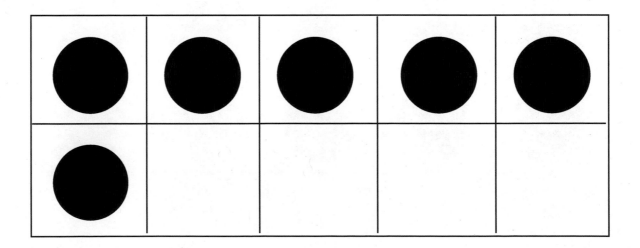

Kemp, Eaton & Poole, 2009

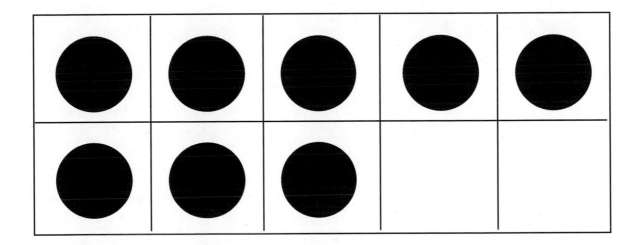

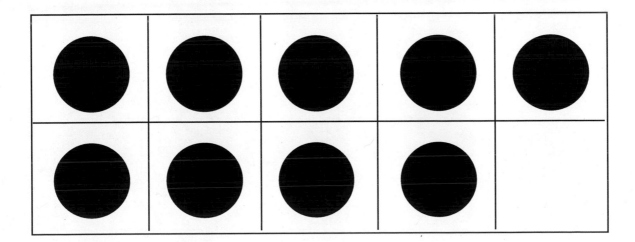

Kemp, Eaton & Poole, 2009

Ten Frames Teen Numbers

Write the number of dots you see in each ten frame set in the box below the set.

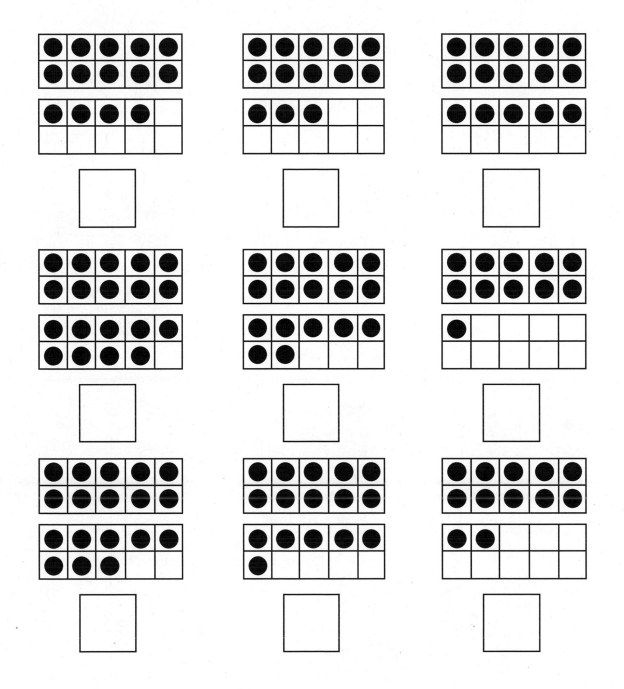

Partner Practice Form

Partner Names:

Score 1 for each match, 0 if no match

?	Match	Topic:	Partner Comments:
1.	1.		
2.	2.		
3.	3.		
4.	4.		
5.	5.		
6.	6.		
7.	7.		
8.	8.		
9.	9.		
10.	10.		
Total Points			

- -

Partner Names:

Score 1 for each match, 0 if no match

?	Match	Topic:	Partner Comments:
1.	1.		
2.	2.		
3.	3.		
4.	4.		
5.	5.		
6.	6.		
7.	7.		
8.	8.		
9.	9.		
10.	10.		
Total Points			

Kemp, Eaton & Poole, 2009

Traditional Hundreds Chart

1	2	3	4	5	6	7	8	9	10
11	12	13	14	15	16	17	18	19	20
21	22	23	24	25	26	27	28	29	30
31	32	33	34	35	36	37	38	39	40
41	42	43	44	45	46	47	48	49	50
51	52	53	54	55	56	57	58	59	60
61	62	63	64	65	66	67	68	69	70
71	72	73	74	75	76	77	78	79	80
81	82	83	84	85	86	87	88	89	90
91	92	93	94	95	96	97	98	99	100

1	2	3	4	5	6	7	8	9	10
11	12	13	14	15	16	17	18	19	20
21	22	23	24	25	26	27	28	29	30
31	32	33	34	35	36	37	38	39	40
41	42	43	44	45	46	47	48	49	50
51	52	53	54	55	56	57	58	59	60
61	62	63	64	65	66	67	68	69	70
71	72	73	74	75	76	77	78	79	80
81	82	83	84	85	86	87	88	89	90
91	92	93	94	95	96	97	98	99	100

Kemp, Eaton & Poole, 2009

Number Strip

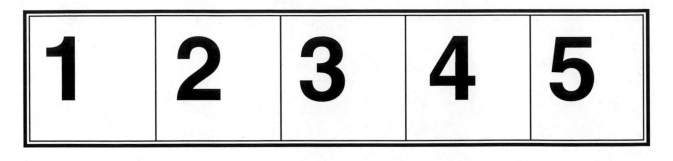

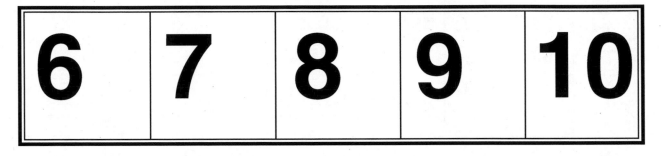

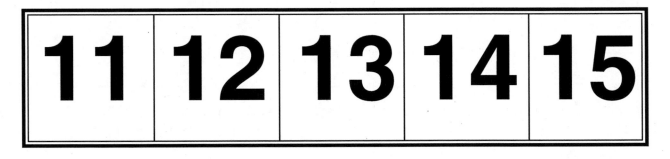

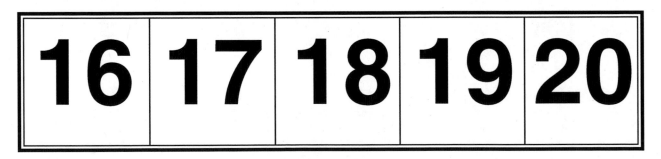

Kemp, Eaton & Poole, 2009

Chip Color Value Chart

Chip Color	Chip Value
Red	100
Blue	10
White	1

Kemp, Eaton & Poole, 2009

Hundreds	Tens	Ones
100	10	1
Red chip	Blue chip	White chip

Kemp, Eaton & Poole, 2009

Restructured Hundreds Chart

99	89	79	69	59	49	39	29	19	9
98	88	78	68	58	48	38	28	18	8
97	87	77	67	57	47	37	27	17	7
96	86	76	66	56	46	36	26	16	6
95	85	75	65	55	45	35	25	15	5
94	84	74	64	54	44	34	24	14	4
93	83	73	63	53	43	33	23	13	3
92	82	72	62	52	42	32	22	12	2
91	81	71	61	51	41	31	21	11	1
100	90	80	70	60	50	40	30	20	10	0

About This Chart: The restructured hundreds chart can be used to aid in identifying placement of numbers, show number progression, number patterns (counting by ones and multiples) as well as beginning addition, subtraction, multiplication and division. More information about using a chart like this can be obtained from the article by Nesbitt Vacc listed in the suggested resources at the end of Chapter 7.

Kemp, Eaton & Poole, 2009

Practice Sheet Template

Kemp, Eaton & Poole, 2009

Math Head Alphabet Template

	Math Head Words
A	
B	
C	
D	
E	
F	
G	
H	
I	
J	
K	
L	
M	
N	
O	
P	
Q	
R	
S	
T	
U	
V	
W	
X	
Y	
Z	

Kemp, Eaton & Poole, 2009

Math Heads Scoring Sheet

Teams						
Vocabulary Word/Term	**A**	**B**	**C**	**D**	**E**	**F**
Team Totals						

Kemp, Eaton & Poole, 2009

Kemp, Eaton & Poole, 2009

See the Story

Name:

Story:

Picture:

VISUALIZE

Kemp, Eaton & Poole, 2009

Story Problems Samples

- Mandy has a pet pig named Big Girl. Mandy took her Big Girl to the county fair. Big Girl won 8 prize ribbons at the fair on the first day. She won 3 more ribbons on the second day. She won 2 ribbons on the last day. How many prize ribbons did Big Girl win in all?

- Karl had 10 balloons. Three balloons popped. He gave 1 balloon to his sister. How many balloons did he have left?

- Mr. Bragger's second grade class had a sack race on the playground. Everyone who made it to the finish line got a bag of M & M's. There are 20 kids in Mr. Bragger's class. Ten kids fell down before they got to the finish line. Two kids' sacks ripped and they could not finish the race. The rest of the kids made it to the finish line. How many kids got bags of M & M's?

- Alex played Whack-a-Mole at the school fair. The moles popped up 25 times. Alex whacked 19 moles. How many moles did she miss?

- Twelve children get on the merry-go-round at the fair. Five more children get on the merry-go-round and three get off. How many children are on the merry-go-round now?

- Grandma and Grandpa were in a pie-eating contest. Grandma ate 5 blueberry pies. Grandpa ate 4 apple pies and 2 blueberry pies. How many pies did they eat altogether? How many more pies did Grandpa eat than Grandma?

- The magician pulled 15 rabbits out of his hat and put them in a box. Four rabbits ran away. Three rabbits hopped back in the hat. Then 1 of the rabbits hopped back out of the hat again into the box. How many rabbits were in the box? How many rabbits were in the hat?

- It takes an artist 10 minutes to paint a picture. There are 5 people waiting in line to have their picture painted. How many minutes will it take the artist to paint all of their pictures?

- Mama bought ice cream cones for Jody and her 4 friends. Two of her friends dropped their cones. Mama bought 2 more cones. How many ice cream cones did mama buy in all?

- There are 7 children waiting for the school bus. Four of the children are girls. How many children waiting for the bus are boys?

- Eagle Elementary school is 3 blocks from Garden Park. Mixed Up Middle School is 6 blocks from Garden Park. Harry Potter High School is 10 blocks from Garden Park.
    - — How many more blocks is the high school from the park than the middle school?
    - —How many more blocks is the middle school from the park than the elementary school?

- In the toy store window there is a display of toy vehicles. There are 16 toy cars, 4 fire engines, 2 buses, 1 dump truck, and 7 motorcycles.
    - —How many more motorcycles are there than cars?
    - —How many toy vehicles are there in all?
    - —How many buses and fire trucks are there?

- The band played at the school concert. They played two songs with a guitar, 2 drums and a piano. They played two other songs with 3 violins, 3 flutes, and 3 oboes. How many instruments did the band use for their music?

- Every school day Carlo and his brother are the first ones to get on the bus. At the next stop, the driver picks up 3 girls. At the next stop, 2 boys and 2 girls get on. At the next stop 1 boy gets on. And at the last stop 3 girls and 2 boys get on.
    - —How many children are there on the bus when it gets to school?
    - —Not counting the bus driver, how many of the riders on the bus are girls?
    - —Not counting the bus driver, how many of the riders on the bus are boys?

- Mario and his father went to New York City. They rode a subway that had 35 seats in the car. The seats were all filled and there were 10 people standing up. At the next stop, 5 people got off and 2 people got on. How many people were in the subway car then?

- The Gardener family grew pumpkins this year. Sally's biggest pumpkin weighed 12 pounds. Cory's pumpkin weighed 15 pounds. And Baby Alice had a pumpkin that weighed 6 pounds. How much more did

Kemp, Eaton & Poole, 2009

Cory's pumpkin weigh than Alice's pumpkin? How much more did Cory's pumpkin weigh than Sally's?

- Mrs. Smiley's first grade class decided to collect pennies to help buy dog and cat food for the Town Animal Shelter. The students asked their parents to help, and they looked everywhere they could think of for pennies that people may have dropped: on the playground, in the school hallways, in the cafeteria, and on the ground when they walked to and from school. At the end of the first week this is what happened: On Monday the students in the class collected 20 pennies all together and put them in a pink piggy bank Mrs. Smiley kept on her desk. On Tuesday they found 15 more pennies. On Wednesday they put 20 pennies in the piggy bank. On Thursday they collected 30 pennies! And on Friday they put in 15 more pennies. How many pennies did the students collect in all at the end of the first week?

- Chayvon had a big bucket of colored pencils, crayons and markers in her bedroom closet. She decided to sort them all out and put them in different boxes. She separated everything in the bucket into three separate piles of markers, crayons and pencils. This is what she found. She had one pile with 15 colored pencils. She had another pile with 30 crayons. She had a third pile with 15 markers. How many pencils, markers and crayons did she have all together?
  —(How many more crayons did she have than markers? How many more crayons did she have than colored pencils?)

- David, Samantha and Jaquel are helping the school librarian put picture books on a shelf in the reading corner. David put 10 big books on the shelf. Samantha put 7 more on the shelf. Jaquel put 15 smaller books on the shelf. How many books in all did they put on the shelf?

- Mary built a tower 10 blocks high. Daniel built a tower next to Mary's 12 blocks high. Kevin built a tower 8 blocks high. How many blocks did they use to build all the towers?

- One day, Monica's grandfather allowed Monica and her three friends to collect flowers from his garden to make a beautiful bouquet for Monica's grandmother. Monica picked 7 white flowers. Tara picked 6 yellow flowers and 3 red flowers. Bobbie found 5 blue flowers. And

Kinsey picked 8 purple flowers. How many flowers did they have to put together for Monica's grandmother?

- Robert's mother made 20 chocolate chip cookies and put them on the kitchen table. Robert ate two cookies when he came home from school. His sister also ate two cookies when she came home from softball practice. Robert's father ate one cookie when he came home from work. Jimbo, Robert's dog, jumped up to the table and ate three cookies before Robert chased him away and moved the cookies to the counter. How many cookies were left?

Kemp, Eaton & Poole, 2009

Problem Type Reference Sheet

Problem Type			
Join	**Result Unknown** Connie had 5 marbles. Juan gave her 8 more marbles. How many marbles does Connie have altogether? $# + # = ?(Unknown#)$	**Change Unknown** Connie has 5 marbles. How many more marbles does she need to have 13 marbles altogether? $# + ?(Unknown#) = #$	**Start Unknown** Connie had some marbles. Juan gave her 5 more marbles. Now she has 13 marbles. How many marbles did Connie have to start with? $?(Unknown#) + # = #$
Separate	**Result Unknown** Connie had 13 marbles. She gave 5 to Juan. How many marbles does Connie have left? $# - # = ?(Unknown#)$	**Change Unknown** Connie had 13 marbles. She gave some to Juan. Now she has 5 marbles left. How may marbles did Connie give to Juan? $# - ? (Unkown#) = #$	**Start Unknown** Connie had some marbles. She gave 5 to Juan. Now she has 8 marbles left. How many marbles did Connie have to start with? $?(Unknown#) - # = #$
Part-Part-Whole	**Whole Unknown** *Connie has 5 red marbles and 8 blue marbles. How many marbles does she have?* $#A + #B = ?(Unknown#)$	**Part Unknown** Connie has 13 marbles. Five are red and the rest are blue. How many blue marbles does Connie have? $#A + ?(Unknown#)B = #$	
Compare	**Difference Unknown** Connie has 13 marbles. Juan has 5 marbles. How many more marbles does Connie have than Juan? $# - ?(Unknown #) = #$	**Compare Quantity Unknown** Juan has 5 marbles. \Connie has 8 more than Juan. How many marbles does Connie have? $# + # = ?(Unknown #)$	**Reference Unknown** Connie has 13 marbles. She has 5 more marbles than Juan. How many marbles does Juan have? $# - # = ?(Unknown#)$

Kemp, Eaton & Poole, 2009

What's Your Problem?
Team Checklist

Team member names:

Check (✓) each task as you complete it for problem #_____.

_____ **We read the problem.**

_____ **We agree that the problem question is this:**
(Write the question in the space below)

_____ **We showed the steps to find the solution using the steps above.**

_____ **We solved the problem and came up with this answer.**

Kemp, Eaton & Poole, 2009

What's Your Problem?
Worksheet

What's Your Problem?				
Team Members				
Problem Type: **(J) Join** **(PPW) Part-Part- Whole** **(S) Separate** **(C) Compare**			**Agreement Initials**	
Problem #	**Type**	**Math Symbol Sentence**		**Answer**

Kemp, Eaton & Poole, 2009

Think It, Write It (Addition & Subtraction)
Worksheet

Think It, Write It
Addition and Subtraction

Name: **Date:**

Problem:	_____ Alone _____ and Me

What is this about? (in my own words – paraphrasing <10 words)

Who?

What happened?

I can solve it this way: (make a plan— math representation and operations)

_____received means add (+)
_____left means take away (-)
_____more than (compare) (+)
_____less than (compare) (-)

What steps do I need to take?
(compute: show all steps and symbols)

What do I know? (facts stated in the problem)

Known: _____ has/had _____

What changed? Someone...
____received ____(has more or add)
____gave   ____(separated or subtract)

What do I need to find? (problem question/direction = the unknown)

Unknown: How many or Find _____
_____ Altogether (Add)
_____ Left (Subtract)
_____ More than_____(Compare)
_____ Less than_____ (Compare)
_____ Part/Part/Whole _____

New Vocabulary:

Connections to Life:

What do I see? (visualize – schema – tally marks)

Check: Does my answer make sense?
(answers the question or follows the direction)

Kemp, Eaton & Poole, 2009

Think It, Write It (All Operations)
Worksheet

Think It, Write It	
Name:	**Date:**
Problem:	_____ Alone _____ and Me
What is this about? (in my own words – paraphrasing <10 words) Who? What happened?	**I can solve it this way:** (make a plan—math representation and operations)
What do I know? (facts stated in the problem)	**What steps do I need to take?** (compute: show all steps and symbols)
What do I need to find? (problem question/direction = the unknown) **Unknown:**	**New Vocabulary:** **Connections to Life:**
What do I see? (visualize – schema – tally marks)	**Check: Does my answer make sense?** (answers the question or follows the direction)

Kemp, Eaton & Poole, 2009

Think It, Write It
Check It Out

| Steps | Work Space |

☐ 1. **Read the entire problem**

☐ 2. **Identify new vocabulary.**

☐ 3. **Paraphrase the problem.**

☐ 2. **Identify what I know.**

☐ 3. **Identify what I need to find.**

☐ 4. **Visualize the problem.**

☐ 5. **Make a plan.**

☐ 6. **Solve: write the steps and operations.**

☐ 7. **Check: compare the answer to the question.**

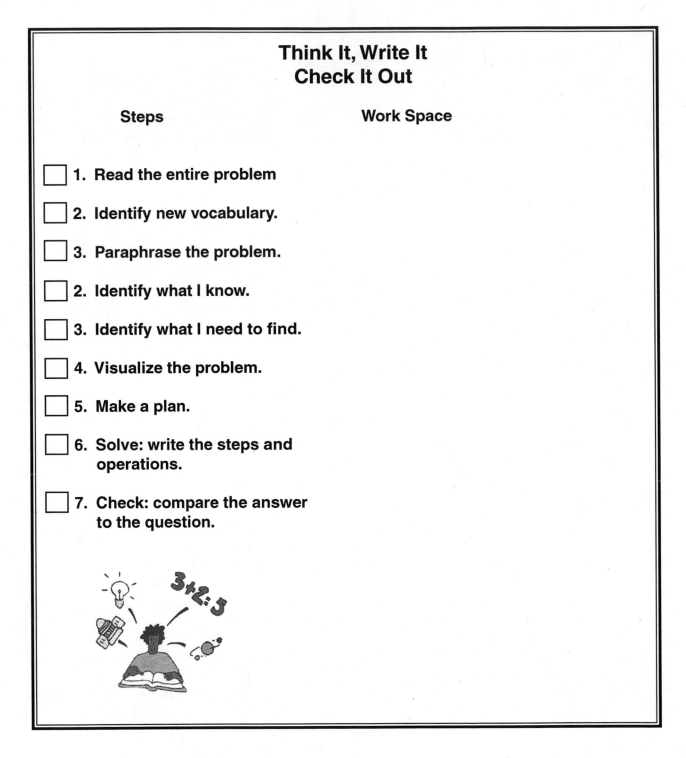

Kemp, Eaton & Poole, 2009

Think It, Write It
Bookmark

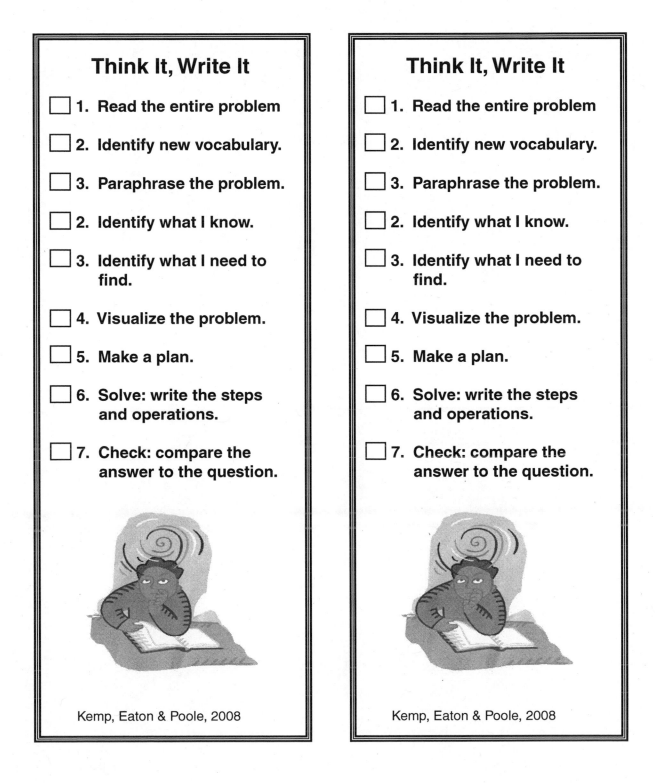

Think It, Write It

☐ 1. Read the entire problem

☐ 2. Identify new vocabulary.

☐ 3. Paraphrase the problem.

☐ 2. Identify what I know.

☐ 3. Identify what I need to find.

☐ 4. Visualize the problem.

☐ 5. Make a plan.

☐ 6. Solve: write the steps and operations.

☐ 7. Check: compare the answer to the question.

Kemp, Eaton & Poole, 2008

Think It, Write It

☐ 1. Read the entire problem

☐ 2. Identify new vocabulary.

☐ 3. Paraphrase the problem.

☐ 2. Identify what I know.

☐ 3. Identify what I need to find.

☐ 4. Visualize the problem.

☐ 5. Make a plan.

☐ 6. Solve: write the steps and operations.

☐ 7. Check: compare the answer to the question.

Kemp, Eaton & Poole, 2008

Kemp, Eaton & Poole, 2009

How I See Myself Template, Page 1

Name:	Date:	Page 1

When I am at school I...	The things I like about school are...
Things I am good at in school are...	**Things I wish I could do better at school are...**

Kemp, Eaton & Poole, 2009

How I See Myself Template, Page 2

Name:	Date:	Page 2

When I read I...	When I do math I...
Some of the things I want to learn about are...	**Things I think I can do better now than before are ...**

Kemp, Eaton & Poole, 2009

It's Okay Not to Know Survey

Date:_____ Boy _____ Girl _____

Please complete this survey. You do not have to put your name on this paper. Please fill in today's date and check off if you are a boy or a girl. Thank you for assisting me.

KEY: Not at all = 0   A little bit = 1   Some = 2   A lot = 4

	Point(s)
1. I like coming to this classroom.	
2. I wish you would give me more time to think before I have to respond or talk in class.	
3. I ask questions when I do not understand something in class.	
4. I am too embarrassed to ask questions in class because I do not want anyone to know I do not get it.	
5. I am too shy to talk in class.	
6. I talk about things I do in school at home.	
7. When I have to take a math test in school I usually panic.	
8. When I am asked to explain how I solved a math problem during class I usually panic.	
9. When I have to read aloud in school I usually panic.	
10. I understand the importance of this survey.	
Total Points	

Comments/Questions:

Kemp, Eaton & Poole, 2009

My <u>OOPS!</u> List Template

Name:		
Topic	**Difficult Concept**	**Solution**
1.		
2.		
3.		
4.		
5.		

Kemp, Eaton & Poole, 2009

Grade My Understanding
Template

Grade My Understanding

Today's lesson on_____
was _____ .

I would give myself a grade of: _____ because I think I understand:
_____ Nothing _____Very little _____Some _____Most _____Everything

I understand: _____
_____
_____ .

I still need: _____
_____ .

Name:_____ Date:_____

Grade My Understanding

Today's lesson on_____
was _____ .

I would give myself a grade of: _____ because I think I understand:
_____ Nothing _____Very little _____Some _____Most _____Everything

I understand: _____
_____
_____ .

I still need: _____
_____ .

Name:_____ Date:_____

Kemp, Eaton & Poole, 2009

Topic Tattler
Template

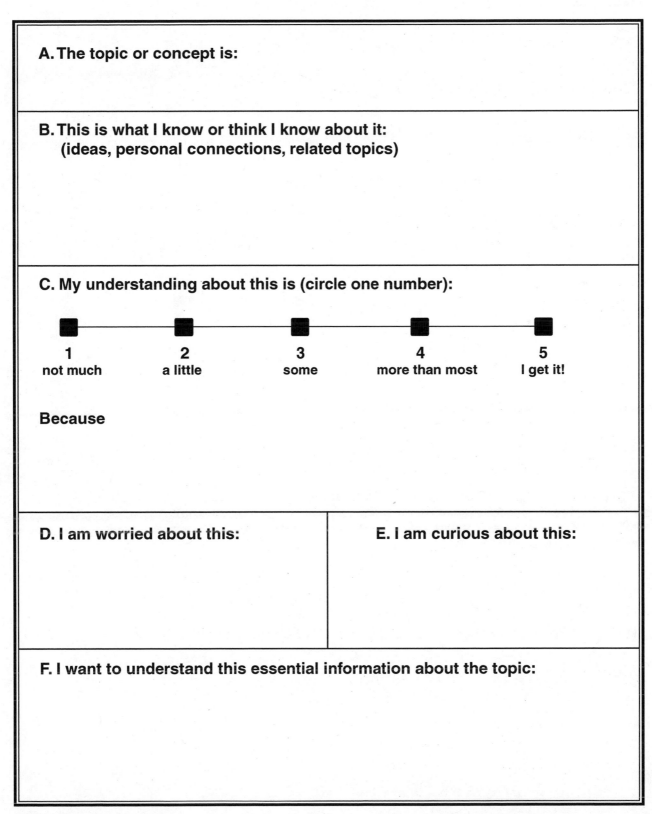

A. The topic or concept is:

B. This is what I know or think I know about it:
   (ideas, personal connections, related topics)

C. My understanding about this is (circle one number):

1	2	3	4	5
not much	a little	some	more than most	I get it!

Because

D. I am worried about this:

E. I am curious about this:

F. I want to understand this essential information about the topic:

Glossary

Acronyms

CAST—Center for Applied Special Technology

CBM—Curriculum Based Measurement

CEC—Council for Exceptional Children

IDEA—Individuals with Disabilities Education Act

IEP—Individual Education Plan

NAEP—National Assessment of Educational Progress

NCLB—No Child Left Behind

NCTM—National Council of Teachers of Mathematics

NRC—National Research Council

PBIS—Positive Behavior Intervention Supports

PISA—Program for International Student Assessment

PM—Progress Monitoring

RTI—Response to Intervention

TIMSS—Trends in International Math and Science Study

UDL—Universal Design for Learning

UbD—Understanding by Design

Definitions of Terms

Algorithms—procedures for calculations.

Cardinal Numbers—the last number counted in a group of objects; it represents the total number of objects.

Cardinal Questions—a set of five question stems that are used as a thinking frame-work to help teachers assess their own and their students' knowledge base.

Probe—a brief, timed sample of academic content that is taken from grade level curriculum and used for assessing or measuring student learning.

Cognitive Process—the mental process of learning and thinking, including aspects such as awareness, perception, reasoning and judgment.

Curriculum Based Measurement—direct, repeated, formative assessments that are administered frequently in order to make decisions about student learning.

Direct Instruction—a teaching method developed by Englemann and colleagues, that is typified by explicit presentation of subject matter (e.g. use of signals), and carefully sequenced (i.e. components of skills are seamlessly and progressively presented) supported instruction with numerous opportunities for students to respond, and frequent review of concepts and skills.

Executive Function—a set of cognitive abilities that control and regulate other abilities and behaviors. They are necessary for goal-directed behavior and include the ability to start and stop actions, to monitor and adapt behavior as required by the circumstances, and to plan future behavior when faced with novel tasks and situations. The abilities to form concepts and to think abstractly are often considered components of executive function.

Explicit Instruction/direct instruction—a straight forward, systematic instructional approach derived from effective schools research merged with behavior analysis.

Extrinsic Motivator—external acknowledgment/reinforcement that is provided to encourage performance of a task, such as positive verbal comments and/or tangibles.

Fidelity Measures—the level of effectiveness of instruction, intervention and monitoring that is provided to students.

Fluency—effortless, smooth and rapid ability to demonstrate number sense, computation and problem solving.

Intervention—an action taken to modify/improve student performance.

Intrinsic Motivator—those things that produce positive feelings, such as love of the task, self-satisfaction, sense of achievement, relaxation, purpose, etc.

Math Literacy—the understanding of math mechanics and processes that enables one to know how to calculate efficiently and accurately, and to know what situations require their application.

Metacognition—the process of thinking about how we think.

Number Sense—a knowledge or awareness of numbers – names, values, and relationships. Children with number sense recognize the relative differences in number quantity and how those differences can be represented.

Ordinal Numbers—numbers associated with order or the notion of position, eg, first, second, third, twenty-first.

Progress Monitoring—a time-efficient, on-going method of assessment used to make informed instructional decisions and quantify students' rate of progress.

Quantity Array—a collection of objects that are sorted and ordered in a certain way.

Rational Counting—counting to determine the number of items in a set or group, i.e. object counting; also known as one-to-one correspondence.

Scaffolding—a system of prompting as a student learns a skill, beginning with instruction and opportunity for practice at the student's comfort level;

once the student has mastered that skill, higher-level content is introduced and practiced, thus building confidence and understanding.

Schema—a diagram, model or plan used to help organize information.

Self-efficacy—a person's belief in his or her ability to succeed in a particular situation.

Strategy—a general action plan focused on the way to perform a task, specifying the sequence of needed actions to reach a goal and including critical guidelines and rules related to making effective decisions during a problem solving process (Ellis & Lenz, 1996).

Structured Worksheet—a tool (cue card) to help students remember problem solving steps or strategies accompanied by direct instruction which may include techniques such as think alouds, visualization, modeling, explicit step-by-step sequencing, and self-monitoring procedures.

Strategic Teaching—instructional processes that focus directly on fostering student thinking; a strategic teacher understands the variables of instruction and the cognitive requirements of learning.

Strategic Thinking—an approach to learning that takes an overview as well as looks at details, asks how things fit together, looks for patterns and connections and thinks ahead rather than just accepts new knowledge.

Subitizing—the ability to comprehend the quantity of a group of four or fewer objects without actually counting.

Technique—a specific action or method used for implementation of a general action plan.

Universal Screening—brief assessments such as CBM probes to identify levels of proficiency and rate of learning in essential academics for each student.

Visible Thinking—promoted by the Cultures of Thinking Project, a teaching approach that helps teachers follow a student's thought process in order to discover student misconceptions, faulty knowledge, prior knowledge, reasoning ability and understanding.

References

Allsopp, D. H., Kyger, M. M., & Lovin, L., H. (2007). *Teaching mathematics meaningfully: Solutions for reaching struggling learners.* Brooks Publishing.

Atkins, M., Duhon, G., Scherweit, S., & Beason, B. (2007). *Response to Intervention: An Increasing Intensity Design in Mathematics,* Oklahoma State University, NASP Poster Session.

Ashcroft, M. H. (2007). *Researchers: Math anxiety saps working memory needed to do math.* Retrieved January 30, 2008, from www. districtadministration.com/newssummary

Barlow, A. T. & Reddish, J. M. (2006). *Mathematical myths: Teacher candidates' beliefs and the implications for teacher educators.* Retrieved on February 2, 2008 from www.redorbit.com

Bell, N. (1991). *Visualizing and verbalizing for language comprehension and thinking.* San Luis Obispo, CA: Lindamood-Bell Learning Processes.

Ben-Hur, M. (2004). *Forming early concepts of mathematics: A manual for successful mathematics teaching.* Glencoe, IL: International Renewal Institute, Inc.

Ben-Hur, M. (2004). *Investigating the big ideas of arithmetic: A manual for successful mathematics teaching.* Glencoe, IL: International Renewal Institute, Inc.

Blakey, E., & Spence, S. (1990). *Developing metacognition.* ERIC Digest [Online]. Retrieved Feburuary 28, 2008 from http://www.eric.ed.gov/

Boehm, A. E. (1976). *Boehm resource guide for basic concept teaching.* NY: Pyschological Corporation.

Boekaerts, M. (2002). *Motivation.* International Academy of Education (IAE). Retrieved 7/1/08 from (http://www.ibe.unesco.org/publications).

Burns, M. (1998). *Math: Facing an American phobia.* NY: Math Solutions Publications.

Carpenter, T. P., Franke, M. L., & Levi, L. (2003). *Thinking mathematically: Integrating arithmetic and algebra in elementary school.* Portsmouth: Heinemann.

Cavanaugh, S. (2007). *Understanding math anxiety,* Retrieved on January 30, 2008, from www.teachermagazine.org

Csikszentmihalyi, M. (1990). *Flow: The psychology of optimal experience.* New York: Harper & Row.

Curtain-Phillips, M. (2005). *The Causes and Prevention of Math Anxiety.* Retrieved January 8, 2007,from http://www.mathgoodies.com

Devlin, K. (2008). *Boys born better at maths than girls "myth."* Telegraph News. Retrieved June 2, 2008, from htpp://www.telegraph.co.uk/news/

Dickman, E. (2008). A *nosology for learning disabilities:A foundation for the bridge between research and practice.* Perspectives on Language and Literacy, Dialogue is important: Language in mathematics classrooms. Vol 34, No. 2.

Feuerstein, R., Feuerstein, R., Falik, L., & Rand, Y. (2006).*Creating and enhancing cognitive modifiability-the Feuerstein instructional enrichment program.* Israel: ICELP Publications.

Fuchs, L. S., Fuchs, D., Hamlett, C. L., Walz, L., & Germann, G. (1993). *Formative evaluation of academic progress: How much growth can we expect?* School Psychology Review, 22, 27-48.

Gersten, R. and Chard, D. (1999). *Number sense: Rethinking arithmetic instruction for students with mathematical disabilities.* Journal of Special Education (1999), 3, 18–29.

Griffin, S. (2004). *Teaching number sense.* Educational Leadership. Vol. 61, No. 6, 39-42.

Griffin, S. (2007). *Early intervention for children at risk of developing mathematical learning difficulties.* In D.B. Berch & M. M. Mazzocco (Eds.), *Why is Math So Hard for Some Children? The Nature and Origins of Mathematical Learning Difficulties and Disabilities* (pp. 373-396). Baltimore, MD: Brookes Publishing.

Hechinger, J. (2008). *Education panel lays out truce in math wars.* Wall Street Journal Article, 3/5/08.

Hosp, M K., Hosp, J. L., & Howell, K.W. (2007). T*he ABC's of CBM, A practical guide to curriculum-based measurement.* New York: The Guilford Press.

Holt, J. (2008). *Numbers guy: Are our brains wired for math?* The New Yorker. July 13, 2008.

Horner, R., & Sugai, G. (1999). *Discipline and behavioral support: Practices, pitfalls and promises.* Effective School Practices, 17(4), 65-71.

Hyde, A. (2006). *Comprehending math: Adapting reading strategies to teach mathematics, K-6.* Portsmouth, NH: Heinemann.

Jensen, E. (1998). *Teaching with the brain in mind.* VA: ASCD Publication.

Jitendra, A. K., Griffin, C., Deatline-Buchman, A. & Sczesniak, E. (2007). *Mathematical word problem solving in third grade classrooms.* Journal of Educational Research, 100(5), 283-302.

Kemp, K.A., & Eaton, M. (2007). *RTI: The classroom connection for literacy.* NY: National Professional Resources.

Light, G.J., & DeFries, J.C. (1995). *Comorbidity for reading and mathematics disabilities: Genetic and environmental etiologies,* Journal of Learning Disabilities, 28, 96-106. Retrieved January 21, 2008, from http://findarticles.com

Montague, M. (2005). *Math problem solving for upper elementary students with disabilities,* Retrieved on February 18, 2008 from www. K8accesscenter.org

Moursand, D. (2006). *Improving mathematics Education: Roles of brain science, information & communications technology (ICT) and the craft & science of technology & learning (C&S of T&L).* Retrieved February 2, 2008 from http://darkwing.uoregon.edu

Moursund, D. (2007). *Computational thinking and math maturity: Improving math education in K-8 Schools (2nd ed.)* Retrieved February 21, 2008, from http://uoregon.edu

National Center for Education Statistics (2003). Retrieved February 22, 2008, from htpp://nces.ed.gov

National Council of Teachers of Mathematics (2005). *Standards and Focal Points,* Retrieved on January 21, 2008, from www.nctm.org/standards/

National Math Advisory Panel (2008). Final Report. Retrieved March 15, 2008 from www.ed.gov/MathPanel.

National Research Council (2002). *Helping children learn mathematics. Mathematics Learning Study Committee,* J.Kilpatrick and J.Swafford, Editors. Center for Education, Division of Behavioral and Social Sciences and Education. Washington, DC: National Academy Press. Retrieved February 15, 2008, from http://books.nap.edu

National Research Council. (2001). *Adding it up: Helping children learn mathematics.* Kilpatrick, J., Swafford, J., and Findell, B. (Eds.). Mathematics Learning Study Committee, Center for Education, Division of Behavioral and Social Sciences and Education. Washington, DC: National Academy Press.

Paulos, J. A. (1991). *Math moron myths.* Retreived February 22, 2008, from http://www.math.temple.edu/

Rose, C. M., Minton, L., Arline, C. (2007). *Uncovering student thinking in mathematics: 25 formative assessment probes.* CA: Corwin Press.

Rothstein, A., Rothstein, E., & Lauber, G. (2007). *Write for mathematics, second edition.* CA: Corwin Press.

Russell, S. J. (1999). *Developing computational fluency with whole numbers in the elementary grades.* Cambridge, MA: TERC (Technical Education Research Center) Investigations in Number, Data and Space Retrieved February 1, 2008 from http://investigations.terc.edu/library/families/comp_fluency.cfm

Shinn, M. R., Shinn, M. M., Hamilton, C., & Clarke, B. (2002). *Using curriculum-based measurement to promote achievement in general education classrooms.* In M. R. Shinn, G. Stoner & H. M. Walker (Eds.), *Interventions for academic and behavior problems: Preventive and remedial approaches* (pp. 113-142). Bethesda, MD: National Association of School Psychologists.

Shinn, M. R., Baker, S., Habedank, L., Good,,R. H. (1993). *The effects of classroom reading performance data on general education teachers' and parents' attitudes about reintegration.* Exceptionality, Vol. 4, No. 4, Pages 205-228.

Siemon, D. (2007). *There's more to counting than meets the eye (or the hand).* Retrieved May 30, 2008, from http://www.education.vic.gov.au

Smith, S.B. & Smith, W. H., (2006) 2nd edition. *Studying math: Pathways to success,* Custom Publishing.

Stecker, P.M., Fuchs, L.S. & Fuchs, D. (2005). *Using curriculum-based measurement to improve student achievement: Review of Research Psychology in the Schools.* 42(8), 795-819.

Tobias, S. (2002). *Succeed with math: Every student's guide to conquering math anxiety.* Interview for Education World, Wireside Chat Series retrieved on January 7, 2007, from www.educationworld.com

Torgesen, J. K. (2004). *Preventing early reading failure: Evidence for early intervention.* American Educator, Fall, 2004.

Tuley, K. & Bell, N. (1997). *On cloud nine: Visualizing and verbalizing for math.* CA: Gander Publishing.

Walsch, N. D. (1996). *Conversations with God: An uncommon dialogue.* New York: G.P. Putnam's Sons.

Wigfield, A. & Meece, J.L. (1988). *Math anxiety in elementary and secondary school students.* Journal of Educational Psychology. Vol 80(2) 210-216.

Wiggins, G. & McTighe, J. (2005). *Understanding by design (2nd edition).* Alexandria, VA: Association for Supervision and Curriculum Development.

Wright, J. (2007). *The RTI tool kit: A practical guide for schools.* New York: National Professional Resources, Inc.

Resources: Print and Video Materials
Available from National Professional Resources, Inc.
1-800 453-7461 • www.NPRinc.com

Allington, Richard L. & Patricia M. Cunningham. (1996). *Schools That Work: Where all Children Read and Write.* New York, NY: Harper Collins.

Andrini, Beth. (1993). *Cooperative Learning & Mathematics Grade K-8.* San Clemente, CA: Kagan Publishing.

ASCD. (2006). *Teaching Students with Learning Disabilities in the Regular Classroom* (Video). Baltimore, MD: ASDC.

Beecher, Margaret. (1995). *Developing the Gifts & Talents of All Students in the Regular Classroom.* Mansfield Center, CT: Creative Learning Press, Inc.

Bender, William. (2002). *Differentiating Instruction for Students with Learning Disabilities.* Thousand Oaks, CA: Corwin Press.

Bender, William. (2005). *Differentiating Math Instruction: Strategies That Work for K-8 Classrooms!* Thousand Oaks, CA: Corwin Press.

Bray, Marty & Abbie Brown, et al. (2004). *Technology and the Diverse Learner.* Thousand Oaks, CA: Corwin Press.

Brown-Chidsey, Rachel & Mark W. Steege. (2005). *Response to Intervention.* New York, NY: Guilford Press.

Casbarro, Joseph. (2005). *Test Anxiety & What You Can Do About It: A Practical Guide for Teachers, Parents, & Kids.* Port Chester, NY: Dude Publishing.

Chapman, Carolyn & Rita King. (2003). *Differentiated Instructional Strategies for Reading in the Content Areas.* Thousand Oaks, CA: Corwin Press.

Coggins, Debra, et al. (1999). *A Mathematics Source Book for Elementary and Middle School Teachers: Key Concepts, Teaching Tips, and Learning Pitfalls.* Novato, CA: Arena Press

Council for Exceptional Children and Merrill Education. (2005). *Universal Design for Learning.* Atlanta, GA.

Crone, Deanne A. & Robert H. Horner. (2003). *Building Positive Behavior Support Systems in Schools: Functional Behavioral Assessment.* New York, NY: Guilford Press.

Dieker, Lisa. (2006). *Co-Teaching Lesson Plan Book (Third Edition).* Whitefish Bay, WI: Knowledge By Design Inc.

Dodge, Judith. (2005). *Differentiation in Action.* Jefferson City, MO: Scholastic Inc.

Elias, Maurice, Brian Friedlander & Steven Tobias. (2001). *Engaging the Resistant Child Through Computers: A Manual to Facilitate Social & Emotional Learning.* Port Chester, NY: Dude Publishing.

Elias, Maurice & Harriett Arnold. (2006). *The Educator's Guide to Emotional Intelligence and Academic Achievement.* Thousand Oaks, CA: Corwin Press.

Flockhart, Dan. (2007). *Fantasy Football and Mathematics/Fantasy Basketball and Mathematics/Fantasy Soccer and Mathematics/Fantasy Baseball and Mathematics.* Thousand Oaks, CA: Corwin Press.

Friedlander, Brian S. (2005). *Assistive Technology: A Way to Differentiate Instruction for Students with Disabilities.* (Video) Port Chester, NY: National Professional Resources, Inc.

Fuchs, D., Mock, D., Morgan, P., & Young, C. (2003). *Responsiveness-to-intervention: Definitions, evidence, and implications for learning disabilities construct.* Learning Disabilities: Research and Practice, 18(3), 157-171.

Fuchs, L. (2003). *Assessing intervention responsiveness: conceptual and technical issues.* Learning Disabilities: Research and Practice, 18(3), 172-186.

Fuchs, L.S., & Fuchs, D. (2006). *A framework for building capacity for responsiveness to intervention.* School Psychology Review, 35, 621-626.

Gardner, Howard. (1996). *How Are Kids Smart?* (Video) Port Chester, NY: National Professional Resources, Inc.

Goleman, Daniel. (1996). *Emotional Intelligence: A New Vision for Educators* (Video). Port Chester, NY: National Professional Resources, Inc.

Good, R.H. & Kaminski, R.A. (2001). *Dynamic indicators of basic early literacy skills (6th ed.).* Eugene, OR: Institute for the Development of Educational Achievement.

Gregory, Gale & Carolyn Chapman. (2002). *Differentiated Instructional Strategies: One Size Doesn't Fit All.* Thousand Oaks, CA: Corwin Press.

Gusman, Jo. (2004). *Differentiated Instruction & the English Language Learner: Best Practices to Use With Your Students (K-12)* (Video). Port Chester, NY: National Professional Resources, Inc.

Heacox, Diane. (2002). *Differentiated Instruction: How to Reach and Teach All Learners (Grades 3-12).* Minneapolis, MN: Free Spirit Press.

Jensen, Eric. (2000). *Successful Applications of Brain-Based Learning* (Video). Port Chester, NY: National Professional Resources, Inc.

Kagan, Spencer & Laurie Kagan. (1999). *Reaching Standards Through Cooperative Learning: Providing for ALL Learners in General Education Classrooms (Tape 2: Mathematics).* Port Chester, NY: National Professional Resources, Inc.

Kagan, Spencer & Miguel Kagan. (1998). *Multiple Intelligences: The Complete MI Book.* San Clemente, CA: Kagan Publishing.

Kame'enui, Edward J. & Deborah C. Simmons. (1999). *Adapting Curricular Materials, Volume 1: An Overview of Materials Adaptations—Toward Successful Inclusion of Students with Disabilities: The Architecture of Instruction.* Reston, VA: Council for Exceptional Children.

Kemp, Karen. (2007). *RTI Tackles Reading* (Video). Port Chester, NY: National Professional Resources, Inc.

Kemp, Karen. (2007). *RTI: The Classroom Connection for Literacy.* Port Chester, NY: Dude Publishing.

Kennedy, Eugene. (2003). *Raising Test Scores for All Students: An Administrator's Guide to Improving Standardized Test Performance.* Thousand Oaks, CA: Corwin Press.

MacDonald, Sharon. (2007). *Math in Minutes: Easy Activities for Children 4 –8.* Beltsville, MD: Gryphon House Inc.

Matricardi, Joanne & Jeanne McLarty. (2005). *Math Activities A to Z.* Clifton Park, NY: Delmar Cengage Learning.

McCarney, Stephen B. (1993). *The Pre-Referral Intervention Manual.* Columbia, MO: Hawthorne Educational Services.

Minton, Leslie (2007). *What if Your ABCs Were Your 123s? Building Connections Between Literacy and Numeracy.* Thousand Oaks, CA: Corwin Press.

Moll, Anne M. (2003). *Differentiated Instruction Guide for Inclusive Teaching.* Port Chester, NY: Dude Publishing.

Munk, Dennis D. (2003). *Solving the Grading Puzzle for Students with Disabilities.* Whitefish Bay, WI: Knowledge by Design, Inc.

Muschla, Judith A. & Gary Robert Muschla. (2008). *The Math Teacher's Problem-a-Day: Over 180 Reproducible Pages of Quick Skill Builders, Grades 4-8.* San Francisco, CA: Jossey-Bass.

National Association of State Directors of Special Education (NASDSE). (2005). *Response to Intervention: Policy, Considerations, and Implementation.* Alexandria, VA: NASDSE.

Norlander, Karen. (2006). *RTI Tackles the LD Explosion: A Good IDEA Becomes Law* (Video). Port Chester, NY: National Professional Resources, Inc.

Overholt, James L., James Lindsey & Nancy H. Aaberg. (2008) *Math Stories for Problem Solving Success Ready-to-Use Activities Based on Real-Life Situations.* San Francisco, CA: Jossey-Bass.

Purcell, Sherry & Debbie Grant. (2004). *Using Assistive Technology to Meet Literacy Standards.* Verona, WI: IEP Resources.

Rief, Sandra F. (1998). *The ADD/ADHD Checklist.* Paramus, NJ: Prentice Hall.

Rief, Sandra F. (2004). *ADHD & LD: Powerful Teaching Strategies & Accommodations* (Video). Port Chester, NY: National Professional Resources, Inc.

Ronis, Diane. (2007). *Brain-Compatible Mathematics.* Thousand Oaks, CA: Corwin Press.

Rose, D. & A. Meyer (Editors). (2002). *Teaching Every Student in the Digital Age.* Alexandria, VA: ASCD.

Rose, D. & A. Meyer (Editors). (2005). *The Universally Designed Classroom: Accessible Curriculum and Digital Technologies.* Cambridge, MA: Harvard University Press.

Salovey, Peter. (1998). *Optimizing Intelligences: Thinking, Emotion, and Creativity* (Video). Port Chester, NY: National Professional Resources, Inc.

Shinn, M. (1989). *Curriculum-Based Measurement: Assessing Special Children.* New York: Guilford Press.

Shumm, Jeanne Shay. (1999). *Adapting Curricular Materials, Volume 2: Kindergarten Through Grade Five—Adapting Reading & Math Materials for the Inclusive Classroom.* Reston, VA: Council for Exceptional Children.

Solomon, Pearl Gold. (2006). *The Math We Need to Know and Do in Grade PreK-5: Concepts, Skills, Standards, and Assessments.* Thousand Oaks, CA: Corwin Press.

Sousa, David A. (2008). *Brain-Compatible Activities (Grade K-2) (Grades 3-5).* Thousand Oaks, CA: Corwin Press.

Stone, Randi. (2007). *Best Practices for Teaching Mathematics: What Award-Winning Classroom Teachers Do.* Thousand Oaks, CA: Corwin Press.

Tate, Marcia L. (2008). *Graphic Organizers and Other Visual Strategies (Grade 1) (Grade 2) (Grade 3) (Grade 4) (Grade 5).* Thousand Oaks, CA: Corwin Press.

Tate, Marcia L. (2008). *Math Worksheets Don't Grow Dendrites: 20 Numeracy Strategies That Engage the Brain, PreK-8.* Thousand Oaks, CA: Corwin Press.

Thompson, Sandra, Rachel Quenemeen, Martha Thurlow, & James Ysseldyke. (2001). *Alternate Assessments for Students with Disabilities.* Thousand Oaks, CA: Corwin Press.

Thurlow, Martha L., Judy L. Elliott & James E. Ysseldyke. (1998). *Testing Students with Disabilities: Practical Strategies for Complying With District and State Requirements.* Thousand Oaks, CA: Corwin Press.

Tilton, Linda. (2003). *Teacher's Toolbox for Differentiating Instruction: 700 Strategies, Tips, Tools, & Techniques.* Shorewood, MN: Covington Cove Publications.

Tomlinson, Carol Ann. (2001). *How to Differentiate Instruction in Mixed-Ability Classrooms, 2nd Edition.* Alexandria, VA: ASCD.

Wall, Edward S. & Alfred S. Posamentier. (2007). *What Successful Math Teachers Do, Grades PreK-5.* Thousand Oaks, CA: Corwin Press.

Wormel, Rick. (2006). *Fair Isn't Always Equal.* Portland, ME: Stenhouse Publishers.

Wright, J. (2007). *RTI Toolkit: A Practical Guide for Schools.* Port Chester, NY: Dude Publishing.

"Life is magic, tricks you never learned,
But you perform them without knowing,
The mystery keeps on going,
And you wonder how you do it all.
Life is magic."
—Gail Sparlin, Life is Funny

About the Authors

Karen Kemp, a 30-year public school veteran, with extensive leadership/administration and teaching experience, has authored and/or co-authored over 30 publications including the books, *Cool Kids: A Proactive Approach to Social Responsibility, TGIF: But What Will I Do On Monday,* and *RTI: The Classroom Connection for Literacy,* and two DVD's *RTI Tackles the LD Explosion* and *RTI Tackles Reading.* Additionally, Karen has presented workshops and professional development seminars in the United States and Europe. She is currently the Director of Special Programs in Cohoes City Schools in New York. Her areas of expertise include Instructional Support Teams, Response To Intervention, Positive Behavior Supports/Social Responsibility, Reading Strategies, Effective Instruction for Inclusive Classrooms and Progress Monitoring. Karen can be contacted at ***karenakemp@schoolofsimilarities.com***.

Mary Ann Eaton, M.S., CCC-S, is a certified Speech & Language Pathologist with over 30 years experience in the public schools of New York's Capital Region. Her vast school-based teaching experiences include pre-school through high school aged students. Mary Ann provides training and consultation to school districts in the areas of literacy, co-teaching, differentiated instruction, curriculum-based measurement and RTI. In recognition of the merits of RTI and its potential for positive instructional impact, she has co-authored a book entitled, RTI: The Classroom Connection for Literacy which provides excellent suggestions for interventions and measurements to substantiate the reality of "hunches out, data in!" Mary Ann is founder of The School of Similarities, an educational enterprise based on the premise that "we are more similar than different." Feel free to contact her at: ***maryanneaton@schoolofsimilarities.com***.

Sharon Poole began her career over thirty years ago as a transition and employment counselor. Subsequently she worked as a high school and community college English teacher, a special education provider, and adjunct in teacher preparation programs. She was instrumental in establishing a successful co-teaching model of instruction at the high school level in English, Science and Math. She is an accomplished staff developer and has provided professional development in a wide array of areas including Data Collection, Progress Monitoring and Differentiated Instruction. Sharon, who has a passion for math, is currently the Assistant Director for Special Programs in the Cohoes City School District, as well as Principal of the Alternative Education Program serving at-risk secondary students.